INTRODUCTION TO LIFESTORIES
VOLUME 1

SHELTERED!

INTRODUCTION TO LIFESTORIES
VOLUME 1

SHELTERED!

RICHARD (RITCHIE) VERNON

"Your story is our priority"

LitPrime Solutions
East Brunswick Office Evolution
1 Tower Center Boulevard, Ste 1510
East Brunswick, NJ 08816
www.litprime.com
Phone: 1-800-981-9893

Published by LitPrime Solutions: 03/19/2025

ISBN: 979-8-88703-464-5(sc)
ISBN: 979-8-88703-465-2(e)

Library of Congress Control Number: 2025902325

CONTENTS

INTRODUCTION

I personally want to thank God with all of my heart for being with me through every situation that I have been through in this life or ever encountered before I even knew who he was, he was there! Maybe in these stories dear reader you come across situations you can identify with that might have happened to you or maybe someone you know? If so I truly believe you will understand as you are walking through these life stories what I encountered! I am truly grateful to God for allowing me to write this first book! After all he is the ultimate pen writer and I'm just one of the many inks he chooses to write with! I'm truly grateful for my publisher who helped me to get this first book published and I'm grateful for my publicist Megan her valuable assistance and help incredible talent that she has In doing these things! And of course the incredible employees and staff that make up this awesome Publishing Company that I know God brought my way! As one of their authors I'm truly thankful and grateful and blessed to be associated with such talented caring people such as Writers Branding! It is my desire to be associated with them for a long time hopefully as one of their many clients, I hope one day I can get together with the other authors under their care and get to know them as well! It is my extreme desire to make God proud through this book as well as my publisher as they are being represented! I also found out couple of months ago when this book was still unedited, that it had received as an unedited book then a five out of five rating on Amazon that's truly remarkable! I truly give God glory for that! As the author I was truly flattered to read that and what they had to say about the book! And now you're looking at the complete first book! If you're an aspiring writer I highly recommend my publisher to you! I also want you to know because I as an individual who goes through life just like you can definitely identify possibly some of your own stories you have been through since I've been through them! And keep in mind this is only the first book!I want you to understand that,and so it is my personal desire to walk you through the pages as if you're walking with me, experiencing what I'm experiencing and feeling it for yourself. It is my desire that you read the accounts to where you maybe identify with them. A lady named Kathy told me that this first book would be a good movie! That would absolutely blow my mind if they made my own story into a movie! I would want a handsome guy like Leonard DiCaprio playing me and I'd like to see Denzel Washington in it as well and as well as other known actors! If that truly happens that would be an awesome honor! But for the meantime it's still a book! I also wanted to let you know that everything that happens in this book is absolutely, 100 percent true. Nothing has been made up or fictionalized, contrived, or conceived, that's why this book is called "Life Stories." and in some stories I get to share the dry sense of humor that God has given me I'm sure some of you have a sense of humor out there as well whether common sense humor or dry like this author's! But regardless all stories are true!

DEDICATION

First, I wish to thank God in heaven, who spoke to my daughter back in September 2013. She called me up the day after I was singing on TV, and said, "Hey, Dad, I think God wants you to write a book." He also confirmed this through a book author who is well-known throughout the world and lived in the same city that I did: Anderson, Indiana. She may still live there today. Ruth Shininess said it to me almost word-for-word like my daughter did, "Hey, Richard, I think God wants you to write a book." That really confirmed to me that I was supposed to write something. But at that point, I really didn't know what I was supposed to have written. I would find out not too long after that. So, I'm very grateful to my daughter, Megan, whom I love with all my heart, to have gotten this started. Without God speaking to her, there would not be a book, nor without my friend, Ruth, who confirmed it on that day. also very grateful and thankful for the East Lynn Christian Church off 53rd Street in Anderson who has been an incredible valuable assistance to the city of Anderson helping with food to give away to low-income families everywhere in Anderson which after 2009 unknown to me I was going to need them as well in a crucial time in my life, and they supplied the food that was needed when I was disabled and married at the time we needed help and they responded extreme blessing these people are and I just want to give a shout out to them how valuable they were to this author's life at that time very friendly great attitude this congregation from this church that help out and volunteer are absolutely amazing and I just want to give a shout out to them and say thank you all over again keep up the good work what you're doing East Lynn Christian Church in Anderson! And their new Pastor Steve! Whom I got acquainted with over the phone!A very nice gentleman!☺⚓☺

I also Thank God from the bottom of my heart, for reconnecting me with my church Shawmut Community Church of God off of Shawmut Street in Boston! And it was another church that watched out for me when my church was going to open up again because I had no idea they were already open I had no contact number nothing to get ahold of them? I am very thankful for Pastor Ron Crosstown Church in Boston where I went a little bit but God dealt with my heart to get reconnected with my old church it was Crosstown Church that kept an eye out for me when my old church was going to be having service again I am totally thankful and grateful for that and I told Pastor Ron of Crosstown that they've got a reward in heaven just because they were looking out for me with my old church! I will always be grateful for Crosstown Church and the time I got to spend with them worshiping and listening to the word of God they are awesome awesome people one of the finest churches in Boston in my opinion! But I'm very thankful for them reconnecting me with my church!☺⚓

I also thank my good friend, Miss Q, who has been a very valuable resource to help get these life stories set up early on which my current publisher has published! I appreciate her with all my heart. and her valuable assistance to me for helping me to stay the course and telling me to keep with it. I appreciate all those God has sent my way to be valuable resources and I appreciate all of them! And I want to thank my friends in Boston, my friends at the Southampton Shelter where I was a resident for two and a half years, the many friends I made there, and all the staff there, including case managers, supervisors, and my former bosses! I appreciate everyone there, I also appreciate former bosses in Indiana I had that I had a good working relationship with,and friendships in Indiana and good friends in Boston now many of them whom I sing with, at different times and their patient support with me trying to get this book done.

I wish to thank my case managers of Hearth and Home Start and of course first of all the Southampton Shelter case managers who handled my life with care and compassion not only as a resident there but also as a working employee later on through them I was able to achieve those things, and for the valuable care they all took in handling my life overall, I myself will always be grateful to them! The Southampton Shelter was a valuable experience in my life,and I'm not ashamed to say that! Without further ado, I, Richard (Ritchie) Vernon, invite you to check out "Life Stories!"

FOREWORD

There I was. I looked around, and what I saw astonished me!

Before my eyes was laid before me a room of the most beautiful colors I have ever seen. I said to myself, *Where am I?* As I looked around this huge room, I beheld what looked like a balanced scale for weighing something, but just what, I didn't know. Looking at this, I was absolutely floored. I said to myself, *What could this be?*

All of a sudden, multitudes of people showed up. They all came in and entered the room, and began to stand in different places. Then I heard this booming voice calling out my name, "Richard Vernon! Please come forward!" I stood there in absolute shock.

How does he know my name? I thought.

Then a very tall man with a stern look peered into my eyes. It was as if he were looking into my very soul! At that moment, I was scared. I felt like I was on fire! He spoke out in a loud booming voice, "Upon your testimony, do you swear to tell the truth and nothing but the truth, so help you God?" I said, "Yes, Sir, I do!" He spoke back, "Please state your name for the record." "Yes, Sir," I said, "Richard Vernon." The booming voice spoke again. He said, "Do you solemnly swear that the statements you are about to give are the absolute truth?" Then he said, "Be advised, you are under oath to God!" I said "Yes, Sir."

Another voice spoke up at that moment. It was the judge, and his name was Jesus! He said to me, "My child, I love you!" He said, "Please give an account of your story." I said, "Your Honor, this is not just a story! You gave me these stories, for these are life stories! And God, because of You, I live these stories! And because of You, I will tell these stories!" And with that, the judge smiled. As I awoke from this dream, heaven roared its approval.

CHAPTER 1

A STORY HAS TO START SOMEWHERE!

One thing I've learned as I'm getting older is that there are developments constantly flowing in my life. And in that respect, I've been through many things that people have gone through, or even are going through now. And I certainly can identify with them! I've seen and experienced different things at different times in life that were good or not-so-good, but you plug away at it, anyway! I was reading a story in the Bible about a man named Job. The devil asked God for permission to make Job's life a living hell, without taking his life. God gave that permission, and at the end of it all, Job got back double what he had before! So, he prospered even more!

Back in June of 2014, and after I'd been a courier for nine years for different companies, I had the biggest test of my life. All of a sudden, things that I thought were secure were taken away from me, one by one. I'm sure the devil must have asked God the same thing over my life, as he did with Job, because before that happened, things were going pretty good. The devil made one mistake in my life, though. He should have asked for my death! Little did he realize that God was going to give me the strength and the energy I needed for the trial I was about to go through! I was determined that I was going to thank God every day for life, even as a homeless man! I trusted him everyday to supply what I needed! And sometimes, out of the blue, people would come up and bless me with food or money or even temporary job opportunities!

Now, keep in mind, I didn't ask those people for anything, all I did was pray and believe. God was the one that laid it on their hearts to bring it to me! And I thanked Him for it, before it happened and after it happened! A lot of what we do in life depends on the attitude we have at the time when we're going through a trial or situation that we have absolutely no control over. And we just have to give it over to God to get us through it. Starting my journey in Lapel, Indiana, was going to be the hardest test that I ever had to deal with. If God could bring me through that, then he could bring me through anything.

And let me tell you something, when you live in an abandoned house where there are many, many holes in the roof, and cracks in the windows in the wintertime, it gets cold like Antarctica, especially for Indiana! You don't know if you're going to live or you're going to die! Yet, I trusted God to get me through it with three heavy blankets, jackets, and extra clothes. It would be so cold in the morning that the living room floor was covered in about five inches of frozen ice and the walls were white as snow, like a winter wonderland. So I had to be careful getting up in the morning. I had to get my footing just getting out the door!

I was extremely thankful for the Lapel Library, where there were nice people that were very helpful. That was where I first would start getting on Facebook in August 2014, and meeting a lot of people, which helped get my mind off that frozen house! Keep in mind, there's no electricity in there, and there's no bathroom that works, so you have to go down the block to the convenience store just to use the restroom! I still had aspirations and inspirations about being a book author. I kept notes and things with me in a backpack to keep them safe. I recalled at that time when my daughter said, "Hey, Dad? I think God wants you to write a book." I recalled Ruth Shinness, world-famous book author, saying the same thing a couple weeks later in September 2013. But did

I really believe what my daughter and Ruth Shinness said, that I was really going to write a book?

It would have taken no faith at all to believe it, back in 2013, because I hadn't become homeless yet. I had what I thought was security! But when you've lost everything, does your mind still believe in what is said? Even in these circumstances, I still chose to believe. Russ Taff sang a song on his album called "I Still Believe," and in the song, he talked about a lot of pain he had gone through. So just like he sang, I, Richard, still believe! But you know what? God has other ideas when we think we can't, because He knows we can! He knew what He had planned for my life, even at that time when it seemed like my only job at that time was to stay alive to fulfill that plan. That's why I'm saying that maybe the devil should have asked for my death instead of putting me through suffering, because through suffering, I was to become even stronger!

A pastor, Jeffrey Johnson out of Indianapolis, once said, "Do everything that you know how to do, and then watch God do everything that you can't do!" That is absolutely true! I'm living proof of that today, and the trials and circumstances that God brought me through. I began to identify more and more with what homeless people suffer through. There were some very sad things that happened in my time in Lapel, and I was constantly mocked by people there who talked about me behind my back, because they didn't have the guts to say what they thought of me or my living situation to my face. It's really ironic, because a few years before all this happened, I was invited to sing in their annual music fest, which I did, and sang about four songs. My, how times had changed! I was being mocked by the same people I used to sing for, the ones that invited me to come.

However, through it all, God gave me the attitude that I was going to get through it, no matter what! (This story about my experience in Lapel, Indiana, will be in another book later on, called *Journey into the Unknown*!) I just want to give you a hint of a few things that happened. Little did I realize that on August 1, 2014, the trial would begin! In September 2015, I was going to go through an even harder trial, the worst month of my entire life! My two cats that I dearly loved for years were taken away from me, when I was working a part-time job and was away one night at work! I came home to a cold, empty house, with no more pets! The pastor of my church and his wife were involved in this, as they owned the abandoned house that I lived in from the former owner. And they had given me guidelines in order for me to stay in that house; I took care of certain things in the yard, and worked around the church, all of which I did, and I worked extremely hard! I was a member of that church for over three years, and once or twice a month, they asked me to sing at the church, which I did. Little did I realize they were going to turn on me.

One day, I went to a CVS or Walgreens, I can't remember which store it was, to send out money to a struggling pastor friend of mine on Facebook. He was in Spain and asked for small donations to help him. I was glad to do it. I hope he reads this book and realizes I'm sharing about him! I knew his life, and he and I had been friends since I first started on Facebook over a year before that! So I was more than happy to help him out, since I worked a part-time job, and I paid my tithes to my church, and was able to eat to survive on what money I had left. I didn't make much, but it was enough to get by. God spoke to my heart to help him, and so I sent him about forty dollars to help his ministry. He got ahold of me about a half hour later at the library, saying he received it, and pronounced a blessing on me. I was happy to help him. When somebody is struggling, you can't just sit back and watch them struggle, you have to get involved! I didn't care what my situation was, he needed help!

When I got back to the house, I received a text from my pastor, and he was very irate with me! I asked him what he was upset about. He said, "I received word that you sent money to somebody and I'm upset about that!" I said, "Why are you upset about that? And what does that have to do with you, when I pay tithes to my own church?" He told me, "Well, you should be paying to your church!" I said, "I do pay to my church, once a week, and I give offerings, as well, when I have them!" I said, "Why would it make you upset that I'm helping somebody else out on my own time? Especially another pastor?" He said, "Because if you're going to give money away, you should give it to your own church!" I said, "Is that what you think about this? A struggling pastor friend of mine needs money, and you think it belongs to you?" I said, "I pay each week to my own church, and what I have left over shouldn't be any concern of yours, because I have faithfully paid since I've been in this church, as often as I could when I was working!" He said, "Well, my wife and I discussed it, and it's just not right that you're doing that, and we want you to move out!" I saw that last text and I was absolutely shocked! I said, "Pastor? First of all, what business is it of yours what I do on my own time, to help somebody else out? I would think you would be happy that another pastor would get a blessing! And who told you that I did this?" He said, "It doesn't matter who told me. The fact is, what you're doing is wrong!" I said, "Wrong to who? You and your wife? Wrong to God? Pastor, it was God that dealt with my heart to help this other pastor! Are you going to tell God that He was wrong for having me do that?" He said, "I'm not going to argue with you, Richard, you have three days to move out yourself and your pets!" He didn't text back.

I was absolutely stunned! I had kept up my word with him about taking care, as best I could, of the house, plus volunteering mowing that huge yard that the church had. Both ways, it was like two football fields connected to each other. But I did it, because I was doing it as unto the Lord as if I were working for Him. And so I enjoyed doing the work, and my part-time job. So there I was, absolutely stunned out of my mind! I thought: *Who in the world could have told him, and what right did they have to do this and try to ruin my life?*

And then I figured out what had happened. The pastor's wife had a sister that worked at the CVS or the Walgreens, and she was there when I was sending the money through! She had questioned me, "Well, where are you sending the money to?" I said, "I'm sending it to a friend who needs it!" I said, "Can I ask what business that is of yours?" She said, "No, I was just wondering!" When I paid for it, she knew exactly where it was going to, and who was going to receive it, because she was the one who processed it!" Now, I'm sure CVS or Walgreens has a privacy policy that protects their customers from employees trying to divulge privacy information about customers. I'm pretty sure that's against the law, but I don't know for sure. So, at the house, it dawned on me, *I know who has done this!* This so-called Christian lady did this behind my back, and gossiped to her brother-in-law, my pastor, about what I did. It wasn't any of her business! If I would have contacted a lawyer, she would have been sued, because she worked there and violated store policy and a customer privacy act, and then would have likely been fired! And believe me, I was seconds away from calling an attorney. And I still had the text on my phone the pastor gave me, as proof that someone talked to him, because he admitted in text that someone from the store had brought it to his attention! And though I knew who did it, I had to turn my mind towards prayer, and get rid of the pent-up anger that I was feeling over what had just happened! I was pent-up with bitterness towards this lady, and now towards the pastor, and his wife. I had to dig down deep and ask God for forgiveness, to forgive those that had wronged me. It took me a week to really forgive! I knew the devil was at work again, using so-called believers against me! After all, we're supposed to be different from the world, not fit into its system.

I got a call from one of my friends who no longer goes to that church, and they told me that the pastor's son from Muncie was going to take over as Head Pastor at that church. I remember meeting him one time, and I can tell you that this son of his had more integrity in his little finger than the pastor did in his whole life! And I mean it. Whenever the town pastors would have a prayer meeting, everybody would show up, except a certain pastor! He cared nothing about prayer meetings! So you're basically telling God that you don't care about revival because you won't even gather with others to pray for it. But yet, you're glad to show up for every prayer breakfast and be the life of the party? That's because the only prayer they do there is praying over the food! I wonder to this day how this guy became a pastor. After all, the word "pastor" means "shepherd!" This was no shepherd! They must have had a lottery, and his name was drawn, and somehow, he said "yes!"

It took me days to let go of the bitterness and the anger that I felt in my heart at that point! I was crying tears out to God to forgive me in my anger and bitterness, and I said, *Help me now to forgive those who have wronged me, because I am hurt and extremely angry!* I wanted to rise up in the flesh! *Please give me peace of mind God, that through this everything is going to be alright, and you have it all under control, because, right now, I don't know how to feel!* I said, *I trust you deeply, God, because I am very much hurting right now over what I'm feeling, and I don't know how to think! I feel numb and I feel angry!* Somehow, God broke through my heart and gave me peace through the situation, even though, unknown to me, the worst hadn't come yet!

I knew I had three days to move out before I was going to be homeless, for real! There would be no abandoned house, nothing to live in, and it was close to wintertime! (I thank God that I had a bike I had bought from a homeless guy who only wanted five dollars for it. I gave him 20 dollars at that time and he cried, he was so grateful. It made me feel bad because I wished that I had more. I still wish I could have given him more. But before I was to leave Anderson, I would return the favor and give it to another homeless guy.) I have never, ever liked the saying, "If wishes were horses, then beggars could ride!" Evidently, whoever wrote that had never met homeless people! I hate that stupid phrase with a passion! I was going to mention something good the pastor and some members of his congregation tried to do for me when I had my van before it went down, but after the stunt he and his wife pulled, not caring whether I lived or died, I'm not going to talk about it. It was my desire to get my van fixed and legally run a taxi service right there in Lapel, but it didn't happen. And I can recall when I was a courier before being homeless, that a few of us offered to take about twenty of the church's individuals with low income out to lunch: our treat! I think we went to the China Buffet and had a really good time. About five of us got together and split the check, including tip, about 60 dollars each! And I had brought about 100 dollars just in case somebody else was short. The pastor even called me on my cell phone while working, one day, and asked me if I could share my testimony with the whole congregation on Sunday morning. And I said that I would be honored! He said, "Ah, very good! I feel it would be a good example of how someone like yourself obeys and follows God!" I told him thank you and went about my delivery work that day.

That was early 2013, when I still lived in Anderson in my apartment.

And now, flash forward to the end of September 2015, and it looked like the end was coming quickly. I said, *Live or die, God, I trust you!* I said, *God? If these are my last days on Earth, I want to thank You for coming into my heart and changing my life so that I can go to Heaven knowing I am forgiven! And hopefully, the people I've told Jesus about will follow You, as well!*

And I got ahold of my daughter on Facebook and said, "Daddy loves you with all his heart. This might be the last time you hear from me. The place I am living at is being taken away from me!" This response shocked my daughter! She said, "Oh, Daddy, what are you going to do?" I said, "I don't know, I just have to trust God through this!" She said, I don't even know this pastor of yours, but right now I think I hate him, Daddy!" I said, "Sweetie? For what it's worth, I had to really dig down deep inside and forgive him, or I wouldn't be forgiven! Because for one moment, I think I would haved hated him, too! And if I don't survive, just know that I love you and I will save your place in heaven, by my side!" My daughter called me on the phone and started crying! She said, "Daddy, I wish there was something I could do!" I said, "There is, sweetie," I said, "Just pray for your dad!" She said, "Dad, you're always in my prayers!" I said, "I appreciate that. I'm broken inside and hurting right now, so please ask God to heal what's broken in me!" She said, "Dad, you know I will, I love you and I'll see you, one day!" I said, "You can count on it, sweetie!" She prayed for me over the phone as I silently cried out to God, *God if this is it, then I want to thank You for Your Son, Jesus, coming into my heart and changing my life! I look forward to seeing You!* And at that point, I thought it was going to be the end!

One night, I received a call from a lady who was with animal control, telling me they had come to my house and took my pets! When I heard this, it absolutely broke my heart! And I thought to myself, *The pets I took care of for three years are now gone!* And about four weeks before that, one of my cats had kittens, and I didn't want those kittens to suffer. I wanted to somehow hold onto my two cats, but I didn't know how, since I was going to be homeless. So I dropped them off on a porch in a basket so that someone could take care of them. I didn't know what else to do. I was ready to panic at that time.

Well, it turned out that the porch I put them on belonged to the lady that came and took my two cats, and called me up that she did that! So I knew exactly who had taken them. My Godmother, Barb, and her daughter, Tammy, who was my Godsister, were furious at this lady, and really wanted to lay into her for doing that to me! With tears, I told them, "No, we can't do that! That would make it worse!" I said, "I'm hurting very much inside, right now! And I have to forgive this lady, the pastor, and his wife that I trusted, and the wife's sister, all four of them that were involved in this!"

Your mind thinks back and you're shocked by what has taken place within a couple of days. Your mind thinks back to how you had been faithful to this church and that you supported them with money and your time and your energy and your enthusiasm and this is how they return it! David Lloyd, the owner of the house before he sold it to the pastor and his wife, warned me a long time ago that all this pastor and his wife cared about was money. The text to my house on my phone a few days before that proved it! All they had cared about was the money. This thought was backed up by one of their former tenants, a good friend of mine who used to rent from them, and this person told me that she and her kids couldn't afford to pay the extremely high rent she paid monthly. And I saw the place where she and her kids lived, and it was a dump. So this backed up the theory that all they cared about was money. After all, you're going to exploit a low-income mom and her kids? This tells me what a sheep in a wolf's clothing that this couple really was, and who, while naming the name of Jesus, basically proved they were phonies who preyed on people's incomes! And to make matters worse, he had a couple of his own people bolt the doors and windows of that abandoned home so that I could not get back in.

At the time I had taken residence in a broken-down, empty van that was courtesy of one of the bar employees. That went sour after a while, when one of the bar's main drunks (and by the way, this comment is not of my own, this is the opinion of those who knew this guy was a heavy drinker) who lived above the bar where I worked in the kitchen complained about my staying there, even though it had nothing to do with him. And he almost challenged me to a fight, which with all the crap I had gone through just a few weeks before, I was more than ready to unleash on him! All the pent-up anger and emotions, I was ready to let it all out! He talked about it, but he never brought it on. He saw me one day eating lunch at the bar, and made this comment right in my face, "You're lucky we didn't fight that night!" I turned to him and said with a stern look, "You're the lucky one!" I said, "I'm almost done with my lunch, and I'm itching to unleash some energy." He just looked at me and walked away. He never confronted me again!

Little did I know that at the place where I worked part-time in a restaurant karaoke bar, as a volunteer dishwasher and busboy, I was going to be approached by two people within a couple of weeks after I'd been homeless! And they spoke to me and said, "We know your situation, and we'd like to offer a solution. We know what a good person you are. My wife knows you pretty well, and you sing karaoke with her! We just wanted to say that we have a little, bitty trailer at the back of the house, and you're welcome to it until you get back on your feet!" I gave him a hug, right then and there! I said, "I would very much appreciate that! I've been through hell the last couple of weeks!" He said, "I heard what happened, and the cold-blooded thing that was done to you!" He said, "My wife and I will never go to that church, especially after that!" The people in that bar had more integrity than some of that church's worship team!

The reason I say that is that, on some nights, I would see about four of those church members smoking and getting drunk in the bars with other patrons! As a volunteer worker there, I sang karaoke on Thursday nights. And that church wondered why they couldn't reach that bar for Jesus? Get a clue! Many of their members, including some from the Sunday morning worship team, were right there, partying along with the people of the same bar that they said they prayed for. So how were these church-goers different from the bar-goers? The point is, they were not! In Scripture, it says to be in the world, but not of the world, meaning Christians are not to be a part of the world's system. I worked part-time in the kitchen, and drank Coke or water, as I had no desire to drink or smoke. I wanted to invite people to the church I was going to, but after I saw church members drinking and smoking and carrying on, I just did my work and kept my mouth shut. Little do these church members realize that not only were they ruining their testimony for Christ by acting the fool, but they were ruining mine, as well, because I wouldn't be able to share anything! Who would listen to my testimony after seeing these fools act like that?

Of course, not everyone there was like that. One of the waitresses in the restaurant part, from the other side of the bar, who had a family in Fishersburg right outside of Lapel, was very sweet to me, and her family invited me over to their house for dinner many times! I was so grateful for that and their company.

That church I went to in Lapel decided to embarass me openly in the congregation one time, but it backfired! The pastor's son who was definitely no Christian with his dirty jokes outside the church called me out after I was clapping to worship songs the praise team was doing. He spoke on the mic to me from the pulpit and decided he was going to chastise me in front of everybody! He got on the mic and said, "Richard? There are complaints that you clap too loud when songs are being presented up here!" He smirked and said, "You're going to have to tone it down a bit!" I was stunned by the comment for a moment and then I calmly spoke back, "I deeply apologize, because I was feeling a preview of heaven!" He said, "Heaven?" I said, "Yes, I was feeling the music so much that I just let my emotions go, and I was clapping like I was in heaven, where they have no complaints in the Department of How Loud a Person Claps!" It got real quiet in the congregation after I said that, and the guy who called me out from the pulpit on stage had a blank look on his face! I continued, "I didn't realize I was in the church library where you are to make no noise. I apologize!" I really thought I was in a church congregation that worshipped God with their hands, as well as their mouths, but was wrong! I continued, "Your argument would hold no water if other members of this church joined in clapping, as well; then you wouldn't even hear me when I clap, because the others joining in would drown out my own clapping." Then I stood up and turned around and said, "Isn't that right?" in a loud voice as I looked around the congregation! They were all dumbfounded except for a few who clapped when I said that! I looked at the Assistant Pastor and said,

"Anymore complaints?" He didn't answer, he just looked at me. I said, "The stage is all yours!" You could have heard a pin drop!

I had faithfully been a part of that church for over three years, and did whatever they asked of me, and supported them in everything they did, including helping build the upstairs gymnasium! And two kinds of gossip went around that small town, where everybody has to know about everyone else's business, because they can't focus on their own. And the gossip was, "That homeless guy in town; what is he doing here?" And, "Did you see those church people carrying on at the bar? Why, they are no better than we are!" And sadly, they were right!

In the end, I was extremely glad to be getting out of Lapel and back in Anderson, again! To this day, I thank God for the homelessness experience, because I identify with what the homeless go through! Being back in Anderson started a new development in my life, where I was to take residency in this cold, tiny trailer that I was very grateful for. It was in their backyard area, and I gave them something a week for rent, to help them out with their three kids, who I got to know very well and loved like they were my own family. I volunteered to do the dishes every night, because they were feeding me, as well, and they would pick me up from my job in Lapel, right before I was to quit. It got to the point where the Mexican restaurant that first hired me full-time cut me all the way down to 10 hours a week! I was faithful to that Mexican restaurant in Lapel, and they treated me like dirt. I felt like it was discrimination, as I was the only Caucasian male that worked there, and everybody else was Mexican. I received a meal on the job and the owner at one point called me "the white Speedy Gonzales" because he said I was faster than anybody he'd ever seen! (God gave me the speed because I used to box in practice sessions with a big guy named Chris, who sharpened what I was to do, until the day of his heart attack. The doctor told him he had to stop, because it was putting a strain on his heart, so he never boxed again. And I had fast hands as a forward in basketball, where I could strip the ball from my opponents that I was assigned to guard, in my early years.) They started me up 40 hours a week and slowly, slowly, slowly, they cut my hours, for no reason at all! I was faithful to that job and worked hard, and this was my reward for hard work? I busted my tail every night I worked there. I regret, even today, quitting my part-time construction job that I'd had previously, to work for those people who acted like that.

Tom was my construction boss, who was great to work for, though he was stern. If I would have known how the restaurant job would end up, I never would have applied there. I was a hard worker and I know the difference between working hard and being used like a pack mule. The only thing I liked about that place was the food. I'm sure that restaurant is still there, today. The food was great, and the waitresses were very nice, but the attitude toward me was horrible.

And the people I was staying with decided I needed to get work in Anderson, where they lived, where I used to live before the Lapel situation! I was more than happy to apply somewhere else! I applied for about five jobs in Anderson, and one of them liked my restaurant ability. And they were impressed with my experience, because I had built up a reputation working for the Mexican restaurant in Lapel. My new bosses couldn't figure out why the Mexican restaurant in Lapel would treat someone with my restaurant ability and speed like they did. I never found out why, either. I mean, really? Ten hours a week? Now, who could live on that?

I worked many hours in my first few days there at my new job; in fact, in one day there, I worked more hours than I had in one week at the other place! My bosses were very pleased with me, and told me so! They told me, "That restaurant's loss is our gain!" One boss told me that I was like a football draft pick that was slated to get drafted in the first round, only to drop until the fifth round, where they would sign me! Another boss on that new job told me that I was lightning fast, and quicker than anybody they had! I was flattered by that, and I told them that God gives me the ability to work fast. My boss frowned at me and said, "I wish God would give these guys that same ability to be that fast!" He said, "We are so glad to have you, you know firsthand how crazy busy it gets back in that kitchen! But you handle everything back there like a seasoned veteran of dishwashing!" I told him, "I have had some practice!" He laughed and said, "You sure did; I'm so glad you're with us, Richard!" And I said, "So am I."

A couple of nights later, they hooked me and another employee up, and he didn't have that speed the other managers had told me about, so we were getting way behind as he insisted that he wanted to wash! What could I do? I couldn't force him to do something else, and like a train wreck, we were getting way behind! Finally, one of the shift managers came back to our area and saw the mess. He wasn't happy, and he looked at me. I said, "The guy you insisted on putting to work with me tonight told me that he was going to wash, and now you see the results of the situation for yourself!" He told me, "I have something for you and him to do real quick that needs to be taken care of! And when you're done, I want you to wash, since you're the fast one here!" I looked at the mess and surmised to him, "It will take me over two hours to get it straightened up!" He said, "If anyone can do it, you're the man that can. Richard, you are the fastest thing on two wheels we got! And don't be surprised, because the other managers have seen your lighting-fast work in such a short amount of time, and all three of us agree that we're going to give you a dollar raise because we think you are that good! No other dishwasher we have ever had, including now, can match this lightning-fast speed we have seen from you!" I said, "Thank you," I blushed, and added, "I hope to do this place proud!"

So before I could finish up the dishes, we were asked to dump some trash into a compactor, which was about a foot and a half over our heads. This meant we had to lift these trash cans from the ground up over our heads into this hole in the wall where we would slide the trash into the compactor. The problem is, these three trash cans probably weighed about 230 to 240 pounds, because they were full, not only of garbage, but of sopping water that was dumped into them. The other guy was a little bigger and stronger than I was, for I was probably about half his size, and he was taller than my six feet! So there we were, from the ground up, lifting these heavy trash cans into this compactor. It was a strain to lift this first can alone, as I put everything I had in it just to get it off the floor. With him on one side and me on the other, we lifted.

It was either the first trash can or the second one when I felt three pops, like the sound Rice Krispies make: Snap! Crackle! And Pop! My lower back popped, my left arm rotator cuff popped, and my lower abdominal area popped! I doubled over as I signaled to the other employee that I was experiencing incredible pain! I was in instant agony, and it was hard to breathe because I felt the huge hernia in my breathing. I had to remain calm. He went and told my employer that I was injured, but nobody came to check on me! I had to get off my knees and go physically tell the employer myself what had just happened! He said, "Can you work?" I looked at him, breathing hard, "No, I can't work, I need to see a doctor, now!" He looked at me and said, "Ok!" And that's all he said! I was shocked, thinking to myself, *I thought these guys cared, but now him and the kitchen staff are looking at me like I've done something wrong!* I looked at them all and just shook my head; they didn't know or seemed to act like they didn't care about the ordeal I just went through; they only cared if I could still work! *What cold-blooded people,* I thought.

The manager told one of the employees to drive me to an all-night clinic, not the hospital! After an X-ray, the clinic told me I was going to need emergency surgery, as soon as they diagnosed a baseball-sized hernia. They said that if I didn't, I could die! I was numb when I heard this, and all I could do was to think to myself as the pain increased, *If a guy has a thing like this called a hernia, then would a woman's hernia be a his*nia? I don't know why this entered my mind at the time, but it did. It got my mind off the pain for a moment, and I relived it in my mind over and over again, like a slow-motion video reel, as I tried to process what had just happened; it made me shudder! I did get the surgery for only the hernia, I think it was the next day, though I can't remember, because I was blacking out on the way to the hospital, and I barely remember anything that happened after that night! I do remember thinking before I closed my eyes and wondering, *Am I going to make it through this?* But, here I am today telling you this: by the Grace of God, it wasn't my time to go!

My lower back was never checked out, and the rotator cuff injury was never checked out, either. Here it is, 2019, and those two things, the rotator cuff injury and the lower back injury, still affect me today! Workman's Comp never took care of those things! All they did was give me surgery for the baseball-sized hernia, and I think that's wrong that they didn't check out everything that was injured. Plus, my former employer was trying to force me with extortion to get back into work immediately after surgery, and if I didn't, they said they would call Workman's Comp and say that I refused to come back to work, which was a total, bogus lie! I have never refused to work at any time in my life when I have been healthy! I have worked after my Navy experience when I was a teen, and of course most of my life. The deviousness of this employer was on full display right before my eyes as I was trying to heal from my surgery bandages!

And so, this employer decidedly was going to have them cut me off my weekly work benefits! Well, what good are a worker's rights if an employer can tamper with your right to receive your benefits and lie against you? This was another situation just like the former pastor and his scheming bunch! I wondered, *Does the employer even care that I live or die by trying to take away money that I really need?* The big boss even called me up one day and told me right on that phone that they were going to lie to Workman's Comp and say I was healthy to work again, after only two days trying to heal from surgery, and that, if I didn't return to work soon, the weekly compensation checks were going to be cut off! I didn't receive many of these. I was trying to follow my doctor's advice after surgery! I bet you my doctor then would have been mad at my employer for trying to extort me to come back to a job that I physically wasn't able to do yet! I told my employer, "Three people will know about this lie you're trying to pull over on Workman's Comp—you, me—" then he interrupted me, saying, "And who is that third person, Richard?" I said, "That third person is the most important one," I said, "for that person is God!" He got quiet for a moment, "And it's Him, on my behalf, you will have to deal with! I'm His child, and He sees your deception, and your lies!" "Nevertheless," he said, "You can either come back to your job or lose out on your weekly checks for what happened to you, and lose your job on top of it! So, basically, you have a choice!" And he hung up the phone.

God, they're trying to force me back to work, this is in Your hands, for I trust You, Lord! I actually could have contacted an attorney at the time and sued this corrupt employer, but at that time, I just didn't think of that; I was still just trying to heal from that surgery. After that, I would be able to return to work, and I would also have loved to have shown the attorney where I got injured and let him see for himself how dangerous that area was where the incident occurred. This would have added more damaging evidence in a court case against the employer, who decidedly put me into a very hazardous situation, a situation that caused injuries I have never healed from! And the employer wanted to deliberately lie to Workman's Comp, saying I'm healthy right after surgery to return back to work! All because they wanted their fastest dishwasher back. They even tried to guilt-trip me, saying that it would take four people just to cover what I do. I was flattered by that, but that still wasn't any reason for me to return! My surgery stitches were still very raw! The doctor had told me it would be about six weeks before I could return back to work, with the limitations of no heavy lifting! Plus it would be a nightmare working in that kitchen, having to recall what had happened before, in that next room over where we dumped that heavy trash that night! I still can't believe that actually happened! But it did happen, and I have to live with it.

What's really strange is that I didn't quit the job and I wasn't fired from it, either; I had every intention of going back to work there again. I was between a rock and a hard place. Without work, I wouldn't be able to eat, either. It was forcing me to go back to work, against the doctor's better judgement. That would be like taking someone who just had foot surgery and telling them that they had to run in a marathon! It can't be done, and that saying that "Time heals all wounds" is possibly correct, but I wasn't given enough time, and the wounds didn't have enough time to heal! What was I to do? At this point, I was homeless and being forced to go back to my job if I ever wanted to eat again! I cried out to God in my pain and anguish and said, *Please, show me what to do?* No answer came that night, so I decided to ride my bike downtown before the weather started getting real cold and go to the library. I felt prompted in my heart to get on my Facebook account, but I didn't understand why. I'd learned to listen to that tugging on my heart, so I clicked onto my account. I had a message!

It was the contact person I had been talking to from Boston since

December 31, 2015, where we met online on Facebook! She and I talked on and off in Anderson, when we first met online, and she had tried to get ahold of me. I replied, "Hi, I heard you've been wanting to talk to me? What's up?" She said, "Richard? You've really been on my heart lately, and I really care about you and your homeless situation! And I was praying to God to help you, and this is what God showed me. He spoke to my heart to ask you: Would you like to start life over again, here in Boston?"

I was speechless. I couldn't say a word! This spoke volumes to me! Not only through this female friend was God saying that, but it was not His will that I go back to the job after being forced to make the decision to be forced to work, or die as a homeless man. God was offering a plan of escape from the city I once loved, and a new start to a city I had never seen! It was scary but intriguing! My eyes were opening to the thought of a new life, a new start, a new adventure in a big city called Boston! I told her, once I was over being stunned, that I had been praying, as well, that I felt that this was the will of God for my life to do this. I said, "You really encouraged me just now!" Being forced to work or die was no longer an option I had to deal with. Instead, God made his own option, and he did it through someone I hadn't even met yet! Within about two months it was going to happen. I just had to hold on until that help came.

She forwarded money to me so that I could eat. I used that 100 dollars wisely with one meal a day at Mcdonald's for almost a month. Eating one meal a day when you're really hungry was a real test, in itself! I was determined not to eat at least two meals a day, because the money would have run out within two weeks. I had to discipline myself to not want another meal on any given day; my life depended on it! God gave me wisdom and it was being tested. When you're hungry, you find out what you're really made of, and the God who made you!

Thank God the water was free at Mcdonald's! It was a little bit of a walk, but it was worth it to stay hydrated. When it got really cold, that water that you got to go from Mcdonald's would freeze within minutes after you went outside! And so you just tried to drink whatever ice would melt in the plastic cup. I would go to different areas and just try to sleep the night away from human eyes, sometimes under a tree! You got whatever you could get and just hoped to hold on until morning, when you'd be frozen, but alive. And I bought a few snacks like peanut butter and crackers to keep me going, which lasted about two weeks. And also I kept a plastic knife from my meal for the snack I had. So for the last month, I was just going to have to dig deep and survive. Another Anderson friend saw me and gave me 30 dollars, and that helped me immensely! I kept telling myself, *One more month to go before Boston, you have got to hold on!* For the last two weeks of that second month, there would be no more food, and stuff would come to my mind to remind me that a better life was coming. *You have got to focus! Hold on, you can do it!*

My mind would flash back as I was freezing in my sleep. Things I used to say came to me, like this: *You know when you've had a major snowstorm in Indiana when the Twinkies and Ding Dongs disappear off the shelves and the generic snacks have been left behind!* And when I was a courier driver in Indianapolis, we would have to dodge giant potholes from the bad weather in the road! I used to call it the Pothole Olympics, where the winner's prize is just keeping the delivery vehicle intact on the road and staying alive! Because if your vehicle fell into one of these giant holes, then they might never see you again.

And then my mind thought of a bizarre but true story that happened to me in the winter of 2013 that I will never ever forget! I was driving on I-65 in Indianapolis doing my deliveries, when the weather started changing to frozen hail. It started to pelt my windshield and I thought it was going to crack my windshield, but thank God, it didn't! I wouldn't have been able to explain to my boss why his employee's face was pink and blue and bruised up from all the iced-up hail. Anyway, thank God that didn't happen!

Before the change in weather, our speed limit was an average of about 70 miles an hour. The sky was starting to darken at about 4 pm in the afternoon, still clear enough to see though; the road was getting real slippery and I applied my brakes slowly to reduce my speed. I started to slow to about 50 miles an hour, and all of a sudden, my front wheels were spinning a little bit. I thought, *That's a bit odd. I have front wheel drive.* Little by little, the van started to turn in different directions, and I couldn't control it. As I turned the steering wheel in the direction the van was turning, it suddenly turned left, where I couldn't see which way the van was starting to spin! I went into panic mode and started praying, *God, please help me! I'm outta control.* I almost said, *Jesus take the wheel!* As the van was starting to fully turn on the freeway, I was well aware there was traffic behind me, and there was nothing I could do about it! I thought to myself, *This might be it, I might die, and end up smashed against a guardrail after spinning out of control, or smashed by vehicles behind me, wondering what is going on!* It didn't look good at all! I closed my eyes to God and said, *Lord! I am yours! In the next few moments, this van is going to wreck somewhere.*

I had my seat belt on, so I tried the brakes slowly, one more time, and hoped for the best. All of a sudden, the van made a violent spin, and I thought, *This is it! Heaven, next stop! I love you, Megan!* I wanted to close my eyes, but I couldn't. I braced myself hard for impact! They always say not to brace yourself for impact before a crash, but who are these people that say this? The van made one violent spin as I saw my life flashing before my eyes! My speed read 45 miles an hour, but the brakes had locked when I tried to use my pedal more! This van was out of control in its final spin and I could see the traffic behind me, then in front of me, as I spun backwards! I was supposed to see where I was going, not where I'd been. The van didn't stop there, and for a brief moment, I thought how odd it would be to hit the traffic from behind, like I was driving backwards! I saw a big semi. But, oddly, the van kept spinning and the next thing I knew, it spun all 360 degrees so I could then see the road ahead of me. I was shaken! I was stirred. But I was alive! And the only explanation I could come up with as to why I was still alive was because Jesus really did take the wheel. I played this scene in my mind back in slow motion as I saw terrified looks on drivers' faces. Was I about to meet my maker? I just knew that I had no control and there was no logical explanation as to why I didn't get killed. Amen...

And then my mind raced again as I was tossing and turning in the frozen weather, trying to get warm. From one night to the next I didn't know if I would survive or not till the next day, it's a hard faith in extreme circumstances but you really have to trust God if you're going to make it out of your situation! I thought about how others had tried to force me to go back to work despite my injuries if I wanted to eat! When I think about that from time to time, my mind flashbacked in the extreme cold I guess it was a way to get my mind off the weather, reminded of Abraham and a difficult decision that he was going to have to make concerning his son Isaac of the Old Testament. In the story, God asked him to sacrifice his son as a token of devotion and worship to God, and Abraham probably had sorrow in his heart for what was to take place. But he obeyed and started to build the altar that he was to use to sacrifice his son. His son Issac said, "Father? Where is the sacrifice for this altar?" Abraham looked at his son, probably with tears welling up in his eyes, and said, "My son? God will supply the sacrifice!" So in obedience, Abraham placed his only son, who was now a young teenager, on the altar. Just like Jesus would do in the New testament for our lives, become a sacrifice for us so that we could live!He would takeOur place on a bloody cross for your sins and mine! Just as Abraham was about to take his precious son's life, God intervened and told him, "Abraham! Do not sacrifice your son Isaac. I see your love and devotion for me!" Abraham probably let out a flood of grateful tears as Issac pulled his only son off the sacrificial altar! God did provide the sacrifice for that altar, after all, when he allowed what I believe was a ram to be caught right next to the altar! And that was going to be the sacrifice that would please God, his heavenly father, that day! And I'm sure Issac was relieved, as he probably went home with Abraham to tend to the sheep! They didn't have Playstation or Nintendo back then, so I'm sure he occupied himself, somehow!

The point I'm making using this example is this: Abraham did have a will to choose from whether he was going to listen to God and obey and follow through painful as it was, but out of his love for God he chose to obey and trust God! He didn't know if God would come through or not, but his devotion to his Creator was strong, and he had great faith! I felt I had the choice to trust God and hopefully make it without going back to work which would have ruined me physically when I wasn't healed from surgery yet! Or do their forced choice I of being forced to go back to work, even through an unhealed surgery. God honored the fact that I was willing to go back, because I, too, had no choice, and so God made a way of an escape for me, because he knew I trusted Him, anyway. I probably would have been injured more going back to work, but I was going to do it if there was no other way out, but like Abraham was going to sacrifice his son, and I was going to sacrifice my body! God gave me a way of escape through my friend in Boston who I really got to know pretty well up to this point from Facebook and I really liked her and I know she liked me! God honored us both! God honors hard faith when you're in a situation and you do the right thing through him Abraham's son Issac grew, and God made a way of escape for me to Boston. He was going to have my friend provide the money for the rest of the Amtrak train ticket needed for Boston! Before my Workman's Comp was to be cut off, God had prompted me to save some money back with each check, and I didnt know why. So, it turns out, the money I saved, along with my friend's money, would be just enough for my bus ride to Indianapolis and eventual train ride, one way, to Boston. I wasn't going to be coming back unless it was to see my church friends outside of lapel and the church in Anderson I got involved in when I was homeless,! After that injury, I wore a back brace to try to ease the throbbing pain in my back as much as possible! I can't tell you who that employer is in this book, but I can tell you this much: they are probably the only restaurant in Anderson, Indiana, that has a chocolate fountain for ice cream and other desserts! Maybe you can figure it out from there, and, yes, it did happen, I did get my weekly Workman's Comp checks cut off, right at the point where, as a homeless man, I needed them the most! But I refused to panhandle and asked people for money, for I just didn't have it in me to do that. At that point, the actual thought of dying without food or just freezing to death had occurred to me! I thought, *This is it, I'm going to heaven before my time, and everything I hoped to accomplish in this life is no longer going to be a possible reality!* So I just prepared myself mentally for that possibility.

I mean, really, just how low can an employer get? At that point, I was really hating being in Indiana. But thank God, the person I met on Facebook from Boston helped everything to change! I didn't hate the people of Indiana, but I hated the corrupt ways, and I have no desire to ever go there again to live, except to visit some of my friends! If somebody rescues you from a burning fire like my friend did in Boston, you dont hop back into that same fire of homelessness! Once I got out of Indiana,I was to feel a real peace and excitement that I hadn't felt in a long time! I was ready to start life anew! And I had an excitement that I couldn't even begin to explain! When I got to Boston and got set up within a few days I was able to get Masshealth Insurance! And it was easy to get EBT, which is food stamps, one day after I applied! If you apply for emergency food stamps back in Indiana, I hope you will have a six-month waiting plan in place, because that's how long it took me, back then, when I applied! You had to be either literally starving to death with your tongue hanging down to your knees, or halfway dead, or both, to get some kind of assistance. To add insult to injury, so to speak, even then they would refer you over to food banks to see if you qualify, just so you could eat! Gee, no thanks! After all that, you're going to put someone through to a food bank to see if they even qualify, while they have no more food? Newsflash to Muncie, Indiana, and your so-called help programs: take an example from a big city like Boston and see how they help people in their own city, and how quick they do it! And keep in mind, Muncie Food Stamps, this city I live in has a lot more mouths to feed than your city does, which makes it even more phenomenal! I would say that Boston does more for their people in this city than the whole state of Indiana does for their homeless! I've been to the capital city of Indianapolis, and I know how they treat the homeless there, like they're some kind of blight on society!

I knew many people who lived under the bridge, because I became friends with them before I was to become homeless. I would try to feed them, whenever my job had assignments in the city. We have many homeless people, as well, but we have a very compassionate mayor and governor, and many, many programs in Boston to help our homeless, our low-income, and our seniors! This is a huge city with way more responsibility! I have never, ever regretted the move to get out of Indiana at that time! And I never will. Boston is this author's home!

My mind sometimes flashes back to that do-or-die situation from my boss and what was going to take place in Anderson, after he hung up on me. I was to lose the place in the basement where I had been offered to stay was now becoming a real reality but I wasn't going to be able to stay there any longer, after I had been there a little while after I first spent a couple of weeks in that little trailer, because they were going to bring their grandmother over, even though they had me move in the house for a little bit before this even took place!

One bright spot during that time was that there was a church next door to their house, and I was curious to check it out, so I did! And I liked this church. The pastor and the people were very friendly! I could worship God in peace there, after all I'd been through! The church was called New Horizons United Methodist Church, and it was awesome. They are on Youtube, and I'm on there with them. What an awesome friendly church they were. I miss them! They are the only reason that I would ever even consider coming back to visit Anderson for about a week. And see my friends in the church outside of Lapel Indiana as well God willing!

Little did I know, my time was going to be up at the house next door soon! But before that happened, I invited the whole family to this church, and three of them came with me. How awesome that was! The mother came down in front and prayed in front of the whole church, and I think her kids joined her as well And in December Christmas 2015, I was invited to do a duet with the music director of the church doing a song called "Mary Did You Know?" What an experience that was! Amen. The pastor also asked me to do "Oh, Holy Night" on Christmas morning there, which was an awesome service! Both of those services are on Youtube. The music director and I, along with another person of the church, were practicing to do another song called "The Lord's Prayer," but alas, it was not meant to be, because the family's grandma needed to be picked up from the airport in Indianapolis, and I had to put all of my things in storage before they brought her back. I never got to meet the grandmother because they have me out of the house before that I think they were ashamed To let the grandmother know who I was and that they rescued Me! and the really sad part is that I saw how they had talked about me to others on Facebook after I left. It wasn't nice, and they spoke of how I used them to stay there. I was shocked when I read that, because it was their offer to have me come and stay there, which I was grateful for, and I offered to pay weekly rent to help them out, Which I did and do the dishes daily, which I did! Keep in mind, I wasn't making much after the Mexican restaurant started decreasing my hours, so I gave them almost everything I had every week, including helping to pay for groceries. And before I was to leave, I helped him and another son to clean out his much-needed car garage.

I don't understand, to this day, how people who took you in can later turn on you? That's really sad to me,the very same people I trusted and who had trusted me Would turn on me later on in Facebook! Why would they lie before God about the truth while I was there? Going behind my back on Facebook when I had been nothing but honest and truthful before them? How do people even act like this? I trusted these people, and I invited them to church! As I'm drifting back thinking about lapel my eyes are almost frozen shut now,as my thoughts are drifting in and out as I'm recalling life in Lapel! And of course how I got to this current situation! For the next couple of months it was going to be a real challenge of life and death survival that's where the real test was going to be! at that point I'm tired and drifting in and out of consciousness I try to stay awake but I'm losing the battle! My mind recalls where I was before Anderson all over again, at that point in my sleep I would have welcomed death, it was so bitterly cold! My mind flashed back to that horrible September month of 2015!

I was homeless for about two weeks in Lapel before I came back to Anderson after I was told to leave that abandoned house in September 2015, and somebody told me about this little church in Fishersburg, Indiana, which I am grateful for today. It is a small Wesleyan Church, just right outside of Lapel. They didn't care if I was homeless or not. They took me in like I was one of their own before I moved to Anderson. They treated me very, very well! They understood my situation and they didn't care! They treated me like gold. And they had me do a song there! I was so grateful for that church, and I hope it prospers today! It's a very small church with the heart of God! And I definitely know that God is pleased with the people there! They were ordinary people like me, but they treated me like an equal! I want to give a shout-out to that church and their pastor, if he's still around, to let them know how much the author of this book appreciated them. They were one of the few bright spots when I was homeless, after they boarded up the abandoned house in Lapel, right before I was to leave! I remember Jesus said in his word, "When you've done it unto the least of these, you've done it unto me!" And they took care of me like I was one of their own! I wish I could have spent more time going to church there. They treated me like family!

Anyway, reality was setting in as I realized it was wintertime in Anderson, January 2016, and I had to think about where to put my things. So I decided to get a storage unit and put my things in there for a couple of months so they would be safe as I tried to survive in the cold! In addition, before I was asked to move out of the home that I thought I was in the presence of friends, it was starting to get extremely cold, wind drifts and heavy snow blowing across my face made life miserable for me! I wasn't the only one in Anderson struggling to survive, there were other homeless people, as well! And from time to time, I would come across them!

To get my mind off the extreme cold when I got up in the morning, I would start running and running and running some more, until I was out of breath! I had first started running in Lapel. The reality of it was about to become as real as it gets, with the frigid cold icy winds and weather headed our way right after December 2015. The weather was to drop past zero, and God told me to run. And run daily, I did, and that's how this homeless person overcame his biggest test of all— surviving that Indiana winter! I hid my bike from sight, since I could no longer ride on it, for I was now on frozen and icy ground! About 15 to 20 miles daily I ran, just to survive, hardly able to see the ground or even what was in front of me, because the icy, windy snow drifts would blind your eyes. So I tried to run smart with my head down, covering ground slowly, but steadily! If I could survive this daily, then I felt I could survive whatever was ahead in the long run! The devil should have asked God to take my life! But he didn't, he just wanted me to suffer, and suffer, I did, a lot! And my hands and feet were frozen with extreme frostbite! I would try to push my hair out of my eyes with frozen hands when it got really windy, and couldn't even feel my hands doing it! And I couldn't even feel my face; my feet felt like frozen logs of wood running on a numb body that couldn't feel any kind of physical sensation. And in Indiana, it became painful and eye-opening to find out that there were only certain people you could trust! How sad was that? Other than God, you didn't know who to trust? I became careful when I would talk to someone.

I kept running up on my days off from work. Little did I know, that would help me in Anderson. So my instinct was to keep from freezing to death every day, I would run! I'd wear a weight belt for my back pain, and because I no longer had a pants belt, God spoke to my heart to go to an auto parts store close by and get a bungee cord! I found a couple that were cheaply-priced and could stretch through the loops, holding my pants up! And I had a homeless friend about my waist size who needed a belt, so that was a no- brainer to get him one, as well! That friend happened to be the guy who asked for five dollars for the bike he would sell me. He loved his bungee cord belt, and I loved mine! I never would have thought of using a bungee cord to hold up my jeans. God is amazing! And I would run to ease up my lower back with that back brace! No matter what the weather was, I ran! I would run, come back exhausted, and prepare for the cold night somewhere, anywhere I could lie my head! So, I know what a homeless person goes through. I know what a person in pain goes through, and there are things that happened in my life earlier that I will share in a later book that I went through. I tried to get into the Christian Ministries Shelter a few times during that time, but they had no openings; everybody was going to stay put in that frigid winter and not go anywhere. I didn't blame them; I would have done the same thing!

I stayed in the discipline of running those couple of months where it was absolutely freezing frigid cold enough to kill you if you weren't active! At night, I would try to find anywhere I could just to survive, just to make it through the night! The person I was talking to in Boston offered a solution one day and said, "If you have any money left from your Workman's Comp check, save it, and I will send over a little bit of money that I can to help you get a train ticket and get you down here, out of that extreme cold!" I was grateful for that! And in those kinds of Indiana weather conditions, you don't know how long you're going to survive! Plus, the money from my Workman's Comp checks were running out. I had to do something! I felt that this was going to be the answer to my prayer! And I thank God to this day, in August 2019, I have never looked back on that fateful decision!So as I was preparing to leave for a huge City I had never been in before in a state I had never been in before kind of like Abraham of the Old testament moving his family I proceeded on a bus with my boxes from Anderson Indiana to Indianapolis Indiana where I was going to catch the train that was going to bring me to Boston! I was extremely excited and pumped! Who wouldn't be? If you had a chance to go from a death situation to a life situation you would be pumped as well where you could start all over again and feel like you have new life,and yout To go from a city that was roughly about 50,000 people to a city the size of Boston! That's quite a shock! But I was ready to take on the new challenge! As I arrived in Indianapolis heading over to where I was to catch my train it was going to be a little bit of a wait and I would sleep in the train terminal until my train was to arrive, as I went to get my ticket and check in my baggage and my boxes which I had four of them I received a rude awakening! It was not mentioned to me over the phone when I talked to Amtrak personnel that it was going to be extra for the four boxes I was to bring on my trip! I went from a complete High to a complete low! Another setback! I thought to myself dear God I'm never going to make it to Boston and if I do I'll have to get rid of my boxes because I don't have the money to bring them on the train I was never told about! I asked for a few minutes with the ticket area and I would be right back as I would now have to assess a new situation, all the money I had was Ford the one-way train ticket to Boston and what little money I had for food on my journey on the train! I had nothing at all left over if I would have known this over the phone call with Amtrak I would have somehow made a way to have the money I needed for the boxes so that I could get them on board safely and paid for with no worries whatsoever! But now this was going to be my stress challenge and it was eating me up inside that if I cannot get my own boxes on this train when it's my time to leave I'll be leaving my only life things left out of my life from being homeless behind! The more I thought about this the more it made me want to cry and I didn't care who saw me because I was that frustrated right now and really about to go over the edge in my sanity after working so hard to get this together! I prayed but I did know what to do I was absolutely stuck! My train was supposed to come sometime tomorrow and if I didn't come up with the solution I wouldn't to be able to bring my boxes with me! I thought to myself at that point one thing after another when is this nightmare going to end? During my time in the terminal I met a nice guy and his girlfriend I can't remember his name but her name was Jessica Knight, and that's the only thing I remember of this couple other than she was seeing her boyfriend off back to Georgia where he lived it was extremely nice I wish I could remember his name? We got acquainted and after a couple of hours they trusted me enough that they asked me to watch her boyfriend's belongings well they went out and had a meal, I told them not a problem at all I'm not going anywhere I'm right here and I even showed them my ID they didn't ask for it but I wanted to let them know I was the person they were talking to! And showing ID shows trust to the person you're talking to because they see your personal information! They were grateful that I was going to watch their things while they went out to eat something, it came back about an hour and a half later and thanked me for watching his things, and I said not a problem I said myself I have a dilemma, he said, what's the problem bro? I let them know that I was told I was not going to be able to bring my boxes on my train because they surprised me with an extra fee that was not discussed over the phone! And so I let them know I was going to lose my boxes and I was going out of my head with anguish after getting so close to getting this done! He looked at me and smiled and said Jessica can watch them for you at her place here in Indianapolis wow you get settled in Boston then you can get ahold of her and get your things back bro and he looked at her and said right? And she smiled and said absolutely! She said you did us a favor now we can do you a favor back! I was overjoyed after hearing this it was like an answer to prayer even though I didn't pray particularly for this! So when it was time for my train to come and the next day I had every reassurance and confidence that his girlfriend would watch my things and that I could trust them and when I'm set up in Boston then I could start sending over a money order or Western Union or MoneyGram or something so I could get my things back at the appointed time! Once I got set up in Boston within a couple of weeks I got a hold of Jessica and I said I'm ready for my things now and I sent a moneygram or a Western Union I don't remember? And she said the money I was sending over wasn't enough? I said that's not true I've had these priced over here in Boston how much it would be! She got a little irritated with me and let me know you have to send more money this won't be enough! Now I was the one getting irritated okay just how much money is it going to take? Is she being honest with me? Or is she trying to extort me for more money then what the price cost? I don't know to this day! I checked on the MoneyGram or Western Union the next day and found out the money had been picked up that I sent even though she said it wasn't enough! I tried to get ahold of her again later in the week her phone had been disconnected! I felt literally sick to my stomach and I was never able to get a hold of Jessica knight ever again I don't know what happened to my things even this day and I had something very special in one of the boxes for the person who rescued me from Boston that she never got to get and everything I had was gone I was stunned and shocked! I don't know to this day if the woman tried to extort and rip me off for my own things with more money? Or perhaps something happened over there I knew nothing about? I'm trying to give it the benefit of the doubt I really am but all I can keep coming up with she said it wasn't enough money but yet she cashed it anyway and she never got back with me again! If she did this against me I want her to know that God saw everything that she did and he holds her accountable for it right now because now it becomes stolen property in the eyes of God that belong to me a believer in Christ! And since she never tried to get back with me it made me very suspicious that she had no intention of getting my things back to me I could be wrong but the evidence is pointing to extortion to me I sent enough money and I also sent extra for her out of appreciation for holding my things and this is what happened when I trusted someone because her boyfriend who was grateful to me for watching his things said she could be trusted? He was very nice and transparent to me seemed like a very trustworthy guy, but to this day I don't know what happened I'm trying to give it the benefit of the doubt, but that ended years ago when she never responded back to me! Jessica Knight if you're out there, I would like it if you'd respond to this author and let me know what happened to my own things when I trusted you? If you don't respond then you're guilty it's that simple and you never intended to get my things to me by trying to get more money out of me! And this is sad because I really trusted you because of your boyfriend! So with that painful realization I was never going to see my things again I just had to move forward the best I could with the little things that I had left on my own person a suitcase full of things and a backpack full of things with a hole in it! Everything else was in those boxes God knows exactly what happened and the intent of that woman! You're on God's time now Jessica if you're still around!

The person I had met online in Indiana and later saw face-to-face in Boston was a real treat. She and I got really, really close, but it eventually didn't work out, because she didn't like the fact that I wanted to seek out a shelter and not stay with her. It would have been wrong for me to stay with a woman I wasn't married to. She was a Christian, as well, and eventually understood what I was saying, but she still wasn't happy about it because we really liked each other. I was developing deep feelings about her within a month, after we met online, that fateful night of December 31st, 2015. Little did I realize then that God was going to use her to save my life in Indiana! I deeply appreciated how God had used her to be able to bring me to Boston, and I repaid that kindness back by helping her out with her bills and groceries, later on in 2016, when I became an established worker working for the Southampton Shelter, up until the time I got knee replacement surgery, Feb. 7th, 2018.

- That surgery not only altered my work life, but my physical desire to continue my training for the Boston Marathon! Do I regret having this surgery? Absolutely! The worst decision I've ever made physically with my body it never got better after that! The only positive thing I took from it was that I can now identify with what a disabled person goes through, and I fight for that cause, as well, wanting to see changes made for the disabled. I never asked for this kind of fight, but I'm in it now! And I will talk about that in the second book and other things as well concerning Boston!

Here it is now, almost three and a half years later, and I still haven't experienced this whole city of Boston. I learned the entire city of Anderson, Indiana, in a year! Even if I had to start over life in Boston at a men's shelter, I would do it, and that's exactly what happened! This author is grateful to God for watching over his life when I really thought I was going to die after September 2015, and I was ready to go to heaven at that point thinking I completed everything I was supposed to do or had tried to do, at that point, on this Earth! I'm sure the devil is kicking himself in the head that he didn't ask God to take my life when he had the chance! Because now it's going to backfire on him! Through this book, any future music, and anything else his spirit wants me to do in this life! You see, God watched out for me through the horrible situations in Indiana and brought me through where I am today, as the author of this book and a songwriter on YouTube, going on a couple of years now! I've been in my place now, almost a full year, and it's been the greatest place I have ever lived in my life! The peace I have here is amazing! God has brought me through a lot of things! And yes, I do miss my pets! It was painful what happened to them! Will I get more pets again? I hope, someday, but not now! God has been through everything in my life with me! There have been more developments, and life continues daily here in my city of Boston, and I can't wait to see the newer things as they come to pass in my life! And if it's God's will to keep the volume series going Book 2 is going to be this, Lifestories Vol 2 The continuation of Boston!

I want to thank my friends: the Garry George family of Anderson, Indiana, for being a blessing in my life when I was homeless in Lapel, and their son, Garri George, Jr. He brought a better sound out of the Gospel rock CD of my own that was completed in 1998, and is in the chapter in this book called, "What is the Purpose?" He did this work in his basement studio in Anderson, and I loved their Christmas party invites! Their Christmas tree in their living room was so huge, it dwarfed everything else! You couldn't even see around it, it was that big! And their Christmas meals were a chef's delight! Nobody went hungry; they stuffed me with leftovers! And I also wanted to mention that Garry George Sr. and his family are extremely blessed with musical talent! Everybody can sing and everybody can play instruments! I had one of their CDs, but I don't know what happened to it, and that bothered me immensely, and one of his daughters I heard has a voice like no one I'd ever heard before, like an extremely angelic-sounding, high alto/soprano voice! I was blown away and mesmerized! And she complimented my voice, as well, which I was very flattered by, almost like being in the throne room of heaven, hearing an angel sing! She is that good! I will never, ever forget them!

They remind me of a group on Youtube that is called the 5 Strings! They are another incredible, big family I heard at Christmastime on

Youtube, and their family plays all kinds of instruments and sings phenomenally. When I was in Lapel as a homeless person, hearing The Garry George Family sing in person, it took my mind off my own situation for a few hours, as we all got together, blending our voices, worshipping God! I will never, ever forget my experience with the Garry George Family! And I got to hear them doing a church concert! Can you say, "Wow?!" What a blessing they were! Also, I want to thank my godmother, Barb Finch, and my godsister, Tammy; I love you both with all my heart. And I truly thank God for my friend, Freedom, and some other friends like Trina, my employer and friend in Lapel at that time, and Max, whom I worked with and his family; others at the Woody's Bar and Grill I worked with at the time, friends from that bar who supplied temporary heat to the freezing cold abandoned broken down place I lived at! The roof had major holes in it! Nothing says winter like a winter wonderland coming down in your own front room from many holes in the roof above your head! Snow fell so hard one day it was about a foot of snow on that living room floorAnd so you literally woke up to an ice skating rink! You didn't know if it was colder inside your house or colder outside your house! And if I had any money I would go to the convenience store up the street and buy a gallon of milk, and I would put it on the living room floor knowing that it would be like a refrigerator freezer! So you knew your milk wouldn't spoil! That was quite a visual experience to behold! To some of my friends from the church I was going to that supplied me with things when I needed them; I never asked for one thing, yet God supplied it all! To the waitresses at Woody's who helped me out while I worked there at no salary for over almost a year: thank you for your tips when I bussed tables or at night waited on customers.

Every little bit helped. Thank God for the head waitress who tried to get me onto their porch by her husband making it into a built-in room right onto their porch! It was to be an enclosed room to keep my two cats and me warm, but it never came about. Her husband had concerns about me. He barely knew me, or anything about me, and I don't blame him for that, after all, he was just watching out for his family! I would have as well, So with that in mind, I had to turn down their offer, which I hated doing! But I truly thank God for all of them that God used to bless my life in Lapel, Indiana, in that moment of time, as I wake up the next morning Frozen I realize my time is short that I won't have to wait for much longer to start life over again in Boston! I started counting the weeks just held on for dear life the best I could! The final two weeks was the biggest temptation test I was going to have to face,you see I had a little bit of money left for food, but if I used it now I wouldn't have anything to buy with on the train so I can eat then, so for the last two weeks I just focused my mind on anything but food, my body was physically weak, but I knew the reward would be being the culmination of being on the train and being able to buy some dinners on there as I would make my journey to a place I've never been to! Just like Abraham and his family out of the Old testament! I'm pretty sure Abraham would have taken an Amtrak back then if one was available!☺ But by the grace of God in April 2016 that day did come,I stand here today as a living breathing testimony of the miraculous power of God! if you don't give up, God will come through, but in my mind even at that time if he doesn't come through I will join him in heaven, just like Paul said to live is Christ to die is gain! but you have to have even a little bit of faith, mine was tested beyond what I thought I could believe in when I'm freezing to death, but by that saving grace that saved me years ago sustained me during that rough time and here I stand today as a living breathing testimony of what God can do in a life! If he did it for me,he can do it for you, no matter who you are! I will never ever forget what he had done for me!

CHAPTER 2

SHELTERED

When you find yourself living in a city the size of Boston, you marvel at how little you know about your own surroundings. After all, you just came from a city where you have lived many years working as a courier and restaurant worker, where it was said by others who knew you that you might be one of the fastest dishwashers in Anderson, Indiana, they know. I was very honored by that, but my goal was not to become the fastest dishwasher. My goal was to become whatever God intended me to be, be it dishwasher, busboy, trash collector, or a courier driver like I had done for years. I had no idea at that time that I was going to end up in a city this big, and when I say big, I mean Boston and surrounding areas that make up Boston have about 5.7 million people! That is a far cry from the 60,000 people I congregated with daily in Anderson, Indiana! But I have never regretted coming to this city. This is my home, and I gladly call it such! I am proud to live here.

"Homelessness" is basically defined as no longer residing in a home apartment, studio, or dwelling place you once occupied, and by leaving through no means of your own! In other words, you had no choice but to go! Living anywhere on the street, or in a shelter, halfway house, or anything like that is considered homeless! So even though I knew I was walking away from one situation to another, I was grateful that I was going to be getting off the frozen streets of Anderson, Indiana, when I left!

I don't know what Boston was like in the past. It might be cold now, but it doesn't compare to Indiana's cold weather season or hot weather season. I've been here almost four years, so I would know how cold or how hot it gets here! Anyways, after being invited up here, I was with my contact person for a couple days, and I really wasn't sure what I was going to do, because this was all new to me! But I knew one thing was for sure. I wasn't going to live with them because that would be wrong! In my heart, anyway.

So, I began to ask questions about shelters around the area where I was temporarily residing, because I was serious about starting life over in a men's shelter! I heard about one that was close to the street where I was staying. The person I was staying with was against me living in a shelter! She felt it would be dangerous, since I was new to Boston, and I didn't know anybody other than her. I said, "Yeah, but my conscience says otherwise, and so does my heart! As much as I like you, and I'm glad we finally got to meet, I wouldn't feel right living together, knowing I'm probably missing the will of God!" So, she shook their head in agreement with me, because she was a Christian, too, and understood that I wanted to fulfill the will of God, whatever that was going to be, right here in Boston! Any thoughts of writing a book were going to have to be on the back table because, now, I just wanted to get established in the shelter where God wanted me to be! I heard about a shelter not too far from where I was, and decided to go there and see what it was all about. Fortunately, it was only about three blocks from where we were. Dragging a heavy suitcase and a torn backpack, we both trudged on the bus and headed there. Once I got in front of it, she had tears in her eyes, and said, "You really don't have to do this! We'll work it out before we get into a serious relationship!" I said, "The whole point, hun, is I do have to work it out, and I won't have peace until I find out what it is God wants me to do in this city! So, yes, I am more than ready to do this!" I said, "I'm very, very, grateful for your part in getting me to Boston, which I truly believe was God's will! And when I do make some money, I will pay back that fifty dollars that you used to get me here! I love you for that, and I appreciate you!" She looked over her shoulder and said, "I don't know if I have a good feeling about this!" I said, "I'm not sure, but I have to find out if this is where I'm supposed to be, or not!" So we said our goodbyes, right then and there, and I walked into the shelter.

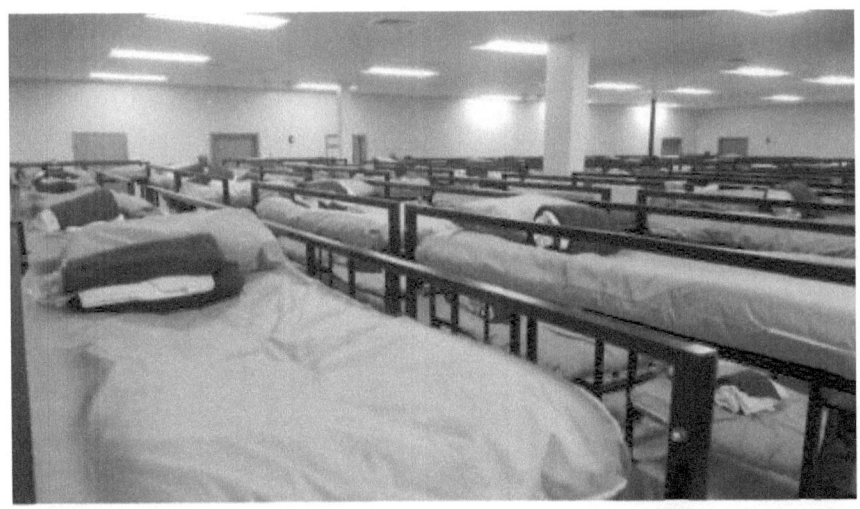

I walked in, expecting to be greeted by someone at the front desk, to find out how to get checked in. I already had gone through their security search, and everything was fine. I was tired, and I was ready to get a bed to rest! Finally, someone showed up at the desk, about 20 minutes later, and gave me a major runaround on how to check in, and told me that I had to wait for another 3 hours before I could talk to someone! I said, "Forget that nonsense!" I said, "I'm cold, I'm hungry, and I'm tired. I'm ready to talk to a human being!" I said, "Can you direct me to another shelter around here?" He said, "One of my supervisors is coming in about 10 minutes, if you want to hang around and talk to him!" When I heard that, new energy arose! I said, "Yes, thank you, I would love that, thank you for your help!" He smiled and said, "It's okay, man!" He said, "Just relax, we'll take care of it!" That put me at ease! Finally, this supervisor comes in, and he's got a very extremely good attitude! I explained my situation to him, and he was very helpful! He said, "I'm very sorry about the runaround you got here this morning, but yes, I'll give you a map, kind of a crude hand map, and I will direct you to another shelter that is walking distance from here! I said, "Thank you, sir, I would love that very much!" He said, "Young man, you have good mannerisms! Are you from around here?" I said, "No, sir, I just arrived from Indiana!" He said, "Well, welcome to you, sir, I hope you find our city a good experience!" "Sir,

I'm hoping so, as well, thank you for your help and your great attitude!" And we said goodbye.

So, with newfound enthusiasm and energy that only God gave, I set off looking for this other place. The snow started coming down, and I had about a 50-pound-or-more suitcase in my hand. It wasn't on wheels or rollers, so I either had to pick it up with me or drag it in the snow as I went! I would alternate doing both. One quick side note: if any of you doubt the validity of what I'm telling you right now in this story, I do have my badge from the shelter to prove it. Anyways, as I started my snowy walk from there, I had to keep brushing off the snow that was coming down in flurries off the flimsy little map, so I could see where I was going. Keep in mind, I'd only been there for a couple of days, so I had no idea what was what, what the streets were, where they went, or anything. I only knew of one or two streets when I got there, so this was a whole different experience, but I was up to the challenge! Talking with that shelter supervisor had renewed my energy, and I was looking forward to finding this other place, wherever it was! I didn't know how long it was going to take me, or where exactly it was, I just knew I was determined to find it! And the funny part is, unknown to me, my destination was only about two miles away. It could have been 20 miles away, for all I knew! But the supervisor did say it was walking distance, and so, I took him at his word. Sometimes, tests come along to see how we respond, and what our attitude is. Are we going to quit? Or are we going to keep going? In order to get to it, you have to go through it! So, I knew I wasn't going to quit, no matter how tired I was getting! I was determined to find this place.

The snow was really falling, then, and I started to run short on breath! I took little rest stops when I could, out of the snow. I wasn't cold, but it was coming down hard! At one of the rest stops, I bowed my head before God and I said, *Dear God, you brought me this far. Now, please lead me the rest of the way to find this place. I have no idea where I'm going, and It's getting harder to read this map! It's starting to smear with the snow on it, please lead me so I can get there. In Jesus' name, Amen! I ask you now to direct my footsteps as I get back on this walk! And I do thank you for hearing this prayer!*

At this point, I don't see street signs that are probably covered by snow, and I had no idea where I was or where I was supposed to go, but I kept saying under my breath, *I trust you, God!* And I meant every word of it! Both my arms were getting tired from dragging that heavy suitcase for many minutes. My body was getting weary from all that walking. When you can barely see in front of you, it's like a scene from a movie, except this was reality! I was starting to get exhausted and a little concerned. *Man, am I ever going to find this place today? And what's more, am I even going in the right direction?* Doubts were starting to creep into my mind.

Just then, I heard footsteps. Some older guy was walking right by me and said, "Oh, son, you look tired! Where are you going?" I said, "I'm beginning to wonder! I'm trying to find a place called the Southampton Shelter." He looked at me and laughed and smiled and said, "My boy, you're almost there!" He said, "I just came from that area, and I was headed out of the snow, and then I ran into you!" I looked at heaven and I said, "Thank you, God, for giving me this sign that I am on the right track of where I need to go!" He looked at me and smiled and said, "I just came from that area, and here you are trying to get there! I can direct you exactly how to get there!" I said, "Sir, that would be awesome!" He said, "Yes, my boy, when you get at the street light, turn left! You don't know where you are, but you're on Albany Street! And you really don't have that far to go now. I know being a stranger, you probably had no idea where you were going!" And he said, "God puts people in people's paths in all different ways so that they can be directed!" He said, "I truly believe God put you in my path so I can now direct you!" I said, "Sir, I absolutely believe that, too, and I thank God that you believe me!" I said, "Are you a homeless person?" He said, "Yes, I am, but God is watching out for me!" I said, "I'm glad God put you in my path today!" I reached into my pocket and pulled out whatever spending money I had left. I had a 20 dollar bill that I gladly gave to him. He was so grateful that he gave me a hug! He said, "Young man, you're a blessing!" I said, "Sir, you have no idea what kind of blessing you are right now! I'm grateful and I'm glad to meet you, because you came along right when I needed you! I had no clue where I was at, even though I had this flimsy map! But the snow started coming down so hard that I couldn't tell my directions on this map! So I believe God used you as my road map! And now, because of you, I'm going to find this place!" So, before I let him go, I prayed with him and I asked God's hand upon him in prosperity, protection, and to provide a place where he can hang his hat one day!

After we prayed, he said, "Most people are put off by my appearance, but you're not? Why is that, son?" I said, "I don't know, I just felt light coming from you, and I felt I could trust you! And now you're leading me in the right path! I hope to meet you one day here in Boston again, but if not, sir, I'll see you in Heaven, and I thank God for the good deed that you did this day. You really were a blessing to me! I couldn't have found the shelter without you!" So we parted company, each blessing the other! With newfound confidence, I was ready to find this place! God gave me a Spiritual Energizer Bunny pick-me-up through this guy that I just met. What a true blessing he was! I wish I could have given him more than what I had.

I followed his directions and came to the light and turned. He told me the street would split off in two directions. He said, "Stay on the left hand side, it's about three blocks down, as the crow flies!" I asked him what crows he was talking about, and he laughed at me and said, "Son, that's just a figure of speech!" So about three blocks down, sure enough, on the left side was the beginning of the Southampton Shelter! It's amazing how God works. Here He was, sending me a messenger coming from the opposite side of where I had to go, and of course there was no way of knowing he was headed where I just came from, and here I was, going to where he'd just been! I said to myself, *How awesome is God? He really is right there and hears your prayer at that point right when you need it!*

So, now, with renewed vigor and energy, I hoisted that heavy suitcase onto my shoulder, determined to get there! Snow was still coming down, heavily, but it didn't matter. God sent me a messenger to get me in the right direction, even when I couldn't see in the snow! I was approaching the shelter, but I was confused. *Where is the doorway entrance?* I thought. *I see a door, but it says 'Do not enter. Emergency will sound!'* And then I heard another voice of a guy close to the building. He said, "Hey, kid, where are you going?" He looked at me, laughing, "You look kind of lost!" He said, "Don't you know, it's dangerous out here in this kind of weather?" I spoke to him, and he cut me off, saying, "Whoa, bro, you're not from around here, are you? I can tell by the way you speak!" I said, "No, I'm not, but I'm trying to get into the shelter now!" He asked, "Kid, where are you from? I kind of laughed about that because I'm a mature adult, or at least I try to be one, and this guy is calling me 'kid?' So I laughed at it and took it with a grain of salt. Maybe a whole teaspoon full. I shouldn't have said anything to him, but I said, "I've only been here a few days, and I just want to get into the shelter that I finally found with the help of a friend!" He kept sizing me up! "Ain't you a long way from home, kid?"

I looked at him, starting to get angry, and said, "This is my new home! I'd appreciate it if you would tell me how to get into the entrance of this place!" Here's a side note. Rule number one in Boston: Don't let people you don't know learn anything about your business! I have since come to respect that. Anyways, the guy finally said, "Sure, kid, the entrance is right around that corner, about 200 feet! "Thanks," I said.

I really wanted to get away from this guy! He had started to aggravate me! And he blurted out, again, "Hey, kid?" I said, "What, now?" "Oh, just letting you know they won't want your kind around here!" I looked him straight in the eye and said, "And what kind is that?" He said, "Oh, I don't know, I just get the sense that you're something different. Some kind of troublemaker!" He said, "These guys will spit you out for breakfast and have your carcass for lunch!" Now, I'm looking at him dead in the eye, he's really got my attention! I pulled my backpack to my side in case he was going to pull out a knife or something so I could block it and try to knock it away, and possibly try to knock him out, in case he attacked me! My adrenaline was high at this point. I said, "Bro, if you want to try me before I even get into this place, then do it, because now you've got my attention, trust me!" I said, "I had a little boxing training back in Indiana! And I'm not going to back down! So if I were you, either let me go in now, and move aside, or try to stop me! The choice is yours, make it now! Because you fully got my attention! If you want to start something, then let's go! Because I'm going to get inside that warm shelter, one way or the other!" He stepped aside and said, "Your funeral, pal! But they won't like you, because I know I don't!"

I looked at him as I walked by. I said, "I've done nothing wrong to you." I said, "I met an angel on the way here who directed me how to get here, and you're acting like the devil trying to stop me from going inside!" I walked by him and said, "Have a nice day, I hope we don't meet again!" I had no idea I was going to run into this kind of aggravation right outside the shelter, just trying to get into it! They had security cameras out there in case there was a fight or something. Of course, there's no way I knew this. I was just trying to defend myself so I could go get warm! Finally, I got to the entrance and I started checking in! My hands were almost frozen after having to put up with this guy for about 40 minutes! The last thing he said before I left him was, "Not only are they not going to like your kind around here, but they don't like friendly guys, either!" That made me angry! I was determined to prove him wrong.

I got my mannerisms from God and my mother, and that wasn't going to change, even though I was coming into a hostile environment on what was considered the worst side of the city of Boston, and possibly the worst area of Boston that I would reside in. Of course, there was no way of knowing that, at the time. And it didn't matter to me. With God in your life, anything is possible, even being able to change anyone or any situation! After all, he did change me, and I was determined to be myself. And I have never strayed away from that! I was glad to get out of the cold, finally. Plus, the guy on the street just now had learned the kid from Indiana wasn't playing, and was not going to be taken down so easily, so easily! I don't like to fight, at all, but when you have to stand your ground, you have to do it. I didn't know if the guy had a gun, a knife, or what, or just a loudmouth, I wasn't going to take any chances, I was going to stand my ground. I think that shocked him, a little bit, and he thought I was going to fold under to him! I said to myself, *He obviously doesn't know this kid! Even though,* I said, tongue-in-cheek, *I am no longer a kid, as far as I know, I'm still an adult! So I will try to act like one in the shelter!* This was to be my first physical challenge since I arrived just 3 short days ago. I'm just glad it didn't have to come down to a fight, because who knows what would have happened? The police could have been called, and I could have been arrested, even though I was defending myself! Any number of things could have happened! I'm just grateful to God that none of them took place. He was really watching my back!

I started checking in everything in security and the security people were a little gruff. I learned later on that they develop an attitude with a hard exterior because of the type of people they have to check in, with all types of attitudes! So I was really not a bit surprised they acted like that! But I was going to be as friendly and cooperative as possible as they were checking me in! I checked in, and they put me in a holding area before they could run information on me, and they told me I had to either sit there or go back outside, it didn't matter to them!

After all, here I am, for all they know, another person off the streets, so they're going to treat me like everyone else. I wasn't surprised by that! So, I handled the waiting area by telling the security people "Thank you," and one of them looked at me and said, "Bro, you're not from around here, are you?" I said, "No, sir, I'm not!" I said, "I'm just trying to find my way in this life, at this point!" He said, "Well, you've got a really good attitude, and we need more people like you in here!" That made me feel warm inside! So much about what the guy on the outside just said about them not going to accept me! I said, "Bro, I have to thank God for that! He's the one who made me how I am!" He smiled at me and said, "Well, looks like God did a good job on you!" So I smiled back and waited in the holding area, which I call "the Holding Tank," or affectionately known as "Section B." I call it that because when people are waiting and stumbling around for check-in, they are often inebriated. I wondered if anybody else was coherent. And of course, I don't drink, so I waited to be seen by someone. Finally, after about 25 minutes, one of the supervisors comes up to me. "Hi, I'm so-and-so," he says, "I already have your information, you're good to go! If you're hungry, you can go eat in the cafeteria, they're getting ready to have lunch there!" He said, "It's a huge room and there's a lot of guys in there, so just be pleasant and everybody will get along!" I looked at him and said, "Yes, sir, I will do that!" He said, "We have your check-in information, welcome to Southampton Shelter!" I said, "Thank you, if it's okay, can I go ahead and eat?" He said, "You and I are going to get along well, you have good manners!" I said, "I'm only as good as the One who created me!" He said, "I like that! Welcome to the place!" He said, "Go get you something to eat!" I said, "Okay, thank you!"

This place was huge! This was not like the temporary shelter that I once stayed at in Indiana, a long time ago. This was a massive place! Unknown to me at the time, there were going to be 500-plus guys in there! That's a lot of people, plus endless staff people, many supervisors, and bosses. A lot of people you say "Yes, sir" and "Yes, ma'am" to, and "No, sir, and 'No, ma'am" to! That's the way I was raised, early in my childhood by my Navy stepdad and my Navy brother, before they went off to fight in Vietnam! So, you learn mannerisms early on. I also found out that my real dad was a service veteran, so there it is! Three people that I knew of were in the military! And I'll talk about that story in another book. As I approached the cafeteria with my new name badge, I asked the staff person if I could go sit down, and they said, "Yes, just as soon as we scan your ID." I said, "Thank you so much, ma'am, I really appreciate it!" She smiled with a twinkle and said, "Hun, you're welcome! Now, go get you a table to sit!" I said, "Yes, I will!"

I was in the cafeteria, and it was huge! I l noticed two TVs on opposite ends of this area ,one on our side of the wall, and the other TV on the other end. Some guys were watching it, others were reading books, some just sitting there. I looked around some more and I noticed a guy painting on something that looked like rocks! This got my curiosity up, so I decided to investigate! I came over and introduced myself to him, and he said, "Hi, Ritchie! My name is Doug, nice to meet you!" He caught me by surprise, calling me 'Ritchie,' because no one had ever called me that! And I liked the name ,and that's how it first started. He said, "I know your name is Richard, but you just look like a 'Ritchie' to me!" And I was flattered by that! So I replied back, "Well, you look like a 'Doug' to me!" He laughed and smiled, and we became really good friends after that.

So much for the outside guy saying, "Kid, they'll eat you for lunch!" It wasn't lunchtime yet, and no one had eaten me! No one even had a knife or fork in their hands to try to snack on me! My dry sense of humor was starting to kick in. I said to myself, *If someone even tries to nibble on this kid from Indiana I'm going to punch them! Here I meet the first guy in the shelter and we turn out to be good friends!* And we are today. These things he was painting on were not rocks, but smooth stones! And he painted incredible designs on each one all different from the other, and the diverse colors he put on these stones were absolutely beautiful! What an incredible talent and steady hand-eye coordination it takes to do something like that! I was amazed because the rocks were only about two inches wide, and to me they looked like masterpieces of art! Doug had a God-given, incredible talent! And I hope he sells some! I watched him a couple of months after we met, and got to see him in action painting on his rock canvas, and I was blown away! You'd have to see it for yourselves to be able to fully appreciate what I saw! Absolutely phenomenal! I said, "I'll talk to you later," and he said, "OK, Ritchie, welcome to the shelter!"

I went back to my area to wait on them to call tables for lunch, and there I met my next friend, Nick. (He and I would later become long-distance walking buddies.) It was my desire at that time to train and to eventually run in the Boston Marathon. And we are still good friends, even today, and he's hoping to walk again with me if I overcome the bad knee surgery that disabled me! Then, I met other guys at our table: my new friend, Billy, who did long-distance walking himself, and was very friendly, and then a black gentleman, whose name I can't recall, who I told, "Hi, I'm Richard from Indiana." He introduced himself, and from that day on, every time he saw me he called me "Indiana," which got my attention when he called me by it, because I knew exactly who was calling my name! Lunch was going to be soon, so I asked the guys to save my seat so someone else wouldn't take it, and I heard, "Sure thing, Indiana!" I looked and smiled back and went around introducing myself to other tables, and got mostly a positive response that I was hoping for. By the time lunch rolled around, I had gotten to meet at least 20 new friends! I was really motivated to start off on solid, good ground in this shelter after what the outside guy said! I felt really good about making a clean, fresh start here in Boston, and wanted to show them what the kid from Indiana was all about!

Our table was called for lunch, and boy, it really smelled good. And I was starving, I practically inhaled my food, and was grateful to finally be able to eat something! After I ate, and it was delicious, I wanted more, and asked when dinnertime was. They told me, and here I was, anticipating what we were having for dinner, and getting hungry thinking about it, when all of a sudden, I hear, "Seconds! Come and get it!" I was out of there like I'd been shot by a cannon! Man, I couldn't believe it! More food! I was thanking God, again, and gobbled it down. You would have thought that I was a thirsty man in the desert who had just discovered water! People were laughing around my table. One guy said, "Man, kid! You sure can eat!" I liked being called a "kid;" it made me feel young! Lunchtime was almost over, and my stomach felt so good. They called us by rows to come up and get our bedcheck stuff for the night on whichever bunk we were assigned to, and my suitcase didn't feel so heavy after that meal! And so I walked to wherever my bed was, with renewed confidence around 500 guys I didn't know.

I learned later on that their dinners were really good there, as well!

But in the meantime, I got to my bed and I bowed my head in silent prayer and thanked God for a really good first day. If I'm going to thank God for something, I'm not ashamed to do it. I didn't care how many eyes were looking at me, I wasn't ashamed to acknowledge Heaven for getting me there safely, and without conflict! At dinnertime, a lot of guys were talking to each other about that new kid who prays at his bed! There were people staring at me from all kinds of tables, but this didn't bother me, at all. I know who I am through God, and that's how they're going to learn me to be! The word of God says to show yourself friendly to even those who don't know you, and I was determined to do just that! I didn't know them, and they didn't know me! So when I got done eating, I went around to different tables, again, and started introducing myself. "Hi, my name is Richard. Very nice to meet you!" I went to as many tables during dinner as I could, introducing myself to all kinds of people I didn't even know! Three-quarters of those people returned my gesture with a handshake, a "Hello, welcome to the shelter," or thing I was going to learn, called the fist bump, where, instead of shaking your hand, your right fist bumps their fist! I said, "I really like this new kind of handshake! I've never seen this before!" I said, "I could really get used to this!" When some people do a fist bump there, they do it to try to intimidate you with the power they put in their bump! Others will just bump you back! It didn't matter who fist-bumped me, I wasn't intimidated by it! I had really hard knuckles from fighting, sometimes, in Indiana, and broke one of my knuckles on a guy's gold tooth after he picked a fight with me. That, of course, is for another story in a later book! So when I fist-bumped back, I got a lot of respect through it, because I was to get the reputation around the shelter of being the new guy with really hard fists! And they said, "When you fist bump this guy, you're going to know it!" I had one hilarious episode of that when a really big guy bumped me with a huge fist and I met his fist and bumped it back. He yelled, "Ow, bro! Not so hard! You've got a really strong fist!" Keep in mind, this guy is about 350 pounds saying this, and I'm just speechless! I said, "Bro? You're a really big guy, yourself, and I'm flattered that you tell me this!" He said, "Bro, I'm serious! You've got powerful fists, and I wouldn't want to fight you!" I didn't know what to say, and there were about 15 guys watching this take place! I was embarrassed by this, and I reached out to shake his hand to extend friendship to him, which he acknowledged. He said to me, "If you ever need a friend, Bro, I'm here for you!" And I said, "Likewise, as well, Bro. Thank you for your friendship!" I never forgot what he said. That was my first reaction to shelter life. And I was excited for this new start.

You couldn't watch TV at dinnertime, so you just headed back to your bed, and even though it was a hard mattress, it was comfortable, and it felt right, like it was the will of God! Through Him, I was ready for this challenge! Guys that I had already talked to in the cafeteria from introducing myself came up and made themselves friendly by my bed, wanting to know who I was, where I had come from, and what a guy like me was doing there. That's a lot of questions, but I was ready to answer all of them! There were about ten guys by my bedside, and I spoke to each and every one of them. One guy spoke up and said, "Bro, we need more of your kind around here!" He said, "You are one friendly dude bro! And I appreciate your new friendship!" I said, "I appreciate yours, as well, and all of you guys!" I said, "All this is very new to me after being homeless for the while that I was, so I'm very grateful to be here with you guys, even now!" One other guy said, "Man, you're all right, you're just like one of us! Misplaced, displaced, but not replaced!" I said, "I really like how you said that!" He said, "I'd like to know more about you, Richard," And the guy who gave me the nickname "Indiana" said, "So would I, Indiana, so would I!" One by one, they took off to watch TV in either the TV Room between Dorm 3 and Dorm 4, or the TV room outside Dorm 2! I didn't care to watch TV right at that point, and in one TV room they kicked you out of there by 7:45 pm, not 8 pm! Even if you're watching *Gunsmoke* and it's getting to the good part where Matt Dillon is getting ready to catch the bad guy? Forget about it! The TV goes off! After you've watched three-quarters of an hour program! And to me, that wasn't fair, and it always sucked! I mean really? C'mon man! Just another 15 minutes? Geez... I just wanted to get cleaned up and ready for the evening.

I was grateful for that suitcase, because it really had come in handy!

I only had a few changes of clothes left to my name, but I was glad to have them. To get your towel when you take a shower, you have to turn in your ID badge, and you get that back when you turn in the towel. That's really simple. They give you your towel, bar of soap, some shampoo, and some razors to go get your shower done! I wasn't going to be able to leave my suitcase with any staff people at the desk, so I had to trust in my new friends to watch my things! I asked one of them that I was really comfortable with if he could do so, Nick, and he said, "Yes."

He and I got along really well, and I also got along with his friends! So much for the kid from Indiana who was told by the guy on the outside, "They will eat you alive, kid!" He didn't know what he was talking about. He never met this kid! This kid believes in treating others the way you want to be treated, that's the way he was raised! I put that into practice in this shelter, so when I think about it today, I laugh at the term, "the kid from Indiana!" It doesn't matter where you're from, it matters what kind of impact you make, and how effective you can be doing it! After all, there were guys from all walks of life in this shelter whose stories I was going to learn as I got to know many of them better, and you learn to care for others.

In the shower, I began to thank God for the new, good beginning. And whatever was going to happen from here, I belonged to Him. The dinner we just had was macaroni and beef and something else, and it was soooo good! Sometimes they served dessert with your meal, but that was rare. I Enjoyed that first day with my new friends that the guy outside said I couldn't make! Anything is possible with God if you have the right attitude and the right motive! This was a very successful first day. And I, for one, was grateful to be a part of it!

At bedtime, you have to be smart with your belongings, because remember, you are in a shelter with 499 other guys! And some of them will be eyeing your things! So you have to use wisdom when you go to sleep. Remember, I had a suitcase. So after I prayed during bed, I decided to put my legs over that suitcase so it couldn't move. And I slept that way, night after night, to keep it safe. The hardest thing was, until I was going to get storage for it, I had to take it with me, wherever I went. At that point, I had one change of clothes to my name. And others there had very little clothes, at all, as well, and I felt bad for them. And you literally had to go into the shower area or big bathrooms to wash your own clothes! And that was mentally hard on me, and not easy to do, because you would have to stand there feeling stupid trying to dry your clothes with a hand dryer located in all the bathrooms! And keep in mind, you have to be smart knowing that you had to get on one side of that blow dryer thing to do that. Remember, there are 499 other guys in this shelter, and you want to keep the peace and use wisdom trying to do just that. And I was doing that for my first month there. But once I got a backpack, that was all going to change. Most of the residents of the shelter had backpacks, as well. That's your lifeline in there, so you guard it with your life. And your cell phone, if you have one. The backpack was a blessing because it was a lot easier to manage than trying to drag around that heavy suitcase. It would be like Linus of the cartoon Charlie Brown, dragging around that blanket of his with weights attached to it! I kid you not! That thing was heavy!

I gladly got rid of that suitcase by giving it away. You just feel like a pack mule outside the shelter when you are hauling your belongings along with you. And if you leave anything by your bed in the morning, you can consider it gone! You have to prepare to eat breakfast, which ends at 6:45 am, and if you miss breakfast you go hungry until lunch, unless you have EBT, which is food stamps, or money of your own to buy something outside the shelter. And you have to be out of all the dorms before 8 am, every morning!

I remember being outside the shelter one day and saw my good friend, Jose, across the street, and I asked him to come over to my side to see me. He proceeded to come across to meet me, a big mistake, because about 12 other guys came over right behind him asking what I wanted. I was confused by this, and asked my friend, "Who are these other guys?" He said, "Ritchie? I have no idea who they are," and asked, "Bro? I thought they were your friends?" I told him, "No, I thought they were your friends?" And they started to introduce themselves, and I was shocked by what they said! It turns out that these 12 other guys were named Jose, too! I looked at them and said, "Wow!" I said, "Guys? I apologize, I was just trying to call my friend Jose over and had no idea that all you guys were named Jose, too?" We all got a big laugh out of that, and I realized that day, if you're going to call your friend Jose over to you, then you better know his last name, as well! Because otherwise, if you call out the name Jose in the shelter, you just might find out that about 200 of them or so are going to be answering you back! And that would be a lot of Joses! I learned that day that not only were there a lot of people named Jose, but you had to be very specific which one you were calling out to! Wow! What a learning experience. Sheeeesh! Also a lot of Hectors, as well!

And they also have this saying there in the shelter, "Have a nice day, and watch your stuff!" That sounded like really good advice to me back then, and I'm sure it still does today...I made a lot of friends back then, including my boss, John, who I was very close to. boss Dave Dolly, who was my boss before John, and Darrel, who was Assistant manager when I worked there, would always put the burden of responsibility on me before John took over. Staff workers, case managers, even supervisors who were in charge daily considered us the best of the best! A shout-out to Serving Ourselves—or as I like to call them, "saving our snacks!" workers, and my fellow WEP employees! We were the WEP Program and we were the best of the best Janitorial Crew everyday, and set the standard for future WEP workers to follow! I will get into more detail about who we were and what we did, in the second book. My boss said we were the best workers he had ever had! And he was the best boss there that we ever had! I was his right hand man, and he trusted me and the others to always get our work done. My job was also to follow up with the other employees to make sure we got everything done. There was nothing we wouldn't do for our boss John Commanski! It was mutual respect and I will never, ever forget that, and neither will he.

CHAPTER 3

FRIENDS THAT BENEFIT

When I lived in Indiana over three years ago, I was a courier and had a lot of friends that I treated to dinners. I didn't make a perfect income, but it was enough to get by on where myself and friends could go out to dinners or movies. I was a runner at that time on my days off, but none of them liked to run, so I would run as if God were right there, running with me! And I would thank Him for His company as He spoke volumes into my heart! After a while when things turned sour, and it was evident I was going to be homeless, all of these so-called friends turned on me because I was about to become homeless. It makes me wonder today: what kind of friends did I really have? Were they just with me so I could take them out to dinners or go to movies together? Is that the only time they were real friends? Well, newsflash! Those aren't real friends! They were just there for the benefits! When I needed them they were gone, and that saddened me. As I started becoming homeless, I developed a friend I didn't think I was going to have. His name was David Lloyd, and I knew him from my church in Lapel, Indiana. David and his family reached out to me within a couple of weeks of me becoming homeless and told me I could stay in his old house. He told me it was broken-down. He told me, "There are many, many leaks in the roof. It gets very cold in the wintertime and hot in the summertime, because there is no ventilation." He said, "You are welcome to that house as long as you need it!" I cried when he told me this, and I realized God would bring friends in times of need! David and his family were awesome!

I thank God for the people that I knew in Lapel, Indiana, that God put in my life from August 2014 up until October 2015 when I moved back to Anderson! And I appreciated my godmother, Barb, and her daughter, Tammy Finch, my Godsister; they were always there for me! They knew me before I was homeless and when I was homeless! It didn't matter to them; they took me on as their Godson and Godbrother! And they were an incredible blessing in my life! And I can't remember the name of the woman and her boyfriend or husband, whichever he was, that reached out to me in Lapel when I was going to lose that abandoned home that David had first invited me to! The problem is, he needed money and he sold the house! (The story of Lapel will be in a later book, God-willing, called "Journey into the Unknown!")

I also met a lady at my church by the name of Freedom. Her and her family were awesome to me when I was homeless! They told me I could sleep in their van, which I was grateful for, until a guy named Paul complained that I didn't belong there, even though it had nothing to do with him! He greatly angered me and wanted to fight. I was more than willing to take him up on a fight. If he started it, I was going to finish it! But that fight never took place. He was one person I truly had to forgive in my heart if I was going to survive! He doesn't know I had boxing experience and I didn't want to be forced to show it. I was trying to keep a low profile while serving God the best that I could as a homeless man!

Flash-forward to April 2016, when I was at the Southampton Shelter, and within a month span I had met quite a few friends! So Nick, who I will tell you more about in a later story, would walk with me on my days off work at the shelter. Now keep in mind, I'm fairly new to Boston at that time, and I barely know the train lines at all. Nick's not real familiar with them, either, so it was an adventure for both of us! We would get off the train and set our sights toward walking back to Boston as far as we could go before we would have to return to the shelter later that day. And since I was a worker and Nick didn't have an income, I would always delight in stopping at a restaurant where we both could fill up with something to eat! We would munch and enjoy each other's company, and talk about future visions we both had! Nick was just a little bit older than I was, but he was in great shape as a walker. We covered close to a thousand miles, walking that summer of 2016! It was truly amazing! At one point in a day, we walked from one city in Massachusetts called Marblehead to a town called Orients Heights, located close off the Blue line train, and that walk covered about 38 miles. Wow! We had never been to the city we had walked from and we had never been to the town we ended up in! I wanted to keep going, but Nick wanted to go back to the shelter, so we did. Man, was that ever an experience! I will never forget that! On that walk we also saw the Atlantic Ocean when we neared a small town called Swampscott. What a pretty scenic area it was! It was a beautiful, sun-shiney day to top it off, and it was hot, so we took a little bit of time there and just looked at the beauty of the ocean. It was breathtaking and awesome!

We went onto the beach where I got into a chasing match with a seagull after he kept flying low, and I mean head-level low, around us. He was probably wondering who was invading his beach. As if he had the rights to it! Of course, I couldn't catch him, and he knew that! He had something in his mouth and dropped it about 15 feet from where we were, and started walking towards us, for what reason, I don't know! Maybe he saw us as a threat and tried to intimidate us. Whatever his reasoning, he was coming! I didn't know if he was coming for a friendly chat or to lay down the bird gauntlet to signify he wanted to go to war. Which, I have to admit, was a little unnerving! I've never been approached by a bird at any time in my life that I could think of. "Ritchie?" Nick said, "What do you think he wants?" "Bro? I have no idea," I said! This seagull wasn't huge, but he was big. This bird is so big he looked like he was either on steroids or he looked like he had one too many happy meals!☺ So, I decided to walk towards him and try to scare him away! Evidently, this bird saw that I wasn't playing, and decided to walk back the other way towards whatever he dropped out of his beak, and scooped it up again and started flying. I decided to chase him away from where we were. He was flying low to the ground with what looked to be like a big oyster shell in his mouth, and he just would not leave us alone. I felt that he was taunting us, even with food hanging out of his mouth! I said, "Ok! That does it, I've had enough!" And I chased this bird for almost 15 minutes. Of course, Nick is watching this scene taking place, laughing and sitting there while I'm doing the chasing. I said, "Really? You can't help, bro?" "No, no, Ritchie," he said, "You're doing fine!" I said, "Thanks a bunch, Nick! You're a big help!"

He continued laughing while I continued chasing. "Something's got to give," I said! And I was afraid that the *something* was going to be me! Keep in mind, it's hot out, almost 100 degrees, and I'm starting to tire, running after this deranged bird! Finally, this bird decided to head out for the ocean. He decided that he made his point clear about taunting us, and threw in a few shrieks just for good measure. He was about 30 feet off the shoreline when he dropped what he had in his mouth into the water, shocked for a moment, just hanging in the air! Then, he desperately made a beeline into the ocean tide to retrieve it, diving again, and again, and again, having no success at all! The oyster he had in his mouth was now gone, nowhere to be found! This bird was panicking and screeching! He surfaced his head above water, hoping that what he had dropped just might be floating! Of course, it wasn't! Heavy shells won't float; he didn't know that because he probably didn't take bird physics in school! You always hear about a school of fish, but nothing about a school of birds! I'm sure his parents taught him to securely close his beak and mouth when flying if he had food, but obviously he didn't listen! After all, how many kids do you know that listen to their parents, bird or otherwise? So, here was his lesson, as he probably started to realize that what he thought was so securely fastened in his mouth was gone! What if he had dive-bombed into the water as soon as he found out that he lost his tasty meal? There is an old saying here that aptly fits: "He who hesitates is lost!" In other words, the bird who hesitates loses out on his tasty food! Would he have arrived in time to fight over the wave currents to keep it from sinking to the bottom? Hmm? Inquiring minds want to know! And he had to think about something else, as well—what about the other birds? Would they laugh at him after he told them what had just happened? Oh, the disgrace and the humility of such an action! Would he be the laughingstock of Birdville? Would they demote him and clip his wings? And to add insult to injury, he had to listen to me taunting him, when he is the one who had been taunting us! "That's what you get for not closing your beak and having food in your mouth!" I said. "Can't find it, huh? That serves you right for harassing us! Hey, bird?" I yelled, "Never taunt somebody with food in your mouth, because then you become the foolish one!" I said, "Did your mama not teach you to chew with your mouth full?" I looked at him one last time and I just shook my head and started walking away!

I felt kind of dumb saying this stuff, but Mr. Big Beak had it coming! Nick was watching this whole thing and continued to laugh. This bird was foggy and soggy- headed, and all from diving so much, and let out a huge screech and started out of the water for the sky and proceeded back to the beach! Nick said, "Ritchie? Look behind you!" I turned my head in time to see that beaked fiend headed straight at me! "Nick?" I said, "Let's get out of here before he decides to get on his phone and call out the bird Air Force on us!" Nick looked at me dumbfounded and said, "Birds can text, Ritchie?" I said, "Bro, I don't know, but I'm not willing to stick around here and find out!" He said, "Good idea, he looks pretty disgruntled!" "Yeah!" I said, "And a few other words that come to mind, as well! You would be disgruntled too, if you lost something out of your mouth while trying to harass someone! This bird never learned that, otherwise he wouldn't have dropped his catch of the day into the ocean!"

Here's a thought: if it's called common sense, then why isn't it common? That's why it's important to close your mouth when you chew your food; the winged, wise one should have known that! But obviously, he didn't get that text! We don't know, to this day, how he would have gotten ahold of other seagulls and bird friends and so forth, but we were not going to find out! We might not have made it out of there alive if the bird tells his bird friends a one-sided story of what we did! Without hearing our side, we were going to be sentenced right there on the spot, even without a trial, by a jury of birds! And it wouldn't take long if we didn't hightail it outta there, right then! So as we hit the road to continue our walk, birdy boy just flew over the sand, circling where we had just been! I said, "Nick, I'm so glad he didn't have a gun or a weapon, or we'd be toast! And I'm glad that we didn't decide to wait on his other disgruntled friends waiting to take us down! I said, "Nick? That bird could have predicted his own weather forecast! After all, he was foggy and cloudy at the same time! And a touch of precipitation of disgruntled anger and rage!" Nick said, "You're so right, Ritchie," and he continued laughing, but probably had a touch of relief that we were out of there, and not victims of massive amounts of bird droppings from the sky from his feathered friends! Otherwise, we would have been painted like two human Rembrandts, as we are being posterized by a bunch of angry birds! And you don't wanna be that guy, trust me on that! Even today, I still think about that, and how bad that could have been for us if we would have stuck around, or what could have happened. And we never forgot that. Would you, if that were you? Probably not...moral of the story, prepare to have an escape plan ready in case your plan all goes south!

A few weeks later, we decided to walk over to South Boston so we could get some shoes and merchandise, because we had completed so many miles that were required of us. We were excited about that, and we were being rewarded for our participation with the Back on My Feet Program by trying to walk to their regional office in South Boston. Neither one of us knew how to get there, and only had an address to go by. It was to be an interesting walk for both of us that day, because he had worn-out running shoes to walk in, and my back brace I was used to wearing for my injured back had gotten stolen the day before! So we were both really laboring on that walk to South Boston that day. Nick had never walked to this part of Boston before, and I had only been in Boston about two months at that time. It would take me forever to tell you this story, so I'll just give you the basics. We walked until we found this place, and it was closed. And this disheartened us greatly! Like a sailboat going along just fine, then all of a sudden, the wind dies down and you're stuck in deep water! We felt like that sailboat! Our energy was gone, our desire to walk anymore was diminished, and we were starving for food! So we walked back to a KFC we had come across, and gorged on some lunch. His feet were killing him because he thought he was coming back with new shoes and running gear, and my back was in agony from a fall I had, and without that back brace, my back was in deep pain! We both knew that we had to suck it up and walk back!

After we ate, we proceeded on our journey back, but unknown to us at the time, we started walking the wrong way! We ended up at a yacht club that we hadn't seen before, and we kind of panicked a little bit. We kept going, then ended up at a place called Carson Beach. We could not figure out how to get back to where we lived. He then said, "Ritchie? If we continue along the coast, we should find our part of Boston!" I said, "I don't know, Nick, we need to rest a minute and think this through!" He said, "I agree, let's rest." So we found a park attached to Carson Beach on the other side of the highway, and decided to rest there. We were getting really frustrated. This was going to be one walk we would never forget! I think of that walk today and I still shudder! We were both physically worn out and hurting. And of course, nobody was around to direct us on how to get back. As we stopped off to rest in that park, I closed my eyes for a moment and let out a silent prayer to God and prayed he would bring to my mind some kind of answer! Little did we both know that the answer was right there in that park.

As I finished that quick prayer, I decided to let my eyes rest for a moment. Nick had taken his shoes off, and was rubbing his blistered feet! I got my mind off my sore back and focused on his feet! He said,

"Ritchie? I don't know how much longer I can go on, I may have to walk on my hands after this!" He smirked, and I laughed at that. I said, "Yeah," I said, "I might have to trade my back in for a good, used one!" He said, "I'll take your back and you can have my feet, okay?" "Okay!" I said. We were saying anything to lighten the load of burden we were feeling! And it was going to be dark in a few hours! We didn't want to be stuck in the park in the middle of who knows where. "Nick? Let me rest my eyes for a moment." He said, "Ok, Ritchie, I'm tired too." So I started to rest my eyes again, trying to think of a way out of this dilemma. As I was resting, I could hear a small voice in my head, and I knew who that voice was, it was God's spirit! He said, "Son? Look around you, what do you see?" I said, "Lord, I see this beautiful park." He said, "Look deeper." So I did, and I still saw the park and the trees! He said, "Son? Raise up your vision!" I said, "Lord? What are you saying?" I remembered the Scripture that said, "Look to the hills or look upon the hills, where does my help come from? My help comes from the Lord!" God was trying to tell me to look further than what I was looking at! I heard His voice again, "Son? Raise your vision!" And so I did just that, and looked above the tree line in the park, and to my wonder, I saw the Boston skyline!

I said, "Oh man!" I said, "Nick? I know where we are! God just showed me where we are!" I said, "Nick? Thank God, we're going home!" With tired eyes, he said, "Ritchie, I don't understand! What do you mean, God told you?" "Exactly what I mean, Nick! God showed me where we are!" I said, "Look!" And then he saw it too! He said, "Ritchie? That's Boston!" I said, "That's what God was showing me when I closed my eyes! He said, 'Ritchie? Raise your vision!' So I did! And now you see it, too!" The problem was, and we didn't know it, we had actually been walking away from the skyline instead of towards it! And God had us rest so that we could see it for ourselves! Thank God! The skyline was about five to seven miles away, but we didn't care, because now, by God's help, we knew where to go! And not a moment too soon, because it was starting to get dark! I said, "Are you good for a few miles more?" He laughed and said, "Ritchie? Just try and stop me!" I said, "Bro? You and me both!" I said, "Let's get out of the land of Oz and head back to Kansas!" He said, "You mean Boston?" "Yes, Nick, I mean Boston!" Without God's help, we wouldn't have made it back! When we finally got back, one of our supervisors joked around and said, "Where did you guys go, on Pee Wee's Big Adventure?" I said, "No, even Pee Wee would have had trouble on this one!" He said, "You guys need to get down to supper before they close!" Nick said, "Sounds good to me." "Me too, Nick," I said, "Me too!" We had unknowingly covered about 35 miles that day. Wow!

Nick never forgot what God did for us that day, and neither will I! Man, we were glad to get back right before it really got dark, and it's an understatement to say that our feet were really sore from our big adventure! Not long after that, we both finally got our running gear, and I think he still has those shoes to this day. Me? I gave mine away to a guy in the shelter who absolutely had no shoes; he loved them! And they fit him perfectly! Amen.

At a later time, we walked up a hill in a place called Nahant. This was a long, steep hill, and we both proposed we would take our time and climb this hill! After a while, we started getting tired, a little bit, and I said to myself, *There's got to be a better way to get up this hill!* All of a sudden, I hear a little voice inside of me speak, "Lean towards the hill when you walk!" Usually when you climb a steep hill, you kind of stand up straight with determination and purpose that you're still going to get up this hill! I believe the voice speaking to me was God telling me a better way to get up the thing! I listened to the voice, and when I would walk I leaned into the hill! The steeper it got, the more I would lean into it, to where I would be pumping my arm so much but using strong leg calf muscles to do the work (When you've run in the biting cold weather in Anderson, Indiana, trust me when I say, you will develop strong calf muscles!) And let me tell you something, it worked! If my knee ever gets healthy again, I now know a better way to climb the hill now! You use your momentum to lean into what you are walking up against. This way, you allow your calf muscles to do the work and you will find yourself getting less tired! But in order to do this, you have to have strong calf muscles! Mine were developed by a trial of fire so to speak, through the blistering cold back then! I didn't have a choice. You either run daily as a homeless person, or you die freezing to death in extremely cold weather! And I believe that it was God that spoke this to my heart that day! So from that experience, I know a better way to walk up a hill now!

And I also found a better way to jog. Most people, when they're running or jogging, pump their arms up high, but I have learned this new running style, that you don't have to pump your arms up extremely high because that will tire you out. If you keep your arms close to your sides, barely pumping your arms, you will find out you will have more ability to breathe better. And I agree with the heel-to-toe running style. I've also learned that if I shrink myself down and put all my weight in my running shoes I have more energy, because my legs don't have to work as hard! I didn't learn all this until I got to Boston! Unfortunately, because I can barely walk means I can't run right now, but I will employ these methods if I can ever run again! You see, when you stand up straight when you're running, you put a lot of pressure on your body and tire yourself out more easily. But shrinking down as a runner putting the weight on your feet you will have more energy if you don't believe me try it! It may work for you! I know it did for me! That's why before I had knee surgery I could go a long distance before I head to slow down and catch my breath! And you breathe in, and then you breathe that out, I was taught that this is the correct way to breathe when you are running! I did this in Indiana when I trained on my own, and believe me, it works! With this new running style that God showed me, and a better way to climb a hill, I hope to use it one day again. It is still my desire to run in the Boston Marathon, someday, God-willing, of course! Nick and I enjoyed each other's company that first summer, and when it was his birthday I took him over to his favorite restaurant, Olive Garden, and let him order whatever he wanted! The amazing thing about Indiana to me was that I had friends when I wasn't homeless! And here in Boston, because I was homeless, I had a lot of friends! Nick and I stay in contact with each other when I see him at visits to the shelter. He's still hoping we can walk again together, someday, and I would love that.

I met another friend when I heard him sing at a Boston Minstrels concert, where I was invited to sing, as well, even though I was working. His name was Russell, and let me tell you something, Russell could sing! He had an incredible singing style that reminded me of the singer from Green Day or one of those groups! I don't know if he's still at the shelter today or not, or if he's back home in the state he came from, but for a short while, he and I both lived there at the shelter and would go to these different karaoke places and sing! I really enjoyed his company and how well he could sing! He was going to set it up where he and I would both sing and this guy and his family would pay Russell and me $400 for the weekend to go do karaoke songs together! Unfortunately, that never took place, and I never understood why! But those things happen! Anyway, I appreciated his friendship. I can't remember his last name, but the memory is there of our friendship!

Kevin Harrison is another awesome friend of mine that I met at the shelter. He invited me to Lechmere to sing at a place called Courtside, (which I will talk about in the chapter called "Hey Ritchie—You're Invited!"). I got to know people there and sang there on and off, even now, when my knee allows me to do a tiny bit of walking! We have sung at different places, as well, and I invited him out to the Hong Kong, one of my first singing spots in Boston! He, time and time again, invited me to go sing at Harvard College where karaoke singers meet on certain Thursdays, but unfortunately, something would always come up with either him, and I never got a chance to sing there. I know I would have enjoyed myself! And listening to other singers, as well! I haven't heard from Kevin in a while. I hope he is well! If you see him, tell him "Hi" for me. He is a very tall guy, you can't miss him, he's about 6"9' or 6"10'. All I know is he is tall enough to look into outer space and see the planets and the stars, and see asteroids as they swing on by! Just kidding, but he is tall!

And of course, there is my best friend, Pops, AKA Donald Flippen! We have been friends since we met at the Southampton Shelter. So April 2020 was four years that Pops and I have known each other. Like any friendship, ours has been tested at times, but we always come back together. We are both believers in Christ, and any problems we have to solve with each other we take to prayer if we can't talk it out, and then God will give us peace of mind about it. Here's what you need to know about Donald and myself: we are out to set the World Record in a card game for the highest score in history. We have been doing this particular card game since September 2016 when we both found out that we loved this game! I've contacted the Guinness Book of World Records, and they emailed me once saying that they are very interested in what we are trying to set. I haven't heard from them, again! Most people play with a lot of cards in this game per hand, but Pops and I have decided to make it tougher on ourselves to score points in the system with fewer cards! We are very, very serious, as we started this at his apartment in Jamaica Plain, and we continued playing it at the shelter, sometimes!

Pops and I spent a lot of time at the Engagement Center when it first opened. And I'm not talking about a dating site for singles or married couples! I'm talking about a place that the city of Boston runs for homeless people on the street. It is a place to come eat, relax, watch TV, get counselors, or use their computers or phones for job contacts and talk with friends for a while! The Engagement Center was fun for me and Pops, and we didn't mind sharing our snacks with people coming around inside the Center! The problem was, we couldn't feed everybody! So we had to use good judgement on what snacks to put on the table, and keep the other ones concealed until we were ready to eat those. We liked sharing our food, but we just couldn't feed everybody! And one guy there saw us playing one time and mocked Pops, because Pops couldn't beat him in a certain card game! And he would constantly be on Pops for it, rubbing it into his face all the time! Finally, I had enough of it! I said, "Yeah, you might be better than him in that game you play! But you couldn't beat him in the game we play!" He looked at me and said, "This game?" He said, "I'm an expert at this game!" I said, "Well, if you're such an expert at this game, why don't you play me! And if you're better than I am in one game, I will let you know! But if I beat you, then you will stop harassing my friend, Pops, over the game you are better at than him!" Pops looked at me and smiled and said, "Ritchie, I know how good you are at this game! I have no doubt you will beat this guy!" The guy got indignant and looked at me and said, "You care to place a bet on that?" I looked at him calmly and said, "I don't bet!" And he said, "Are you afraid you're going to lose?" Then I smiled and said, "No, I'm not afraid I'm going to lose! Because I look at it this way: I'm not only playing you for myself, but I'm playing you for my friend here, as well, because he is also good at this game!" The guy looked at me and laughed and said, "Well, I'll beat you both, then!" I said, "Okay, anytime you're ready to play!" He looked at me and said, "Let's play now!" He said, "I have to warn you, I am an expert at this game!" I said, "Remember how I said, if I beat you, you will stop harassing my friend Pops?" He said, "Okay? Deal!" And he said, "What if I win, what do I get?" I said, "If you win, whenever Pops and I play, you will be the first one welcome to the table to enjoy our snacks!" He said, "That's a deal! You guys have great snacks!" I said, "Okay. We play to a thousand in this game." He said, "Okay, your funeral!"

Pops just looked at me and smiled! We had pretty much learned the ins and outs of this game! After all, we've been playing together since September 2016 and have learned each other's style! So we began to play, and he talked nonstop like he was trying to distract me or something! But I didn't let that bother me. I just concentrated on what he was doing, and I concentrated on what I was doing! He won the first hand, and looked at me and said, "I told you I was better than you!" I said, "Bro, the game isn't over, that's just the first hand! You may have an early lead, but we play to a 1000!" He said, "Okay, I'm just saying, I'm going to whip your butt!" He was leading 130 to 45! So he swelled up with bravado! He said, "You might as well give up now!" I said, "Bro, I'm just now starting! I watched your hand and I have seen how you play!" He said, "So?" I said, "I've caught on to your style! Now you will see my style up close and personal!" From that point on, I won the next nine hands! I ended up beating him 1070 to 620! People around the table saw the beatdown and cheered when I took this braggart down! He said, "Oh, the cards must be fixed!" and, "Oh, the light was in my eyes!" I said, "Bro, the light was in my eyes, too! And no, the cards aren't fixed! You just can't admit you were beaten by a better player!" And to this day he never admitted it! Pops was extremely happy! Because now, this guy couldn't bug him anymore! A much better player had beaten him in the game that he thought he was an expert in! Pops looked at him at the end of the game and said, "Now who's the master?" He glared at Pops and left! I said, "Pops, I guess he won't be bothering you anymore!" "Yeah, yeah, yeah," he said, "he won't be! You not only took him to school, but you ate his lunch along the way!" "Yeah, something like that," I said to Pops.

Anyway, since September 2016, up to my birthday, August 11th 2019, I have kept accurate records of all that time my friend Pops and I have played! It is our desire to set the world's highest record in history of this particular card game, and I'm hoping the Guinness Book of World Records recognizes it! Because he and I have really played hard to get to where we are today! And one of our friends Mario, who is (or was) the manager at the Engagement Center remembers when we got our first record-breaking moment in a score when we played cards in there! Mario not only remembers us, he wants to take us out to lunch and see us two guys from Boston get our names in the Book! This would be an incredible feat! So, Pops and I play as much as we can, and Mario's going to get us a verification letter stating what we're doing! However, even if the Guinness Book of World Records doesn't get back to us, Pops and I will have pride in knowing that we have probably set the record already, but we just want to set it higher and higher! After all, we benefit from our friendship!

CHAPTER 4

HEY RITCHIE,
YOU'RE INVITED!!!

It was May of 2016 and I was invited to participate in a thing called the Soar Program, which I will explain more about in another book. As the months went by, I was talking to a few friends in that program, and they referred me to a guy there that liked to sing. Since I like to sing, as well, it was a good match; so he told me that once in a while, he goes out to karaoke in Boston!

This got my attention, and he said, "Hey! Let me introduce you to a place called Kings in the Back Bay area. They have great singing on Thursdays, and we should go!" So that Thursday was my first karaoke experience since I moved to Boston. As we went there, I got excited, and I'm sure he was, too! And let me tell you something! I can't remember his name to this day, but I do know this, he had a really nice singing voice! We put our names on the list, and to our surprise, there was nobody there but us and the DJ! What a real letdown this was! So, anyway, we picked out our songs, and we were going to sing a lot since none of us were there except the DJ, my friend, and myself! Kind of like doing karaoke's greatest hits by yourselves! I had just got done doing the first song when a lady came into the room and she was screaming my name, "Hey Ritchie? Great job on that song! Woooo! Woooo!" I tell you, I just looked at her, a little dumbfounded and thoroughly embarrassed! I didn't know who she was, but the DJ smiled and told us that it was a drunk lady who heard my name called. I looked at my friend and he didn't know what to say. The DJ said, "Every so often, she comes in and she'll just clap for anybody!" When I heard that, it didn't make me feel any better! I looked at my friend and said, "Your turn!" And he didn't take his eyes off that lady the whole time he did his song, wondering if she will make an outburst on him. I wondered, too. Right on cue, at the end of the song, she screamed his name! About 10 minutes later, she left. We did about five or six songs each, thanked the DJ, then decided to cut out of there and head back to the shelter.

He and I were talking on the way home, and thinking, *Boy, what a let-down!* I told him, "Remind me not to go there again!" He said, "You said it, Bro!" He told me he was shocked that there was no one there. When we got back, he did let me know that there were other karaoke places in Boston that he knew of, so I was interested in finding out where they were.

A group I was to learn from called The Boston Minstrels came and played and sang for everybody one weekend in the shelter cafeteria. I had to work that day, so when passing by, I got to hear them as they were performing in the cafeteria. And that's when I first heard a guy by the name of Russell sing! He was a resident, like I was, and I had seen him in passing before, but I didn't know he sang, and I said to myself, *oh man, this guy's got a really good voice! He is incredible!* I was headed up to the room to do more work when two of the staff approached me. "Ritchie?" They said, "We know you sing, you get up there and sing right now so they can hear you!" I said, "I can't do that, I'm at work!" And both of them took me arm-in-arm like they were two prison guards assigned to escorting a prisoner. Here we were, up on the stage with the crowd looking at us, and probably wondering, *what in the world are they doing up there?* At this point, I was a little red in the face, and there was nothing I could do about it! Up on the stage where the band was about to do another song, one of the lady staffers interrupted him. And she said, "This is Ritchie! He's one of the workers and a resident here, and he sings! He does music on YouTube and he shares it with us!" The guy smiled at her and said, "By all means, let's have the young man sing!"

I was really nervous, as there were a lot of people in the cafeteria, and this kind of caught me off-guard! I had my mind thinking about work, and all the sudden I was getting recruited into singing a song? He asked me, "What song do you want to do?" I said, "If it's okay, I'd like to do the National Anthem!" This got roaring support from the cafeteria crowd. Some of the men in the crowd were veterans. "All right Ritchie! Go get 'em, go get 'em," the crowd shouted back! As I was singing it, I could see the other employees walking by, stopping to listen, including all the staff! And my boss John walked by and smiled! He had never heard me sing before. I was a little embarrassed, but I gathered my wits and poured out my heart into this song! I did it an octave higher than it's normally done, and when I got done singing, I got a standing ovation from the crowd! I was a little embarrassed! The head guy of the band said, "Wow! Bro! You can really sing!" He said, "I want to talk to you after we do our concert here!" I said, "Okay," and I said, "by the way, I heard you guys before I came up here, and you are really talented!" He said, "No, my friend, you are the one that's really talented!" And I was embarrassed by that.

After the concert, he said, "Man! I'd really like it if you could join us when we do different concerts, maybe teach some of these guys how to do some harmony parts?" I said, "I would love to!" And so from that point on and off, I sang with The Boston Minstrels! They were incredible band players and really good singers! I sang with them, up to the point where I couldn't sing with them anymore, because after I had the knee surgery, I could barely walk. So it would be nearly impossible to stand on stage for an hour and a half or so. He told me I could sit in the chair while the others stood. I tried it two times after the surgery, and I said, "I'm not comfortable with that at all, plus, I feel it would disrespect other members, and like I would have special privileges!" I said, "I'd like to do my part singing standing up. I just can't, because I can't stand for more than 10 minutes."

I really enjoyed my time with the Minstrels! I sang with them all the way up until about July 2018! Five months after I had the surgery, my knee couldn't take it anymore. I could barely stand. I had to tell them all a heartfelt goodbye, they were really good to me. They took me in as their own, Tim and Jane McHale and the rest of the Minstrels! They had me doing solos at different times! And they always paid for my meal every time we went out to eat. They were really really good to me. Tim gave me a bike, which I'll have to tell you about in another story, to help my knee rehabilitation. But I no longer have that bike, and I will tell you why, in another story chapter in the second book. I stay in contact with them, through Jim, by email. They let me know how much I am missed, and I let them know that I miss them, too, even to this day!

They always had a curious saying: "We're spiritual, but we're not religious!" I can identify with that saying, because as a believer in Jesus, I have a spiritual nature, but I'm definitely not religious, either! There's a big difference between religion and relationship! Religion is man's way of getting to God! But a relationship through Jesus is God's way of getting to man! And I had a relationship.

So, Russell and I decided that we were going to go to the Limelight. He didn't have any money because he wasn't working, and I was, so it was a no-brainer, he was too embarrassed to ask for some snacks, and I felt that, so it was going to be my treat. I felt that the people would like our singing, and they did! He and I never got down there again to sing, and that always puzzled me! I kept inviting him, but he never came, so I continued there at Limelight, on and off for three years, and I enjoyed it immensely.

I came to Limelight one night, minding my own business, and this guy approached me and said, "Ritchie, I think you have a really good voice, and I want you to come and sing in my studio!" I was excited about that, because I wanted to get some more music done! I had one CD not completely finished at that point, and I wanted to get it done, so it would be nice to start working on the second CD! So he said, "No problem, bro, I'll draw up a contract, and you give me $200, and we'll work in the studio until we get your first CD done, and then start on your second one! I thought, *Wow, this is too good to be true!* So I paid him the money the next Thursday, and he gave me the contract! We were going to be recording later the next week, I just had to wait on his call! Of course, I was very pumped and excited! Well, he texted me about mid-week and said, "You know what? We're not going to do this, I'm giving you too good of a deal, and I want you to tear up the contract. I'll make a new contract and we'll do each song for about $100!" If your math is correct like mine, that's $800 for the full CD, instead of $200, which to this day, I still have that contract! I said, "Bro, you're breaking your word with me, and you even gave me a contract with your own idea on it, which I agreed to, now you're going back on your word!" He really didn't have much to say! So I told him, "When you can, just give me the $200 back that I already paid you!" He said, "Don't you want to do this new contract with me, Ritchie?" I said, "Bro, there is no way! After all, you broke your word on a contract you made up yourself, and now you want me to do a new contract? I said, "There's no way!" I didn't trust him after that. Would you? I don't think so! And he was trying to give me a hard time about giving back the $200, insisting we could do another contract! I called him a week later and said,"You know what? You give me $100 and you can keep the other $100," which he did! I said, "I should have known better than to trust him after he said that he'd keep his word!

I have a friend, Tim, who worked at this guy's studio, and he came up to me and said, "Ritchie? Bro, I apologize for my friend, I hate to say this, but he's nothing but a liar!" I told Tim, "Thank you for that, but he couldn't admit that he had done something wrong! And I forgave him for what he did, but that I want nothing more to do with this because he didn't keep his own word!"

A radio producer I was working with at the time from ITNS radio out of Las Vegas told me that he was very upset with this guy, and wanted his attorney to sue him! I was a music client of this radio station, and they still play two of my songs, to this day, on his station, and other stations. His name is Sam Watkins, and his wife's name is Tina, and together they run ITNS radio! They are awesome people! They first contacted me in December of 2018 to be a part of them. In

January 2019, they had me do a live broadcast over the phone radio with their listeners. What an honor that was knowing there are radio listeners listening to your own songs, as well! To this day, I am still considered to be one of their clients, and they are on Facebook. I want nothing more to do with Facebook anymore, because I've had my fill of my accounts getting blocked and scammed! I have no desire to get on there. After the contract incident, I told Sam to let it go, and that I was going to learn a lesson from that! I was really bummed by that, and discouraged, thinking we were really going to record!

That was my first bad experience at the Limelight. I went there later on, and I never saw this guy again! About February 2019, I started coming back to Limelight frequently, up until about May 2019, and the reason I stopped going was because of the pattern of things that happened three times in a row with a certain song I wanted to do, and the DJ just did not want to play it. The song was "My Way" by Frank Sinatra. He said it would wreck the mood! I said, "What do you mean 'wreck the mood?' Considering the person who sang before me did a really slow song! It was the last song of the night that I wanted to do! But he talked me out of it three straight times! I mean, just how many times can you sing the song 'Africa?' I mean, C'mon, man!"

The funny part about all of this is that after I stopped going to the Limelight, I was asked to get into a karaoke music contest in July of 2019, which I wholeheartedly agreed to do! Now here's the ironic part. That song that the DJ of the Limelight refused to play three straight times for three weeks in a row actually won the karaoke contest at a place called Sissy K's in Faneuil Hall in Boston! I was shocked! Because there were ten other really good singers there! I was so happy that I went next door and I tipped the Hong Kong karaoke host $20 in her jar! She was shocked! She thought I was trying to move up the song list that I wasn't even on that night!And when she calmed down, she said, "Ritchie? You might as well sing since you're here." And so, I did! She got more excited when I told her that I had just won the first prize singing next door! And I wanted to share my joy of winning my first karaoke contest in Boston by tipping her jar!

And what's even more shocking is that I was invited to sing in another contest the next month in August, and won that one, as well, at a place called The Wild Rover! And both of these places are on each side of the Hong Kong bar, as well! I feel that it's by the grace of God that I won these contests! And I was invited to take part in a huge contest called the Best of Boston! This was to be a major karaoke contest. Only, for what they considered to be the 10 best karaoke singers in Boston! Because I won two of these contests my name was attached to this contest! I, in no way, consider myself to be one of those 10 top singers! Maybe in the top 1000 singers in Boston, but not the top 10! Sadly enough, I never got a chance to enter that contest of a big money prize because, in August to December of 2019, I was to come down with a major cough tickle in my throat where I just couldn't restrain myself! So, to this day, I don't know who won that contest, because I wasn't there to be a part of it! And it was also my friend, Jermaine, a worker and great singer from Limelight, who suggested that I learn the song, "All of Me," by John Legend. The funny part about that, now, is that I did learn the song before I entered the contest, and that song won the second karaoke contest at The Wild Rover! And now I sing it at different places. And Jermaine never got a chance to hear it. But I shared with him how it won the contest at The Wild Rover, and he beamed with pride!

Now, I look back on that night in the first contest at Sissy K's. The cool thing about it was that there were some really good singers there that night, and I clapped for every one of them, and believed any one of them were good enough to win. And then when I heard my name called at the end, I was in absolute shock!

I had no idea that it was going to meet a need back then, because unknown to me at the time, a friend of mine in the Philippines had injured her ankle, and was going to need crutches for her foot in order to get around. Her hospital wouldn't supply those crutches, and so, the right thing to do when you win this money is to share it, so that your friend can get her crutches. She was almost crying when she found out that she was going to have the money in order to get them. She was so happy. Her name is Miss Q, the woman that got these stories over to the former publisher, the very book you are reading now!

Now, let me back up a little and tell you about this other place that I was invited to sing in September of 2016. It is called the Hong Kong in Faneuil Hall, where I still sing as a regular, today! They have treated me like a family member there, to this day! I love the staff there, the other singers, and the camaraderie! They won the Karaoke Bar of the Year in 2018, and I was there on the night they won it! When five of the karaoke hosts first heard me singing there, they told me, "Bro? You need a stage name when you get up and sing! Something really original that will catch people's attention! Because in our opinion, we think you're a really good singer!" So I thought about that, and the DJs said to me, "Ritchie, don't you do music on YouTube?" I said, "Yes, I do, why?" "Because we think that would be a perfect stage name for you with your own music channel, here as a regular. We will call you 'YouTube Ritchie!'" And the name stuck, even to this day! I want to thank those five DJs: Jazzy Jeff, MC Soy Sauce, Dan the Man,Eddie and KJ, and they all sing awesomely! And I've gotten to sing duets, as well, with some of the female DJs such as Smurfette, Captain Rad, Tiz, Tall Drink of Water, and others! And they all are great singers! When people see that you care about them, they let you know! There are nice bartenders there to get your Cokes or your snack meals! When people hear my name when I sing there, they know who I am! And I also have YouTube business cards that I get to share openly with people who are interested in what I do in music! When they hear you sing and they like the song or they like your voice, it's an open invitation to share the music card with them, which I do! And many of them have checked out the songs on YouTube!

Every time I come into the Hong Kong bar, it is like going to visit your own family! They have treated me so well. And the food is good there, also. So, whenever I'm out singing somewhere else, I feel like I am one of the singers representing the Hong Kong karaoke bar! Some of the DJs have come and gone, some are still there, and I've met some new ones, as well!

It was God's idea for me to enter back into the karaoke scene that first started in Lapel, Indiana, September of 2014, when I was a homeless guy, believe it or not! So I love to share openly the music that God has given me to do on YouTube under Richard Vernon uhi. I'm only using that as a reference point, so you know who I am music-wise.

Now, some Christians have criticized me and said, "Oh, would Jesus do something like what you're doing?" And the answer to that is a wholehearted *yes!And I would ask these same christians, when you're not busy criticizing people, what are you doing for God?* It was God that dealt with me to come and sing in the bars, and he also dealt with my heart to get a music card ready for anybody who wanted one. A lot of people have taken that card and checked out the music! I've had positive feedback from most of them! And I would say to these Christians, who criticized something that God put in my heart to do: You wouldn't go in these bars, but how else are you going to reach the people inside the bar, unless you meet them for yourself! Why criticize it if you are not going to utilize it? Find something to do for God, and do it well! Even Jesus' own disciples asked him one day, "Rabbi," they said, "we see others who are not with us that are praying in your name and doing things, should we tell them not to do this?" And I can just imagine Jesus shaking his head at them when he said, "If they are not against us, then they are for us, let them be!" And I am one of those who are not against other believers when they criticize me, because I'm doing what I feel God has proposed in my heart to do! Yes, Jesus would have done exactly what I'm doing. He put it on my heart to do it, and it has had positive results! You see, it takes more than prayer, it takes action to be where they are! And not come in there preaching at them, try to share with them, actually being friendly like Jesus would. I really care about the people and I invite them to check out the music that I do! As I said before, there's a difference between religion and relationship!

On the opposite side of the Hong Kong place is a place called The Wild Rover, which I've mentioned already, where my friend Kevin and I have received a good reception at different times! He and I were also invited to sing at the Kinsale, which is located over by the Government Center on the Blue Line. At the Kinsale, the DJ's name is Scooby, and he has a really good voice and a nice selection of songs. He is awesome.

The food is good there, and they sometimes have really good crowds. One night we were singing there, and one of the bar patrons liked the songs we were doing so much that he gave Kevin and me both $10, because he said he appreciated the music! That was a trip. Kevin mentioned to me, "See, Ritchie? It really does pay to sing here!" And we both laughed. I now have a relationship with different places that I've been invited to sing at in Boston! I sing old and new songs. I get over to the Kinsale whenever I can.

There was a place in Lechmere called Courtside, which I had been a part of on and off for about two and a half years! They had, in my opinion, some of the best fries I've ever tasted! And since I don't drink, I had Cokes or water! And people would come to me after I did a song and tell me they liked the song. That was an open opportunity to share a card with them! Unfortunately, Courtside is no longer there, because of the owner's health. He had to quit, and that was sad. I don't know how his health is today, I haven't heard any more.

There's also a place over by Fenway Park where the Boston Red Sox play, and it's called the Lansdowne Bar and Pub! The unique thing that sets this place apart from most other karaoke places—other than a place called the Sons of Boston—is that it has a live band, as well, that will do live karaoke music for you! And I have received some great results from that, as well. The band members at both places are extremely nice and accommodating there to help you get started. If you've never sung with a live band before, it is an experience. I have been there a few times, and I hope to go back there again! In Maverick, Massachusetts, there is a karaoke place called Mavericks! And they have good food there, as well, and the karaoke DJ there is someone that I used to sing with at the Hong Kong. Her name is Diana, and she is awesome! We like doing singing duets, as well. I try to get over there when I can! The crowds pack in and there's some good singers! I really enjoyed my first time singing over there. I hope to do it again sometime!

There are a couple more places I want to mention. One place is called Bell in Hand where they do a karaoke contest every Tuesday. I've never won there, but I've come close a few times, as the DJ told me! It has a great atmosphere, and the people are really nice there! And a place not too far from that is now called The White Bull Karaoke Tavern, which I guess is the oldest bar in Boston, if I'm understanding that right,It was named the Cornerstone bar & grill which means they have quite a history! The karaoke atmosphere on Thursdays over there was electric! Great sound system and the DJ Michael is awesome. He has an awesome voice when he sings! Up to this day, I still visit and sing in there despite the pandemic. the days now or Tuesday and Wednesday over there and it is electric and I've met some really nice people there employees and singers! The other singers are really nice over there. There's an old saying: what would Jesus do? He would do the same thing that he put in my heart to do! I also received an invite from one of the singers from the White Bull tavern and he invited me to sing at where he sings at on Monday night! It's in Sullivan square off the orange line train and this place is called, tavern at the end of the world! What a unique name! The first Monday he invited me I couldn't come, so out of friendship for him and he is a another singer I was determined to make it over the next Monday and I did! It's a smaller place singing wise than the white bull, but it has the same atmosphere and a fantastic music system, the microphones are awesome to sing with, DJ over there is named Scotty and he is awesome he's a funny guy as well he also sings, and there was quite a selection singers really good singers, that I had the pleasure of listening to and making new friends with while waiting my turn, I had a fantastic time with these new friendsAnd I thank my friend Ricky for the invite, we've known each other about two years, and I was able to share quite a few YouTube cards,and I believe they were truly interested in checking out the music! I had an awesome time with new friends and I also got to share my gospel YouTube channel at the same time! People were very friendly and talented as well! I had an awesome time there and I look forward to going back! I'm making friends there and I want to follow up on that! The word of God says go out to the highways and byways the hedges and compel them to come in!Some of them don't go to church and chances are you're not going to see them their!So I feel It's my job to go to them in their own territory! This is why God dealt with my heart about 5 years ago to get some business cards made of the music on YouTube that he gave me to write! So I've been sharing the cards all that time and a lot of people I had talked to actually responded and checked out the music! So it's been worth it! If a Believer doesn't want to go into their environment and compel them to come in,then it's not meant for them to do that, and that's perfectly fine if that's their conviction! What I would ask the same believers, instead of criticizing why don't you try praying? Pray for us who are doing the work trying to compel them to come in! Because people like us are out there trying to compel them to come in! Since I have the tool using the YouTube card with the gospel songs on it, this is a drawing point to invite people to come in!And the results are that some of the people do check out the music on YouTube! And when they see and listen to the music they will feel God's presence through the songs, because it was God's idea in the first place to have the card made! He used my homeless friend Anthony to do it! So I just share music it's a good witnessing tool,if they like your voice they will check out your card information! And then from there God can do the rest! What would Jesus do? Probably would do the same thing I'm doing and others would do!Since he is the one that compelled me!You see, I'm not out to make my name great! I'm out to make God's name even greater! Even as a disabled man who can barely walk, my voice is not disabled! So if any managers of any karaoke spots read this chapter and you want to invite me out to where you are, to critique you, just send me an email which will be at the back of the book. I would love to definitely come out to where you are!

There's a place called The Charles Playhouse which houses the world-famous Blue Man Group! If you've never seen them perform, then trust me, you need to go! Before I came to Boston from Indiana, I caught their act, and they were phenomenal! As you first walk in, you will find that there are some people who come on Friday nights after 10 pm that go drink with their friends, sing, and listen to the singers. The lady bartender is very polite and the DJ is awesome! His name is Jimmy, and he and I have become good friends who do some songs together. His sound system is really good, and he is a really good singer! I will take over his singing spot in the rotation when it starts getting busy, and I really respect that about him! He has a really quiet humility about him, and it shows, even though he has been doing what he does for a long, long time! I also like doing a few duets, as well, with a new singing friend, Alex. The really cool thing about singing there is, some singers are very theatrical on stage when performing songs! And I enjoy watching them. It makes perfect sense, since they also work concessions for the Blue Man Group!

Almost last, but not least, is Cathay Pacific in North Quincy, another awesome place to do singing when I can get over that way. And their Chinese meals are fantastic. Over at this place, you get a really great value for your money! I always order the number 12 Special on their menu, and this is no joke, when I take it to go, it takes me almost three days to eat the whole meal! I am not kidding! They give you a lot of food.

I have really connected with a lot of people since August 2016 up until now from all these different karaoke spots. And the karaoke DJs are awesome! There's a few places that I don't sing at anymore, but I already explained that, it's a personal preference for me. So I think in my mind, what would Jesus do? Exactly what this author is doing! Because He is the one that placed it in my heart to do it! And I have never regretted that decision. My friend Kevin also told me that we should sing at Harvard sometime. I would love to sing with him there, since he's graduated from Harvard. I miss my time with the Boston Minstrels; it was a great experience for a little while, singing with them and developing friendships at different places! The leader, Tim, has told me that they miss my voice. That's very humbling to hear, and I will never forget that!

CHAPTER 5

A BIG BOOST!

One thing I learned about living at the Southampton Shelter is that they not only give you a bed that you sign for daily, and feed you three meals a day and snacks, if they have any left over, but they also supply you with case managers. These case managers have been very beneficial to me since I've been in Boston over 3 years now. When I first got checked in at the shelter, they immediately supplied me with a case manager. Her name was Sue, and she and I got to know each other really well. She was awesome and very professional at what she did! I'm very grateful for Sue's compassion and professionalism in doing her job. I will always be thankful for her, as she was a real blessing in my life.

One month after I had already been in the shelter, Sue got me a job with a thing called the Work Experience Program (WEP). In this program you can either work in the kitchen or you work in janitorial. There was no opening in janitorial at the time, so they had me work in the kitchen, and let me tell you something. When you have to get up early in the morning, and I'm talking at 4 am, to feed 500 guys, you better be not only awake, but you better be ready to serve with a good attitude! When I first worked in the kitchen, I worked with this guy whose name I will not mention, because the whole time I was there, he had a horrible attitude towards the staff and residents of the shelter, and very few of the residents even liked him! He was favorable with others, and stingy with many! The only reason he and I got along was because we were both hard workers. Most of the residents we served from 5 am to 6:45 am were very grateful for what we gave them, yet some tried to demand other things. Many tried to bargain with us, and we had to stand by the guidelines. Some would try to force me to give them an extra pastry or muffin, and I'd tell them, "I cannot do that," and I'd stick by my resolve and shelter rule guidelines!

I even had one of the residents threaten me over a muffin if I didn't give him an extra. I told him, "You can threaten me all you want, but I have to stand by the guidelines!" He said, "I'll see you outside, bro." I said, "Okay, when I get out of work, if you want to talk more about it, we'll talk!" He glared at me and said, "We won't be talking," and I said, "Ok, your choice!" He really aggravated me, but I didn't blame him for being upset, because it wasn't my rule and I had to abide by it! So later on that week, I went looking for him outside, to see if we could resolve this peaceably, and pretty soon, he came up to me. I prepared myself defensively, just in case, not knowing what might happen. I had my hands raised in defense, in case there was going to be a fight, but he surprised me. He came up and apologized, and said, "Bro, please forgive me, I had a really bad morning," I said, "Bro, that's not a problem, I forgive you!" I said, "Please understand that if I had it in my power to give you an extra muffin, I would have done so, but I have to follow the guidelines, as I am a new employee there." He said, "I totally get it, Ritchie! You are one cool dude, and you really had guts to try and find me and resolve it. Most guys would have run away from me and I would have had to find them!" I said, "I understand, Bro, but I felt that I had to get it resolved. I was hoping to talk to resolve it, so thank you very much!" From that point on, he and I became really good friends for the two and a half years I was there!

After Sue came along, another case manager took me over, and her name was Patti. During my time in the shelter, she was very instrumental in finally getting me a place in October 2018. At one point before that, I had told her, "Look Patti, I'll take a broom closet if it's available!" She laughed with me. Somehow, four months before that October month happened to get a place, my name had been left off a thing called the Chronically Homeless List that I didn't even know existed! Walter, another case manager, found the issue with this, and added me to the list. Sarcastically, I said, "Great, I wonder what's going to happen now?" He said, "Trust me, Ritchie, now that you're on that list, I believe the process of finding a place will move more quickly, because your name is at the top of that list, where you should have been over a year ago, but somehow, your name got accidentally replaced. You have an excellent record here as a worker and a resident, and we want to try to reward that!" That made me feel better when he said that! I thought, *wow, they really do care!*

There were workers who worked both inside and outside the shelter. We all had a thing called contract beds, which we had to sign in for before 1 pm each day, otherwise we would lose our bed that day. If you somehow lost your job, you would lose your contract bed, as well, and you would have to go into Community. Community is where everyone else is at the shelter who doesn't have a contract bed. At 1 pm, the staff would assign the beds that the residents would receive. Not every resident would get the same bed, every day, only the contract bed people would get the same bed every day. I will talk more about the contract beds in another story, sometime.

I have to tell you about something that happened in Dorm 1, which was considered the workers' dorm. One night, I was asleep and there's a guy that slept above me, who had many, many shoes. This guy was crazy about shoes! He had enemies and friends that tried to buy his shoes. He didn't want to sell them or give them away. As we were asleep one night, somehow, someone came into our dorm and took a few of his shoes from under the bed! When he woke up the next morning, he found two shoes gone! And when I say "two shoes," I'm not talking about a *pair* of shoes. Somebody had taken a right shoe and a left shoe from two *different* pairs of shoes. So when he looked at them, he found either a left shoe, or a right shoe, and he held them up to us. We started cracking up, laughing, about that. Understandably, he was very mad, but that didn't stop us from laughing. He never got them back!

After that, about June of 2018, the heads of the shelter decided to tear down that very same dorm, and make it just a dorm for anybody! This really aggravated me and other workers, immensely, because I worked with other guys that were good, hard workers. I thought we were going to be rewarded by having Dorm 1, but instead, it was taken away from us, which means we would be reassigned new contract bed numbers in either Dorm 2, Dorm 3, or Dorm 4.

And you won't believe who was assigned bed number 1 in the whole shelter! Don't ask me how that happened, but I was the one that received that bed, before Dorm 1 was reassigned. The only thing that I can attribute that to is that I was under the grace of God the whole time I was in the shelter! So, I received a really good locker and the number 1 bed in the whole shelter, at that time. Keep in mind, there were 500 residents there!

When we were in Dorm 1, we got special privileges, like if a basketball game or a football game came on, the workers from Dorm 1 got to go into the cafeteria, watch the game, and have snacks! Staff person Terry was really good to us, and made sure when he worked that we got to see these games. I had a really good relationship with him. He treated me as a respected worker, and I treated him as a respected staff person! Anyways, back to June 2018, after we lost Dorm 1, which I still don't understand to this day, we were scattered about in the other dorms, which meant that the new, number 1 contract bed would be bed 54 in Dorm 2, and just who do you think got that bed? Once again, I did, and I was astounded by God's grace really working things out in my favor. I didn't ask for bed 54, I just asked God to get me a decent bed when they moved us, so what does He do? He gives me the best bed in Dorm 2! We also got to keep our footlockers, and we had a regular locker, as well. I was grateful for that.

I also have a really good friend by the name of Gary, and when we were together in the Soar Program, we became really good friends and helped each other out immensely. So, for a couple of months, the newly-replaced worker living quarters were scattered in the other three dorms, and I kept wondering to myself, *when are they going to change this? They might as well take away our contract beds and throw us back into Community!* After many broken words in that shelter, you tend to get cynical! But that's where the case managers really quieted the storm! They are the go-between between insanity and reality! Having God in my heart helped get me started a long time ago, and it translates into how you're supposed to treat others! I knew that if I lived there, with the residents, I might as well get along with them the best I could! Having peace in my heart with God Allowed me to get along with most of the people who were really good to me, because I treated them like they were human beings! I have never forgotten my friendships with the guys that I stayed with in that shelter, and I have been invited back at Thanksgiving and Christmas to spend more time with them, which I really enjoy doing! For Christmas in 2018, I was invited to sing some Christmas songs there, which I was very honored to do! And I look forward to Thanksgiving in 2019!

Four months dragged on in the Dorm 2 situation, and one day, I heard my case manager, Patti, say my name over the intercom. "I'm really excited to hear her voice, and I'm wondering what's going on?" She said, "Ritchie, you remember when we put in this application for you to get a place?" I said, "Yes, I do," and she said, "Well, guess what? I'm taking you over to that place today, so you can look at it!" I fell out of my socks when I heard that! I didn't really fall out of my socks, I don't think that's even possible! But you understand what I'm saying, it felt just like that! I felt like my life was getting ready to turn the corner again in a good way. I was very excited that it was going to be close to the downtown area! Nearby trains, buses, restaurants, you name it! So we went in there and got the paperwork all filled out, and one day not long after that, I heard my name called again over the intercom. It was Patti! On the way up the stairs to her office, I ran into Walter, again. He was smiling at me and said, "Ritchie, I heard your name called, this could be it for you!" I spent a few minutes before those stairs, telling Walter how much I really appreciated and respected him. And thanked him for finding out that I wasn't on that list and putting me on there, for without him doing that, I don't think I would have had the opportunity to get housing! I wonder to this day if I had been put on that list after my first year of qualification, if I would have gotten a place sooner than now? I always pondered on that. But then again, maybe it wasn't the right time to leave back then. Maybe God had more for me to accomplish at the shelter, and I wouldn't have received the place I have now. That's a lot to think about! But? Now on this day it was all coming to pass! I was absolutely elated! I couldn't stop thanking Walter! He told me he didn't hear that very often! I said, "Well, Sir, you're hearing it from me." He said, "Ritchie, from what I know about you, you have earned this, young man!" This made me beam with humility and it humbled me right to my very core! I said, "God really does have favor on me, and even though I feel I don't deserve it, I'm very grateful for it!" See, the bottom line is, when you trust God, He makes a way for you!

Patti was very excited to meet me in her office, and she said, "Ritchie, it's happening, you're moving today!" I was just about ready to cry! At times, I believed it was really going to happen, and other times, I believed the shelter was going to pass me by! This is why it is important to have faith in God! A lot of the guys put their faith in the shelter system to come through for them. But the system does fail sometimes, case in point, like when my name was left off that list that I was supposed to be on! That's why my faith is in God because He knows what to do with my life, and His system never fails! Amen...

By the time I was to leave from there, it had been almost two and a half years to the day. Patti said, "Have you got your things packed up?" I said, "Yes, ma'am, I do, I've been anticipating this since last week, I just didn't know when it was going to happen!" There were times I had told her that I was ready to take a broom closet if one became available! And I would just hang myself upside down like a bat at night, and sleep there! And I had started previously saying goodbye to my friends, and told them I would be back at Thanksgiving to see them. They asked me, "Ritchie, when is this going to happen for you?" I said, "I don't know, exactly," but I could feel it in my bones that it's getting ready to happen. I think that was God preparing my heart for that particular blessing that was going to come that morning. I said my goodbyes and was feeling good about what was starting to take place! Excitement is an understatement to describe how I felt! And what's hilarious is, when we got there, there was no place to park! Oh brother! So Patti dropped me off and parked on another street, then joined me. I kept saying to myself, *Please, God, don't let this be a dream and I wake up either still homeless in Indiana or waking from my shelter bed!* But it was real this time, and I was wide awake to experience it. I kept pinching myself to prove it; my left arm had the pinch marks to show that it was real this time!

After we got into my place, there was absolutely no furniture or anything in there, but that didn't matter to me. I was ready to kiss the floor. I gave Patti a big hug and told her "Thank you." She laughed and said, "Ritchie, you're welcome, I will be in touch." I was grateful to have the place, and I would sleep in a corner of the room for about three weeks, with no blankets, no pillows, with just my jacket on that floor. It didn't matter to me, because I was just so happy to be there. And I adjusted, from that point on. A few weeks passed by, and Patti, Sue, and another case manager named Javonica stopped by. "Ritchie? We came by to see how you're adjusting to your new place, and we have a surprise for you!" I said, "A surprise? For me? Oh wow! What is it?" They brought in two big boxes and a big bag. I said, "Patti? This is all for me?" She said, "Yes, Ritchie! We wanted to give you some things for your place!" And boy, did they ever! The two big boxes had kitchenware, including pots and pans to cook with and plates, cups, and silverware! I felt like I was in Shopping Channel Heaven! I was so thankful! God knew what I needed, and I didnt even have to pray about it; he brought it via delivery service, courtesy of where I used to live, the Southampton Shelter! Wow! And no less, through case management! This is an example of how the shelter not only works hard to get you a place, but they follow up on you to see that you're doing ok! That, my friends, is called compassion! Ahe shelter and its caring group of case managers really do take care of you! I'm living proof of that care and concern! How I truly thank God for them! Isn't it just like God to surprise me in this fashion? Because He knows I love surprises, big or small!

I had another case manager by the name of David Cabral, who was very instrumental in working alongside Patti to help get me my place. I would go to his office, quite often, and fill out paperwork for an endless amount of places to move into. He worked for a place called Hearth, which was very good to me, as well, and they helped me to get my birth certificate again, by paying for it! And I can't say enough about them. They were phenomenal working with me. David no longer works there, but I hope he reads this and it lets him know just how much I appreciated him.

After he left, I received another case manager from Hearth by the name of Isaiah, who was very instrumental in getting me furniture from a place called New Life in Walpole, Massachusetts. We went there by bus, and I got to pick out anything I wanted to complement my new place! Once again, I was about ready to cry, as I didn't want to get too greedy, and give someone else a chance to get things as well, but I was very grateful that I could pick out something. New Life Furniture Bank was a blessing, and I believe a very Christian-based resource for this author. There were extremely sweet people there that were very nice to me! Isaiah smiled when he saw me jumping around like a little kid in a candy store, like I was waiting to get a big piece of chocolate! Well, chocolate time had come for Ritchie! Isaiah looked at me after we picked out everything that I have up until today and said, "Bro, God has been good to you, I can see it in your face, and the music of yours that you do on YouTube, as well! I'm so glad to be a part of this to help you out!"

Isaiah is no longer my case manager; I have Demetrius now. Demetrius is another one of those guys who is another blessing! He has been really good to me. When I first moved into my place, it was the first time in over four years that I wasn't homeless, and I thanked God for the blessing he had just bestowed on my life!

When I first became homeless back in August 2014, I was to experience things I'd never experienced before, and every time I kept saying to God by faith, *Lord I love you, I trust you, I believe in you, I have faith in you, and I know you will more than come through for me, awesome Abba Father God!* That was my prayer of faith for over four years that I would speak daily! And God saved the best for years to come in Boston! At the time when I moved in, there was another case manager from a place called Home Start that was assigned to me. Of course, I wasn't even aware of this, and I was very surprised when that new case manager, by the name of Megan, came over to meet me for the first time in my new place! And she was very instrumental in first getting me food in this new apartment so that I wouldn't go hungry, because at that point I had nothing to eat, and I thought to myself, *If food doesn't happen here, at least I'd die happy in my new place!*

At that point, I had applied for my Early Retirement disability after a botched knee surgery, something I did not want to do until I was actually ready to retire, and not be forced into retirement! But that kicked in, as well, and I'm grateful for that today, as I draw on that disability each month! Social Security has been very good to me, and the disability benefits, as well. Patti, the Shelter case manager, also made sure that I was to get some things at another furniture store, which I didn't pick out, but the one thing I appreciated from that place is my dining room table and chairs, since the couch I first got from there was hard as a proverbial rock! And I still have it today, but they refused to take it back unless I paid them a fee to remove it! What a bunch of nonsense that was, a real learning experience! I wanted to exchange a mattress after the 30-day trial period. With the new bed from that same furniture store, they told me it was free for 30 days and if I didn't like it they would come and get it and give me another one. Well, I didn't like the mattress, because it was hard as a rock, too! Now, keep this in mind, I'm grateful for this stuff, but I also had a back injury and a knee injury that caused the surgery, and I can't sleep on a hard mattress like that one! You see, this furniture store gave me a really hard time about coming to get the other mattress and exchanging it. If I knew they were going to be that difficult, I would have gotten a bed at New Life Furniture, instead! And they weren't going to come and exchange it unless I paid them something to take it away! If their manager knew how I felt about this place, they would have taken care of me immediately, knowing I am a disabled person from the knee surgery! But nothing was done about the bed, and so I had to live with that, for a while! I won't mention this furniture store by name, all I know is that they gave me such a hard time over the bed and the hard couch! The difference between New Life Furniture and this other place is miles apart. New Life is not well known except in Massachusetts and maybe some other places. But I thank God that, somehow, I found a place online called Wayfair Mattress and Furniture! And through a misunderstanding with them, I got a free futon mattress! I was absolutely shocked because I paid for it, and then my money was returned! I am, to this day, absolutely shocked about Wayfair Mattress and Furniture, because in my book, they are way fair! If I ever order anything again, I will order from them, because they have been so good to this author!

I now have a new case manager named Mary coming to visit me soon! She's from Home Start and she has a very pleasant voice, like Megan! ☺ So I look forward to getting to meet with her, as well, and I appreciate Demetrius from Hearth! God made sure from Day One in the shelter that I've been well taken care of! So, yes, case management definitely gets my vote! Trust me, they would get your vote, as well! I just wanted to share that with you; they've been nothing but a blessing! Another case manager who worked behind the scenes, Javonica, was also a blessing! And you now see why I highly endorse these people, because of God who made all this possible.

I used to be a long-distance runner before I had this surgery, but now I do a different kind of running, and it's all for God! He is my source for all resources. The case managers of the shelter were a real blessing, and Hearth, and Home Start. This author will be truly grateful moving forward! Amen.

CHAPTER 6

JUST FOR THE RECORD!

When you have been a resident and worker in a big shelter like Southampton, you realize that you live in the big city of Boston, and no longer do you reside in the small city of Anderson, Indiana! On my first day in the shelter, it was a reality culture shock! In Anderson, the population is about 60,000, and as I mentioned before, for Boston and surrounding areas that make up Boston, we are talking close to 8 million people! And so, your eyes are opened up the very first day you're in the shelter and learning you are about to become roommates with 499 other guys! There's one of two ways you can approach your experience. You can see it in the most negative way possible, or you can use it as a very positive thing that happened! I agree there was a lot of negativity there, and drug use, as well. But that isn't what makes Southampton Shelter unique. What made it different for me in the two-and-a-half years I was there were the people that cared! When you approach people with a good attitude, chances are, you are going to receive a nice attitude back! I got along well with my supervisors and bosses that I worked for. I was called on to train about ten people to work. I will document that at a later time, for another book! I got along with most of the staff there, even though there were some that had really hard attitudes towards the residents of the shelter! And those people and I didn't see eye-to-eye on how they treated people! They had this attitude that they were so much better than the residents. One made a comment in Dorm 1 one time, that the workers in there were getting too comfortable with their stuff, and needed to downsize it! Just a very cocky attitude from a staff person who was absolutely clueless when it came to what a homeless person feels or is going through! A very cold-hearted and self-righteous attitude from a person who has never been homeless and who will never understand!

The contract bed workers in that dorm stood by each other and watched each other's stuff when they were not by their beds! And we learned what staff would treat us right and which ones didn't like us! And so I decided to share with the staff person who made that comment about our stuff, "I hope you realize you only have a job because of the residents that are here. That doesn't make you better than them, you're supposed to be able to serve them on this job with at least dignity and respect!" She looked at me like I was crazy! And said, "Well, who are you to talk to me like this?" I said, "I say this because I am a future book author and I will be writing this story!" I also shared this with fellow employees, some who thought they were better than the residents because they had a job! I also told them the same thing, saying, "You need to be nice to the people living here who envy your position. Just because you work here now doesn't make you better than them! And keep this in mind, as well, you're one paycheck away from being where they are!" And so, most of the employees listened to me when I said that! I had no desire at that time to be a leader in the WEP program! But I found myself later on becoming a spokesman for them and the residents of the shelter! I will document that in a later book, a position I didn't want as a leader but found myself unwillingly being qualified for! And I had many residents as friends throughout the time I was there! I went back there and visited them and a lot of them are still there, and remembered me and smiled! They said, "Ritchie? You're one of the lucky ones that got out of here!" And I told them, "I was one of the most fortunate ones, learning from my experience here, and I am grateful for it! God was not only watching over me at the shelter, but was giving me favor, as well, in my time there."

I heard that HBO was going to be doing a documentary on life at the Southampton Shelter and supposedly calls it the "worst shelter they've ever been in!" The sad part is, I've met the guy doing this documentary, and the title of this chapter is called "Setting the Record Straight!" As the author of this book, I plan to do just that! I will agree with the HBO documentary, there is a lot of negativity, and there was some violence when I lived there, and there was drug use rampant outside and inside the shelter, as well! I saw those things for myself. But I'm also here to declare that there was also positivity. As one who lived the experience, I'm here to tell the full truth! And I'm here to share the positive side of my experience there! I have never seen a place like this that helps 500 people with Thanksgiving parties and Christmas parties as I experienced there as a worker and a resident! The case managers, as I mentioned in another chapter, are awesome, as they are out to help those who are willing to not only get work at the shelter, but to get a place outside the shelter, as well, and I'm living proof of that since I now have an apartment through my case managers! They also had days where they would give away a lot of clothes that were donated, and these were very nice clothes! There were many days where outside departments would come in and volunteer their time and cook for the residents! They also had people on staff that were almost like a cross between a counselor and a psychiatrist that would be willing to talk to you at any time over any situation! Yes, there were some not so good people there who worked as staff! And a supervisor who is no longer there, and I'm glad she's gone, because she treated the residents like crap! But I also wish that Jason Lee was still there. He was an incredible supervisor, very compassionate and friendly towards the people under his care! But Jason also heads programs to get the residents fed through outside organizations at different times, serving special meals at lunch and dinner!

And they would have music programs coming in there to entertain them, as well. I became a part of one of those bands called the Boston Minstrels, who invited me to be a part of their band as a singer with them! On Christmas Day of 2018 at the shelter, I was asked to sing there, as well, doing some Christmas songs, which as a songwriter on

YouTube I was very honored to do! And I've met a lot of homeless people on the street who don't want a handout, they just want a hand up! And I became friends with many of them. It's true there is a huge drug problem in Boston and around the shelter, and some people use it inside the shelter walls! Sometimes fights break out, but in a place that size, that's also a testament to how well the staff like Terry, and Big, and others, who would take care of things. When I think of them, I think of how we'd sometimes play catch with a football with each other, and there would be almost 20 people watching us play back-and-forth. And those are some memories I have of the staff and the environment there, and I still have that ball, today.

Sometimes, people do overdose in some shelters. Southampton Shelter is no different from that! But what really sets it apart in my mind is the programs that they have and the awesome case management! Many of the staff are nice. I got along with all those in authority over me except one night shift supervisor who was an absolute jerk! Nobody liked him, and I could see why, up close and personal, because one morning, he and I got into it, and he provoked me into anger! My boss found out about it and had me report him for harassment! The head supervisor over all the supervisors found out about it and really laid into that guy! And then she called me into her office and said, "Ritchie? I know you are one of the best employees we have, and I'm telling you now, he will never bother you again!" And he never did! I never did get reimbursed for the full day I was supposed to work, and that bothered me! I lost about six hours of pay from that incident. And I never forgot that, I was so upset. If John would have been my boss at that time, I guarantee you he would have made sure that I got paid for it, because that's the kind of man he was. Unfortunately, my boss at the time told me, "It's only six hours, Ritchie! Don't worry about it!" What an absolutely stupid thing to say to a hardworking employee! If they did that to his paycheck, I guarantee you he would worry about it! Are you kidding me? Before John became my boss, he told me this one day, "They should put you in charge of the WEP Program, because you make sure all of you get everything done, whether you're shorthanded or not! You guys are the best workers this shelter has ever had!" And I was proud to hear that, and shared it with the other guys! They loved hearing that!

Unfortunately, it was going to strike a nerve. supervisor Ben came by a few minutes later to check on our progress, and was smiling with pride at how clean everything was, and told me, "Ritchie? You guys do an excellent job, and I never have to check on you!" I said, "Thank you, Ben, we always try to do it right." He smiled at me and said, "Yeah, it shows!" I said, "That's the second compliment we have had today!" He said, "Oh?" I said, "Yeah, John came by earlier and said the place was so clean, he said, 'Ritchie you should be the head of the WEP Program!' " I thought he would smile when I said that, but the color drained from his face! I said to myself, *what did I say wrong?* He gave me a stern look and glared at me and said, "I am the head of the WEP Program!" I said that I didn't think anything was meant by the comment that John told me, and that I was flattered by it! And I believe to this day that this is why I never got the Assistant Manager position that I had trained months for. And to prove his superiority over me, he called me into his office one day and told me in front of three other supervisors, "Ritchie? We all agree you have managerial skills, and you are one of the best WEP workers we've ever had! But you can forget about it, because Darrel is our Assistant manager, and has been for a long time, and he's not leaving, so forget about it!" Then I spoke up. I said, "You're wrong! Because he told me himself that he was quitting! And I would know because he puts me in charge after he takes off every day!" They all said it wasn't true. I looked at each one in the face and I said, "It is true!" Ben glared at me and said, "You can go now!"

So I left the office knowing what I said was true, wondering why he said this in front of three other day supervisors? Was it to humiliate me? I wonder even to this day! But, the bottom line is, within 3 weeks Darrel did quit, and they couldn't believe it! The day he quit, they eliminated the Assistant Manager position! Was this to spite me? I'll never know, but it left me with a bad taste in my mouth. And before I had the fallout with Ben, he used to ask me to do cleaning around the shelter after my shift ended. "Don't punch out, Ritchie, stay on the clock, and I will make sure you get paid to do what I need to have done! A little extra money for you to have in your pocket." He smiled. I said that I would like that, and showed up about 3 or 4 weeks straight doing intense cleanup, about 2 or 3 hours more after my shift ended. And I never let him down, and he would compliment me on my work! But all that stopped after I shared the compliment that I had received from my soon-to-be boss, John! And Ben put another guy in my place for the extra work that I used to do.

They would also have days where my former boss, John, would spin 45 records for people in attendance to try to guess the music they were hearing, and if they did so, they would win prizes that they could keep! There were also, and still are to this day, outside organizations that will come in and cut your hair when you put your name on a list! So, as you can see from this author's point of view, there's a lot of positivity to the shelter, as well! Beth, who was the head of the shelter, I believe, at that time, was very nice to me. I appreciated her friendship and she always encouraged me to fulfill my potential. Even looking back at that today, I had no idea what that was, or would turn out to be. I'm pretty sure through this first book that some of that desire and potential is starting to seep through! And at the shelter, they also have an area called the Southampton Clinic, which is located close to security check-in before you hit the cafeteria. There are nurses, an excellent doctor named Dr. Chatterjee, who I always got along with, encouraged me in my potential. I guess I was just too dumbfounded at the time to see it, because I hadn't opened my eyes mentally or spiritually to see what was there.

They had a case manager by the name of Max who was really good with people, and we got along great. He now knows what I know about the doctor who had the attitude with me, that he was still smug over his so-called perfect surgery on my right knee that never healed! Max came with me one time to my appointment with this doctor and saw exactly what I had told him before, for himself, that this doctor was a real piece of work! And I also warned other residents at the shelter at that time to not have any operations with this doctor, and many of them listened. They saw the results when they saw how I could hardly walk. And keep in mind, they saw how quick I moved at work before that surgery.

The clinic had a receptionist named Jackie who was very good with the residents! And I don't remember the one she replaced, but that female receptionist was good, too. One of the head nurses was a very talented painter who had some of her paintings on the office wall, out front! And if things got out of hand in the clinic or the shelter with some people's bad attitudes and fighting or whatever, there were also campus police to take care of any situations! And one of the positives for me was, as a person who learned a little bit about boxing in Indiana before I came to Boston, I got a crash course from a resident in martial arts! Before I was to become disabled, I was still able to teach some basic defense moves to a few people being picked on there, and a staff person who wanted to learn how to defend himself if he needed. So I was able to pass the training along just about two weeks before I was to get my place, to teach them some of the basic moves that I learned from my friend. If I was physically able, I would have taught them more, and, fortunately, I haven't had to use it near where I live. Incidentally, the guy who gave me a crash course of training in martial arts is named Jose. He's in his own apartment now, but I will never forget what he taught me! When you receive something good or beneficial, you pass it on!

In the Soar Program, I was treated very well, and respected, as well, for the 80 guys living up there, including myself. It was one of those programs which was supposed to be a go-between between life in the shelter and life in their own apartments, or situations they were to encounter on the outside after they left the shelter!

When you treat other residents and co-workers with respect, chances are, you get that back in return! I received the nickname "Ritchie" from the residents. I truly love that name, today. How I got the nickname was my friend Doug and by guys who saw my work ethic and decided they were going to call me Ritchie, as well, and not "Richard," anymore! And so this author loves that name! When I sing at karaoke places, I am Ritchie! And I have truly embellished that name!

Another of the positives this place has over many shelters is that from 7 am to lunchtime, the residents go to the dining area of the cafeteria and get to watch TV, read books, draw, color, or talk with other residents. They can stay in there all the way up until bed check time, which is 1 pm, even in bad weather or good weather. Most other shelters will kick their residents out all day long until it's time to come back in for lunch or check-in time. Some guys from other shelters actually come over and visit the Southampton residents in the cafeteria, since they were kicked out of their shelters, they have somewhere else to go until check-in time!

The one thing I didn't like is that they kept calling residents "guests" of the shelter! To me, a guest is someone who stays for a little bit, and then leaves! But a resident is someone who lives there for a short time or a little while! That "guest" tag always irritated me! But as you can see, not everything that goes on in a shelter is negative. I have pointed out many positives to you that happened to this author while I was there! You can hear it from an outside source or a documentary, but until you've lived it and seen it for yourself, you won't know the truth! This author saw both sides of living there, as a resident and a worker. And now you know the story. Whoever the readers of this book are, need to know what truly happened in the time I was there for two and a half years! There was bad and there was good! A man with an argument is no match for a man with experience! And I experienced it, so if this person who claims to work for HBO that lives in the shelter wants to carry out his threat trying to sue the city because of the documentary, well, I'd like them to know that I will be more than happy to be a witness for the defense, for the shelter and my city, because I saw it all! So I say, take that documentary with only half-truth, because their argument doesn't hold water! I lived there, so I know! There's more good things I can share with you, but I think you get the idea, that this author was treated well and with respect in my living time there, and I will never forget the people that were there nor my experience!

CHAPTER 7

POWER SOURCE

When you're like me, and live alone in a building with many residents in a big city, you tend to feel a little bit lonely. It's hard to communicate those feelings with people that speak different languages, so the only thing you can do, and the first thing that I do each morning, is plug into the Power Source! People with cell phones can identify with this story because when their phones get low on power, they have to get them plugged in and recharged, otherwise the phone will have no power! And it will become useless, because you won't be able to use it! That's how it is with my life when my spiritual energy or my spiritual batteries are running low. I plug into my daily Power Source, and that Power Source for my life is God! Without that power, I wouldn't even have a life! Because I get daily guidance when I reach out to Heaven, either to thank Him for even a little thing, or a big thing, or if I have a concern or prayer request, He listens!

But like most any father, He hopes to hear praise first as I speak out His name! Like an earthly father would have a son or daughter come up to him or his wife, and they might have a need to ask their father or mother for, and they may want to hear something good that either one of them has done, before they hear their need! I know if I'm that father, and a son or daughter comes up to me with a need, I hope they first acknowledge that their father did something good for them, and has helped them out in the past! So any earthly father or mother would want to hear some kind of praise first from that son or daughter, before they tell the parents what the need is ! I know I would! Well, God is likened to an earthly father; He wants to hear me praise Him, hopefully, before I bring a concern before Him! And make no mistake, He wants to hear our concerns! His word says He knows our needs before we even ask! So He knows what I'm about to ask Him, but what He's longing to hear from me is praise for what He has done in my life! And when I go before God in prayer in the morning, after I wake up, I remember the good things He has done in my life, past, present, or future! The best part of waking up is not Folgers in my cup, as the commercial says. No. The best part of waking up is knowing God can fill the portion of my cup. In other words, He will supply my daily needs. Folgers, I don't think, can do that. And I can feel His presence inside of me when I'm welling up with thanks unto Him, and things he has done, for the different things He has brought me through! And He has brought this person through a lot! He is my Source! And I plug into Him every day.

And no, it's not perfect every day. Is a marriage perfect every day? No! Some days, you have to work at it! Christianity is the same way; I have to get my thoughts out of the way and try to focus on Him. Early morning prayer time is not the easiest thing before I start my day. So, some days I have to discipline myself to concentrate on God. Having some chocolate milk helps, too! So, some days, I really have to talk to Him, even though my mind may not be focused right then and there. But I'm telling you now that it's worth it, because once I start praying and praising Him, my mind thinks of Heaven. I remind God every day that I am far from perfect, and I get down on myself sometimes, but He lifts me up when my thoughts are centered on Him. And I can't even describe what it feels like when you center on God at that time; it feels like your body is lighter than air! That's the only way I can describe the sensation I feel at that point! It is a sensation your mind can't comprehend, yet your body feels it, and I can truly say in the years that I've been on this planet, that I have never ever felt anything like that, anywhere and anytime, on this earth! You feel at peace, and your mind isn't racing with the day's activities, but calm, you can't explain the peace of God!

I watched a Star Trek show one time where a man on a planet was being absorbed by a lifeforce when he called on its name! That is a great example to me of how God's presence fills me up inside when I call upon His name! And God is not impressed by big flowery prayer words that are trying to impress him! You know what I'd say to that? Forget about it! All God wants is a sincere heart with no pretense! He knows we're not perfect, because if we were, then Jesus would never have had to give his life on the cross for our very lives, because he was the ransom that became our sacrifice! So there is no way I can describe in words what it feels like when his presence is inside. You really can't describe it unless you experience it in prayer. And that's where I find Him. Not every day do I feel His presence, but that's why it's called faith, but His word says that He never leaves us or forsakes us once He's in our hearts, and His love is the down-payment for our lives, to be paid in full one day when we see Him face-to-face! When I'm really drawing close to Him and telling Him how much He means to me, and I open my heart in pure sincerity to Him, that's where I find Him! And you'll find that Heaven is never closed. And He knows my needs before I even ask, His word says, and I learned a long time ago, that when I come to God in prayer, I should just be honest before Him! Keep in mind, He knows what I'm thinking, anyway, so if I'm honest before Him, then I would not be trying to hide anything, anyway. I mean, after all, how dumb would that be? He loves when I am just open before him, and do not try to hide my feelings or my thoughts. I mean, just try to hide something from your spouse and see how long that lasts! God is like that; there are many similarities between a relationship with God and a relationship in marriage! And there is no answering service awaiting you to go through about fifteen prompts before you reach Heaven, like the phone does when you're trying to reach, oh, I don't know, maybe a human being? Heaven is always open, and it doesn't matter what mental state I'm in at that moment, whether I'm happy, sad, angry, or frustrated, or whatever my mood or faith is in, I tell him, "God, I can't live this day without you, why would I even want to try?"

There was an old saying that they had in the seventies, "let it all hang out!" And with God in prayer, I daily let it all hang out! I tell him, you have done so much for me, and you continue to bless my life! And I praise you for it! Even when I'm getting ready to get myself cleaned up, I remind God daily just what he means to me! The iron bars they have on the far side wall of the bathtub are a real blessing, because without those to lift myself out of the tub, I'd be toast! For without those bars, I couldn't use my arms and lift myself out of there without some kind of strong support to hold onto! So yeah, it is a blessing when you are handicapped or disabled! Even the toilet lid is cool! You're probably thinking to yourself right now in your mind, *Now, Ritchie? Hold on! The toilet lid?* Yes, the toilet lid! And I'll tell you why! A lot of you reading this right now are probably thinking, *Ritchie? You obviously must not get out much, because you're entertained by a toilet?* No! I didn't say "entertained!" I said that the toilet lid was cool, and here's why: most toilet lids need to be lowered gently, or they will slam, and you might wake up Grandma, and she won't be very happy! But with mine, it acts like it's on some kind of hydraulic brake and lowers gently to the seat! I can get up from there after doing business on it and let the lid fall onto the seat, and not my seat, the toilet seat! And even if I tried to slam it down, it would still gently slowly fall. Now, how cool is that?

I'm sure some of you are thinking, *Bro? You're easily entertained!* And I would say, yes, I am! It doesn't take much for me to appreciate even the littlest things! Now, that doesn't mean that you get mad at your own toilet lid, if you have one and have a chewing-out session with it, because it still slams. Just be mindful, and don't let the toilet lid slam when you're done, or you're going to have to deal with a very cranky, angry Grandma that you just awoke, almost like a very disgruntled bear you have just interrupted from hibernation! I say Grandma as an example, because when I was much younger, I would be invited some weekends to stay with my grandparents, every so often. Whenever I would use their restroom, that toilet lid would clank down so hard that it would have awakened their next of kin! Keep in mind, my grandparents had high-velocity hearing aids that were turned up so high that hearing the toilet lid crash with a huge thud must have, to them, sounded like a sonic boom blast! And it was a deafening sound! And after I'd washed my hands, I could hear them both chewing me out while I was leaving the bathroom and I was still in the hallway, while I was wondering what it was going to be like when I had enough nerve to finally enter the living room! I didn't have to wait long to find out! For the sake of the readers here, I will let you draw your own conclusion of what was being said! I don't want to go into detail on that! There might be kids in the room, so please use your own imagination! Put it this way, I thought my life was over! They did get over it, finally, in about a week or two, long after I had left! It took me a while to recognize that you don't tick off the grandparents! Otherwise, they might develop a sudden memory lapse sometime around Christmas or your Birthday! That's one indication for when you knew they were upset!

Back to being an adult now. Anyway, as I get older, I do know God is there, I feel His presence daily! I can't say enough about Him! I can't make Him wait until Sunday to talk to Him in a church! Would you make your wife have to wait a whole week to talk to you? Of course not! You might find yourself divorced, or sleeping on the couch, or in the garage! Just like a wife, God wants a daily relationship with me! And the more I want to share my life with Him, the more He shares His presence with me! Daily, I feel that presence because of the relationship I have with Him. He didn't force me, He asked me to allow Him to be a part of my life, and I said "yes!" He took me just as I am! And like a good, earthly relationship, I have never regretted it, even when I was homeless, because I knew God was there! Amen! He filled my heart with gratitude and joy! He has given me a saying that I want to share with you, and it goes like this, "Our attitude of gratitude through God will determine our altitude!" And that is ever so true! He loves a cheerful giver, but He loves cheerful praise, as well, with a good attitude! And He loves good intentions that come out of the heart, out of something I want to do for Him! As a believer in Christ I totally get the giving part, that says there's a Scripture that reads, that it is better to give than receive. When you receive something, you're grateful and thankful for it, but, when you give, you feel able to do something with gladness from your heart; that's the difference! And it feels like fulfilled satisfaction knowing you made someone else happy even for but a brief shining moment! That, to me, is joy!

I disagree with Pastors who say that God only rewards our works and not our intentions, because when I intended to get my friend a birthday gift he wanted, I found myself five dollars short of buying his gift, and they couldn't hold it for me, even though his birthday would be the next day. With sadness, I watched them put the item back in stock. I left the store rejected, because I knew my friend wanted that gift, and there I was, without enough money to pay for it! So I made a silent prayer to God, asking Him to please make sure that someone else could get my friend the gift he wanted, since I couldn't! I'd have to think about getting him something else before the store closed in about an hour. My heart sank, but God knew my intention of getting that for my friend, and I'm sure heaven smiled, anyway, even if I couldn't smile at that point.

As I started to go back in the store, I heard some noise commotion that caught my attention, and so I went over to investigate. It seemed two dogs were having an argument, and the owner couldn't get his dog away from the other one, and it was stressing him out! I accessed the situation and decided that I was going to grab the other dog by the back of his collar, to pull him away from the owner's dog, and the trick worked as the attacking dog was startled by someone grabbing his collar. The dog tried his best to bite me, but I had a really strong grip on that collar and I wasn't about to let go! This infuriated the dog to no end as he desperately tried to take a chunk out of me! The more he resisted, the more tired he got, as his frustration was giving way to exhaustion! His loud barking became almost a whimper now, as he couldn't get at whatever was holding him back! And as he started whining, I saw this as a good opportunity to pull him away from the other dog, grabbing his collar tight and making him walk with me, away from the scene! The dog was too exhausted to resist me anymore, and gave up fighting! I now had the attacking dog about twenty feet from the owner's dog, and let go of him slowly, which I'm sure surprised the dog, but he was in no condition to attack. I yelled in a loud voice at him, "Get out of here!" And you would have thought that dog's butt was on fire! He hightailed it out of there as quickly as he could go, and he never looked back! I thanked God that I had the arm strength to hold him back! He was about a medium-sized German Shepherd, and the dog he was attacking was much smaller, so I held his collar back with all my strength, and it had worked! The owner was so relieved he was almost crying.

He was so happy his dog had survived! My arm was throbbing, from trying to hold the bigger dog back, and I looked at my watch and saw the store would be closing in about 25 minutes, and I had to hurry! The man smiled at me and said, "God bless you, young man, for your bravery! If you hadn't come along when you did, that bigger dog would have torn Couch Potato to pieces! I said, "Sir? You named your dog Couch Potato?" "Yes, young man, that's his name!" I wanted to burst out laughing, but I just let it well up inside of me! I said, "What do you call for him for short if you're upset with him? Do you call him Couch? Or do you call him Potato?" I couldn't believe the words that were coming out of my mouth!I said to myself, *Am I really saying these things? And yes! I guess I am!* He said, "You'll have to ask my wife that one, she's the one who named him!" I said, "Let me guess, is it because he likes to watch TV a lot? On the couch?" I couldn't believe what I was saying! He spoke back, "Yes! That is exactly right, how do you know that?" "Oh? Just a lucky guess!" In my mind I was formulating the equation. *Let's see now...Dog laying down- watching TV- plus couch- equals Couch Potato! Ding ding ding! Brilliant!* What a deduction!

I looked at my watch now, I had 17 minutes to go before the store closed! I said, "Sir? I apologize, but I have to leave now and do what I was trying to do, before I heard the commotion!" He said, "Young man, before you go, I want to reward your bravery!" I said, "It's OK, Sir, I did it out of instinct." *My brain started screaming at me, Richard? You idiot! Let him reward you!* So I said, "Sir? It was no big deal, I didn't do it for a reward." He said, "Young man, hold out your hand!" So I did, and he gave me a $20 bill! And I could not believe it! But, there it was! I was ready to cry! I looked at my watch, 12 minutes to go! Sir? I

"Gotta go now!" I said, "Thank you very much," and said goodbye to Couch Potato! What a great name for a lazy dog! And I hightailed it back to that store before they closed. Maybe Couch Potato would be safer on the couch? Oh well...

I was able to get my friend's gift, and because I exerted a lot of energy pulling back that big dog, I was hungry, as well, so I got a quick sandwich. My friend was very happy on his birthday, and so was I! So this saying that God rewards our works only but does not reward good intentions is baloney! God knew I needed the money, because my intention was to get my friend's gift! And He made a way to make that happen! So God rewards not only our works, but if our intentions are good according to His will, He also rewards our good intentions! A big Amen on that! Scripture comes to mind, and I think it's in the New Testament, I can't remember word-for-word, but it's something like this, "And he heareth us according to His will, and He will supply our need!" So, did God hear my need that day? Yes, He did! When I acted in Faith, He answered the prayer! But, I had to put my legs to my faith and try to act on it! So praise God for an answered prayer with 12 minutes to go!

And even now when I pray, if I've had a bad day, I try to come into reverence in His presence because He's Holy! I might have to cool down a bit after being upset, but after that, I talk to Him and either ask for forgiveness, or to forgive whoever or whatever the situation was. Words are powerful, so what we speak can either make us or break us. A New Testament Scripture says that there is life or death in the power of the tongue. And being human, I still make mistakes when I might say something I didn't mean to say at the moment, so I need to own up to it and ask for forgiveness, right then and there, or at least later on when it weighs heavily on me to make it right! And that's not always easy, but God gives me the power to do it. I could easily say like any person, "The weather is horrible today, looks like it's going to be a miserable day today!" And because I spoke words into action, guess what? It's going to be a miserable day!

I learned long ago in a freezing weather test like Indiana, that I wasn't going to let bad weather dictate to me how I was going to feel that day, or any day! And even to the point where many times I could have froze to death, faith and hope kept the dream of living alive! Believing the impossible when it didn't look possible! And even today in Boston, I've heard people tell me, "Oh, Ritchie! Your surgically-repaired knee is really going to feel it when winter starts getting cold!" Oh, really? Newsflash to those who think this way, I've had this knee messed up now for almost two years, and it doesn't matter if it's winter, summer, or spring, it feels the same way no matter what the season! And why is that? Because I decided that the weather is not going to dictate to me how my knee or myself is supposed to feel! It just ain't going to happen! I'm pretty sure my knee isn't smart enough to know what the weather is doing, and my brain doesn't send text to either knee about what the weather forecast is! Bottomline is: the change of weather does not own, dictate, or dominate how I'm supposed to feel that day! God dictates my thinking!

Now, you might be reading this and maybe you don't believe in God, but that's okay, no one will force you to. But that doesn't change the experience I had with Him when I asked Him to come into my heart and change me. I still have rough edges about me, and in no way claim to be perfect, but the closer I draw to Him, the closer He draws to me! Here's a thought you can write down if you want: God wants us just as we are before Him, He wants us to be real before Him and not religious! I knew a lot of people in Indiana who would put up a so-called holy front in church and act like heathens on the outside! Am I judging them? No, they judge themselves by playing and acting like a fool! And they bring reproach on the name of Christ through these actions! Here's an example. If I represent my family at home as a good kid,then why in the world would I act like I have a bad attitude away from the family? I would bring embarrassment, shame and reproach on my own family until I try to make it right! God is like that, so If I know Him in church, then it stands to reason that I would know him outside the church! Unless it was just nothing more than a religious front inside the walls of the church! God wants me to be real with Him and others.

I tried to be real every day of my life when I lived with 500 guys and staff in the shelter, because it wasn't a religious front, these guys would have seen right through that! Because God lives inside of me, I was able to be the real person He made me to be with no pretense! If you're real, then you're not going to be anything else but real! Jesus said to his disciples one day in a parable that two men prayed in a church and one said, "I thank you, God, that I am not like those other men!" And the other man said, "God please be merciful to me, a sinner..." So, who was self righteous, and who was seeking to be made righteous? Whose words do you think God honored? Jesus came against the religious teaching of his day because they didn't follow the law of God! Jesus was the law of God! And he tried to show them and they wouldn't listen! That's why I'd rather have a real heart than a religious heart, because with a real heart I become real and open before God.

The Christian life is not all bed and roses, because you are going to encounter some thorns along the way, and He navigates me through life's troubled waters, because He is my lighthouse! There is an old saying that says "God is my co-pilot!" I highly disagree with that! He *is* the pilot! In fact, He owns the whole airline! If I try to be a co-pilot and fly the ship with Him, I might wreck the plane! He can fly the plane, and I know, as many passengers would as well, that He will get me and them to our destination! A big Amen! He knows what He's doing, my job is to trust him and He will get me where I need to be... That's called Faith! Believing in what we cannot see and believing God with the hope of what we ask him for, or hope will bring us through! You might have an argument in your belief and why you feel that way, but you see, He has given me the experience, and nothing will ever change that! There is nothing compared to feeling His presence come in, when I asked Him into my heart years ago and said, "Take my life, God, and use it for your glory," I signed on His spiritual dotted line! This was before I became an author, and he has allowed me to be a singer-songwriter on YouTube, as well! I have connected with many other singers throughout Boston, and I've really enjoyed their company! He was with me when I was homeless for years! And He was right there encouraging me daily that He had something better for me down the road! When the opportunity to come to Boston through my friend came up, to be honest with you, I was a little scared, but ready to believe this is where God would have me to be, and so I took a leap of faith and believed! And if I would trust and believe Him by faith, it would come to pass, and it did! And look where I am today! This author is living proof of God's love, favor, blessing, patience, temperament, and long suffering with my life, waiting for me to be the person He's molding me to be now! If I would have stayed behind, I would have perished in Indiana! Absolutely, no doubt in my mind on that, and I would not have been able to fulfill whatever will He was going to accomplish with purpose in my life!

There's an old saying that comes to mind that I heard a long time ago, and it goes like this: "Please be patient with me. God is not finished with me yet!" And boy, how true that is! I feel as I'm getting older that I'm just getting started! Even with the pain I suffered from the botched knee surgery, how I remember what it was like when I used to be a long-distance runner! When I was invited to come and live in Boston, the one desire I had as a runner was to run in the Boston Marathon for my age group! And I can guarantee you, I would have done really well because I trained really hard in Indiana in some of the worst weather conditions I had ever been in! Including five-below weather with snow gusts everywhere for many days! You run or you die! So I learned to discipline my body and my mind, with God's help, of course, I didn't do it on my own! He gave me strength during those times when I was homeless in some of the coldest weather imaginable! And I drew my strength from Him! And instead of thinking about homelessness, I would run like the wind, daily! Feeling deep down inside, there is somehow a greater purpose! If I didn't leave Indiana at that time to go, I am convinced to this day that I wouldn't have survived the arctic chill weather there much longer and would have died as a homeless person, never fulfilling whatever I was called to do. And when I was invited to live in Boston, I thought that purpose was going to be fulfilled running the Boston Marathon! I was in really, really good shape!

And I also ran with a club three times a week called Back on my Feet! This was a walking club that would meet together three times a week to walk or run, and being the runner I was, I enjoyed the freedom of running! But looking back on it now, even though I'm disabled, my mindset is still of a runner. I just have to do a different kind of running now! I try to run for God, getting this book done, getting more music done, trying to get many things done. And yes, I do think of those days when I think about if I never would have had this knee surgery, I feel I would have been in the Boston Marathon in either 2019 or 2020! And I was also looking forward to doing a thing called the Veterans' Run, where you run for veterans who served in the military! That would be a great honor, since I did a little bit of Navy time myself when I was much younger. But I can't dwell on that, I have to dwell on what's ahead and not what's behind me! Will I ever run again or even walk normally again? I can't answer that! But this much I do know: God will be there every step of the way, whatever He has me to do!

I have been invited to the Philippines next year, and as an author, I hope to fulfill that, God-willing! If it's His will, it's my will to do His will! I'm getting ready to have a birthday in August 2019, and I look at that as another year of opportunity, that I could do something for God! I take nothing for granted. I was hoping to try out for the National Anthem in 2020 for the Boston Red Sox and the Boston Celtics, since I was asked for July 4th, 2014, to sing the National Anthem before a good-sized raceway crowd in Indiana before I was to become a homeless person! Unknown at the time, they put the video on YouTube, and it's still there today! I found it by accident in early 2018 when I was still living at the Southampton Shelter! I was shocked to see my picture on YouTube, so I hope to use that video as an audition video! That is one of my desires to sing the National Anthem! If it doesn't happen, then I'll move on to something else! As I'm getting older, God is keeping me quite busy with different projects, which I am very grateful for, because it keeps my mind off what I can't do.

When I was younger, I injured my right hand in a car door accident, and every now and then when I try to start writing, it will shake uncontrollably! I also found out one of the symptoms of knee surgery is body-shaking. I looked it up on Google because my left hand would shake, as well! I've had problems with my eyes at different times, with a thing called flashes and floaters, that would come across my eyes like you're seeing little specks as you try to blink them away! That was a shock when it first happened, that also was in 2018 at the shelter! It looks like sparks of lightning out of the corner of your eye!Maybe some of you can identify with that? My eyeglass doctor explained what it was, that it could be temporary or permanent, and he said, "Ritchie, you'll just have to live with it! There's no medical surgery that can be performed on this!" So I took his advice and I do live with it! When these things come into my eyes, I close my eyes and thank God that I still have vision!

The hernia surgery I had years ago started acting up about four months ago with the same symptoms I first had when I first got a hernia. It had to be operated on to save my life at that time, in 1998! But they didn't operate on me at that time, they gave me some kind of medicine to temper the pain, and it worked for a while before it became a full-blown hernia, and at that point it had to be operated on! Where half my side down below is very numb from the surgery! And of course, my lower back injured at the same time as my knee that eventually resulted in what they felt to be knee replacement they said would make my life better but that never happened! And both my hands are very stiff now, they weren't like that before I had that knee surgery! And my rotator cuff on my left arm gets very painful sometimes when I try to move my left arm! The hernia, lower back, and rotator cuff were all injured on the job in Indiana before I came to Boston! But legally, I can't tell you the name of the restaurant I worked for that caused this issue! And this is a very popular restaurant. They worked on the hernia part with an operation, but they never worked on the lower back that got injured or the rotator cuff all in the same motion, doing what they had me to do at this restaurant at the time! And the way I would get my mind off of that at that time would be I would wrap one of those back brace belts around my waist and I ran, even when I was in pain!

When you're a runner, you try to train your mind to do what your body needs to do! And of course, I've had setbacks in 2019 as I continued to work on this book with my phone acting up, the voice-typing thing acting up, and oh, don't get me started on spellcheck, because it needs a hearing aid, and it can't hear the words that are coming out of your mouth! And that annoying Google Assistant thing constantly interrupting when I'm checking email or trying to text someone! It would be like someone planning a nice dinner with their wife or girlfriend and all of a sudden an annoying person shows up at your table and refuses to leave, and you have to get up from your seat and escort them out of the room! That, to me, is Google Assistant in a nutshell! I'd love to escort it out of my life and off the planet!

Another setback was a stomach virus that almost took my life, but God got me through that, which I'm very grateful for! That was December 2017, when I still lived at the shelter. One day, my body shook like I was having a panic attack, and I was cold and couldn't get warm! The shelter clinic checked out my condition and immediately set me up to go to the hospital, but I was going by way of Uber! You know I had to wait for a stupid ride to get me there for almost an hour? If I'd known that was going to happen then, I could have walked there myself or died trying! My clinic was extremely mad at the Uber driver and told him next time, they would call Lyft, instead! They told him, "You're gambling with a patient's life here, and if something would have happened to him here while he was waiting on you, we would have sued your company down to the ground!" I was too weak to put in a verbal argument with the driver, but I'm sure he got a real indication of how I was feeling when my expression was not that of a satisfied customer! The nurse warned him, and said, "If I were you, I'd go now!" And said, "Your boss will hear it big time from me!" This guy put his head down and looked like a person who had just gotten a thorough whipping on his behind! Within minutes, he got me to the Emergency Room, and they had to put a lot of fluids in me because the virus, whatever it was, was dehydrating my body! And these life-saving fluids at the hospital, I am convinced, possibly saved my life! I also believe if I didn't go to the hospital that day, that I would have passed away inside the shelter! So I knew God was watching over me at that time! I had to wait two days before that condition went away! Yes, there's been a lot of setbacks, But the positives are this: the stories are getting done! I have a go-to person in Ms. Q, who I send the stories over to, and she prepares them all together when they're done to send over to my publisher! I look forward to seeing where this book goes when it's completed!

There's an old saying that goes, "Count your blessings and name them one-by-one! This author has counted his blessings, many times more than one-by-one, daily! I think of where my life was, where it is now, and what God plans to do with the rest of that life. I'm very excited for the opportunity to accomplish things, even though I'm disabled! God has given me a very sharp mind. A never die, never quit attitude! And that's not easy, considering I was once a long-distance walker and runner, who used to swim, used to be a courier delivery driver, who can't do sit-ups or push-ups anymore, and deals with constant knee pain. Because of the injury in 2017, I deal with back issues,and neck issues as well. So, yes, now life is an adjustment, from one life story to another.within one setback my back my knee and my neck all in the same injury it was horrible because of a little pothole sticking out from the street that my foot went into never knew it was there all the times I crossed that street but this time it was to get me! But, I am alive with a clear mind, where I can focus! I owe my life to Him. For you see, daily, I plug into the Power Source! And I run like the Eveready Bunny, spiritually and mentally speaking. I just keep going, and going, and going, because He gives me that power! I don't have a religion. I have a relationship with God, there is a difference! It's like being married! A husband should do more than just say "Hi" and "Goodbye" to his wife each day! If he's any kind of husband at all, he has a relationship with his wife! He would know her, and she would know him! That's how it is with God! He knows me! And because I know Him is reason enough that I love Him more and more daily! For He, indeed, is my Power Source!

CHAPTER 8

WINTER WALK

It was November 2018 when someone asked me, "Ritchie? Are you going to be doing the Winter Walk in January?" I said, "I don't even know what that is! But it sounds intriguing!" At that time, I was going to a place called Boston Warm, and it's one of those awesome places in Boston that is a church that reaches out to the homeless. What's so unique about this place is, they'll feed you lunch, give you activities to do, and counsel you, if you need it. There's about three or four pastors that run it, and every one of them is very nice! They even had me sing there a few times! They really have a vision for what they do in the city of Boston, and that touches me deeply, because the homeless are the forefront of what I hope to see eliminated in our city and be an example city around the USA. Since I was in a homeless situation for over four years, I totally identify with those that are in that predicament!

I decided to find out more about this thing called the "Winter Walk." And what I found out about it really touched my heart, deeply! It turns out that this is their first year doing this event, and I feel privileged to be a part of it, as it turns out there were many businesses that got involved and jumped on it! It is a two mile walk that starts at Back Bay, then goes downtown through the Boston Common and winds back to

Back Bay! And when I found out what they were sponsoring, it really touched me! This walk is dedicated to the homeless situation here in Boston and to bring awareness about everything that has to do with homelessness! And there are funds to raise exactly for that cause! So as you can see, this really got my attention, and even though I'm either permanently disabled or temporarily disabled, I still have the mindset of a runner! I ran on my own for many years, no matter what kind of weather it was, in Indiana! And winter in Indiana can be downright nasty cold! But when you're committed to running, you do it, anyway! I started training on my own, even before I became a homeless person! So yes, I definitely wanted to do this to walk, especially for my fellow brethren of homeless people! I don't remember exactly which month it started, it was either January or February, but once it came around, I was ready to go! They knew I sang at Boston Warm because they had me sing there, many times. And so, I had the great honor of singing The Lord's Prayer! As they were doing a prayer before the run started, more and more walkers were gathering together in the Back Bay area, and as I began to sing this song in front of a huge crowd, I just envisioned heaven looking down on us all. And so, I poured my heart out into the song. I nearly cried as I was trying to focus on what I was singing, because I knew there were so many homeless people in the city of Boston that really needed help! The weather was a little bit chilly, and a lot of people heard me do this song for the first time that morning, letting me know how beautiful the song was. I told them that I was honored to be a part of it!

I noticed there was a lady in the crowd who kept rubbing her hands together. She didn't have any gloves, and it was very cold! I looked around at the people that were by her and nobody reached out to help her! And keep in mind, it's not freezing cold, but still, it is cold! So this really bothered me that her hands were freezing! So I did the only thing a person could do in that situation, you give them your gloves, and I was glad to be able to do that. I bought these gloves about two months ago downtown at the Boston Common, so these were very warm gloves. She had a tear in her eye of thankfulness, of just being able to keep her hands warm, and I was grateful that she could do so now. So, for the remainder of the walk, I just smiled and put my hands in my jacket pockets, where they stayed warm! When you're in a city this size and you see a need, you just try to reach out and meet that need, if you can! I was very grateful to have bought the gloves at a cheap price, but I was even more grateful that they could be put to better use. She let me know that she was one of the homeless people and that she didn't have any gloves. I had a little bit of money in my pocket, so I said, "Get yourself something to eat later," and I reached in and pulled out what I had in my pocket. She just about cried, right then, and I almost cried, as well! I looked up to Heaven and I said in my heart, *This is exactly why they are doing this Winter Walk! And now that I'm aware of it, I want to do it every year no matter what the weather is doing!*

It was sunny out yet cold, and even though I can barely walk now, I was ready to do this! If you ask any disabled person if it's hard to walk, I guarantee you they would say, "Yes, it is!" So let alone just walking, walking two miles is a real task and a challenge for a disabled person. But as I said before, even before I had the surgery where I am now disabled, I still had the mindset of a runner, and I was going to do this, no matter what it took! They did a quick little prayer and then everybody got together and started walking. It was really awesome! I had not seen this part of the city yet, especially walking into the downtown area! It took my mind off the knee pain I was experiencing and I concentrated on just simply being able to walk! Which, if I was a normal walker, I could do this in my sleep! But it was going to be a challenge. We're all walking together now, enjoying each other's company, and I invite you, the reader, to come along and walk with us! It was such a beautiful morning for the walk we were embarking on. People were in wheelchairs, as well, as we made our way to downtown Boston Common! Some people were jogging, some people were walking, and it was a huge crowd that morning. Everybody was polite, not getting in anybody's way! I was grateful for that, because it would be hard for me to sidestep anybody with replacement knee surgery pain! As we started approaching the backside of the Boston Common, I saw just how huge this park really was. It was absolutely magnificent!

I noticed that there was an incline once I got into the park. I was a little bit tired, but we had reached the halfway point of our walk, and I knew in my mind that I was going to do this! Seeing this incline made my heart sink, and looking at it, I knew I had to get it up in order to get outside the park and start our descent to Back Bay. With renewed determination, I said to myself, *I don't care how much it hurts, this is for a cause and I'm not going to quit now!* So I put my head down and started walking up that incline. It was very, very painful! I said to myself, *I'm not going to stop now, I'm going to do this!* Just how do you think I would have felt if I would have quit at that point? Nobody would have blamed me, but I definitely would have blamed myself! So no, I was not going to quit. As I started walking up the hill of the park, I felt like I was faltering a little bit, but I was very determined. My knee was in great pain and I didn't care if I had to crawl, I was going to get up that incline! That's the mindset you have to take in order to do something like that! I was really struggling by now, but I was determined to make it! I kept saying to myself, *I've got to do this, not only for myself, but for the homeless people in the city of Boston!* I can tell you by now, the pain was excruciating, and I was struggling.

All of a sudden, a guy came right up next to me and said, "Friend, can I give you a hand?" I reached out my hand to him and I said, "Yes, I would love that!" God knew my need and determination right then and there, and I was not going to quit, so he brought along another walker, a very healthy walker, to help me get up the rest of that incline! I was so grateful for that! So arm-and-arm now, the guy, Gregory, helped me get up the rest of the way! he was talking to me as we almost reached the top, and it got my mind off my knee pain, and I was very grateful for that. As we reached the top, I told him, "Thank you, thank you so much! You are a Godsend!" He said, "It's not a problem, at all." He told me that he noticed me laboring trying to get up that incline and wanted to lend a helping hand, and I was very appreciative to God that he was there! It was a straight walk returning to Back Bay. He said, "If you're okay now, I'm going to catch up with my group, okay?" I said, "Absolutely, do that, thank you for being there!" He said, "No problem, Ritchie, you enjoy the rest of your walk!" We exchanged email information and we are in contact, even today! This just tells me that God knows your needs before you even ask! God knew I was going to struggle going up that incline and he sent a helper to be an encouragement to me! And you know, if I were a healthy walker, I would have done the same thing if I saw someone else struggling! You have to have a certain mindset in the city and a compassion to reach out and help people, because there's a lot of people that are homeless that definitely need our help! Some don't want a handout, they just want a hand-up! This is another reason why this author is doing this book, to be able to help accomplish that aim!

FeaturePics.com - I1301737

As I started walking back, I was grateful that it wasn't too much further to go, because my knee was totally exhausted, but I was glad to be able to do this! As I started approaching the finish line, people were actually there cheering the walkers as they came across the line, as if we'd been in a huge race of some kind! I was absolutely shocked. *Wow, they really do care!* So with the walk finished, I sat down to rest for a minute and catch my breath. Right then, a guy came up to me and said, "Sir, can you help me? I am homeless! And any little thing you can give would really be appreciated!" I looked at him and I said, "I'm not sure what I have left in my pocket, but you're welcome to it." I thought in my heart, *I don't have any money left because I gave that girl those gloves and what money I thought I had!* I said, "Let me check my wallet, if I have something you're more than welcome to get it!" He said, "Sir, that would be very much appreciated." So I stood up, still in pain, and told him to hold on a second. I reached into my pocket to grab my wallet and I didn't see any money in there at all. I was very disheartened by that. Just as I was about to put my wallet back in my pocket, God spoke to my heart and said, *Ritchie look again!*

I spoke under my breath to the Lord and said, "Okay, Lord!" As I looked again, there, in the crevice of my wallet, was a bundled up $20 bill that I didn't know I had! I pulled that $20 out and gave it to that man! He was about ready to cry, and I was shocked that I even had it. I could have sworn I had no money left! Now to this day, I don't know if God put that in there or if I just overlooked it in the crevice of that wallet. I don't know, but I'm glad it was there and I thank Him, anyway, that it was there to be given. The man said, "Thank you sir, so much, I haven't eaten in a few days, and this, plus the lunch that they give after this Winter Walk, will really help me out!" I just looked at him and said, "Bro, I'm just glad to be a part of all this! I was homeless for over four years, so I know exactly what you go through. Every time I see you, I will do what I can to be able to assist you."

All of a sudden as we were talking, another one of his friends came up and had this look on his face like he couldn't believe what he was hearing! He pulled his friend aside and said, "Don't listen to this guy, this guy is a liar. He just wants something from you!" His friend told him, "Bro, he just gave me a $20 bill!" His friend argued with him and said, "Maybe he's just trying to get rid of you!" After he talked to him, he left! I asked, "What in the world was that all about?" He told me that his friend didn't believe I was homeless and called me a liar. That really made me angry. I was having a really good morning, but that set me off! Because you see, I had been telling this new friend how I was also a new, upcoming book author in the city before this guy interrupted our conversation! And I was telling him a little bit about what the book was about before this person entered the picture! Now, I don't know who this guy was, but I would love to talk to him in person, and let him know that the person he called a liar is now an author of this book, and indeed, was homeless as they both were! I would love to talk to that guy and show him this book when it's completed and say, "You didn't believe I was an author or homeless! You didn't find out my story. That's why I wanted to talk to you in person, I was trying to tell you the truth!"

Of course, I forgave him for this, but I'd still love to talk to him today in person in a friendly way and tell him to be careful who he judges at face value, because he was in no position to judge anybody, or tell any of his friends that someone is a liar, just because he didn't know them. Well, let me introduce myself to you, I am Richard 'Ritchie' Vernon, the author of this book. Your friend told you the absolute truth and you wouldn't believe it, and now you're hearing it from this author in this book! You know, I could make that same speculation about you, that you weren't really homeless, that you were just trying to warn your friend! I understand that! But I was homeless,and I'm real! That's all I have to say about that, anyway.

When the walk was over, they served us lunch and had bands and singers come up to perform on a platform, and the mayor of the city spoke, as well. I first met him when I came up to Boston, in May 2016 when I was on a job assignment. He was a very likable guy, and had heart and compassion for his city. I was taking all of this in, and I look back at it now as an awesome experience. I hope to see my friend, Gregory, again, for the 2020 Winter Walk. I have renewed vigor about the Walk, as well. I hope you, the reader, enjoy this story, because it is true, and I look forward to doing the Winter Walk again next year, God-willing!

CHAPTER 9

SAY WHAAAT?

When you live in a city the size of Boston, your mind reflects back to the city you came from over three years ago, Anderson, Indiana, and that city is way smaller in comparison, size-wise and population-wise, it is much smaller. I've always thought of Boston like a giant arena where different sideshows are going on. What I'm about to share with you now is a compilation of stories that took place between 2017 and August 2019, so let me get started on that.

My friend Pops and I were on our way back from the train station headed to my apartment, when we passed a hotel. There was a guy that was getting ready to cross the street. I looked at him, and I immediately recognized him. I told Pops, "Pops, you know who that is?" He said, "I think I do, who is it?" I said, "Pops, that's Jet Li international film star, he does karate movies and different films! Hold on, Pops, I'm going to try to say 'Hi' to him real quick!" Before he crossed the street, I said, "Hello, you're Jet Li, aren't you?" He looked at me and stared intently for a moment and said absolutely nothing! And then he ran across the street! Now I know film stars when I see them, and that was definitely Jet Li! But for whatever reason, he didn't say anything! Well I guess Mr. Li didn't know that it was an author who was speaking to him. And now he gets to read his name in this book! Jet Li, all I wanted to do was say "Hi" to you! But you just looked at me and walked across the street! I don't know if that's how you act in real life or not but I was trying to be friendly to you! Anyways, Pops just shook his head and said, "Why didn't he say 'Hi' back, Ritchie?" I said, "Pops, I don't know! Maybe his stardom is too big for this world!"

I was on the Blue Line train one time, going to Wonderland, and a few foreigners got on, about Maverick I think, and as they got on, they asked me since I was sitting right there, "Does this train go to Wonderland?" "Yes, it does," I said, "It is the last stop on the train!" They said, "Okay, great, we got on the right train." I said, "Yes, you did! Because I, too, am going to Wonderland!" So the train got going, and immediately, the voice prompt comes, "Next stop: Wonderland!" I looked at that and said, "Whaaat? Wonderland's the last stop, not the next stop!" The husband-and-wife foreigners looked up and saw that, and were very confused! I told them, "It's okay, when I get off, that's when you know you're in Wonderland!" They said, "Thank you. We appreciate that!" And then on the next stop, it spoke a normal stop, which would have been the airport! But then again, it started acting up! This time it said, "Next stop: State Street. Change here for the Orange Line!" The foreigners looked up, seeing that again, and just shook their heads! They probably wondered what kind of train this was. I was shaking my head and wondering too: what is going on with the train prompts? State Street is where I got on about five stops back! Now the voice comes on again and says, "Next stop: Revere Beach. No smoking, please!" Of course, Revere Beach was about another three stops ahead! We're not even close to Revere Beach yet! At this point, I'm laughing! But the foreigners are holding each other very tight now, probably thinking, *Are we going to be able to get off this crazy train?* I laughed and I assured them this has never happened before, that this train has never done that. But it just happened to do that when they got on. And you're probably thinking, *Are we on a weird train?* I was beginning to wonder, as well! The voice came on and said again, "Next stop: Revere Beach. No smoking, please!" And believe it or not, they got it right this time! It was Revere Beach! The foreigners looked at that and were relieved! The train leaves from there and says, "Next stop:

Airport!" He looked at his wife and she looked at him, and he said to her, "Airport is where we got on! This is nuts!" She looked at him and asked him to remind her to never get on this train again! He looked at her and said it was a deal! He said they would take an Uber back to the airport! I looked over at them and said, "It's okay. The next stop for sure is Wonderland, no matter how many stops it says it is! Just ignore the voice prompt and know that the next stop is Wonderland!" She looked around and probably thought they were on Candid Camera! They said, "Thank you for guiding us, we wouldn't have known where to get off!" He said, "We will not be taking this train back from Wonderland to the airport! We will take our chance on Uber, instead!" I looked at them, shook my head and said, "I don't blame you! The voice prompt insisted that Airport was next! Even though I knew Wonderland was next!" He looked at her and she looked at him. "Let's get off this train as soon as possible!" I said, "I don't blame you!" and I laughed.

I got on the Blue Line another time and was headed back from Wonderland to Boston. I had done some shopping at Walmart to get some food in Lynn, which requires a train and a bus. I can't remember which stop it was, but I met an interesting teen when I headed back towards Boston. We started chatting to each other immediately from across our seat. He said he had just gotten off work and was headed to soccer practice! I said, "Where is soccer practice?" I think he said Maverick. I'm not sure to this day, but that's where I think it was! I said, "You have a pretty good team? He said, "Yeah, we do! The practices are very interesting!" I said, "Oh? Why is that?" He said, "Whenever we kick the ball out of bounds, we have to decide who's going to go after it!" And I looked at him and shook my head and I said, "Okay, how is that interesting?" He said, "Bro! This isn't a normal soccer field we're talking about! This one is close to the ocean! Whenever we kick a ball out of bounds that way, we have to decide who's going to swim for the ball!" I looked at him and laughed, and said, "Oh man, that would be an interesting practice!" And he said, "Yeah, depending on the current, we have to swim fast, or we may not get the ball! We've lost about ten balls to the ocean!" I said, "Oh, man, I hope you guys carry a lot of balls with you!" He looked at me and said, "Yeah, bro, we do!" I said, "I hope your games aren't near the ocean?" He laughed and said, "No, there was more inland, otherwise the referees would have to swim after the ball!" I said, "That would be very interesting!" He said, "Yeah, you'd have a lot of disgruntled wet referees!" I looked at him and laughed, and I said, "Yeah, you're right!" I said, "Could you imagine football being played by the ocean? Who would have to go after the ball?" He said, "Yeah, that would be funny!" He got off at his stop and said, "It's been a pleasure talking to you, Bro," and I told him the same. "Don't get wet out there at practice!" He said, "Don't worry, I'll get someone else to chase the ball!"

I was on the Blue Line again when I heard the sound of a baby crying. This rapidly got my attention, and I noticed that the cry was about four seats down from me on the left side of our train compartment. I glanced over to see why this child was crying. She was in a baby stroller having a fit, possibly hungry, tired, or needing some attention. I glanced up further and I saw the mother, or whoever was taking care of this child, doing nothing but taking selfies. And I saw she didn't have earphones on, so I knew she heard that little girl crying and did nothing to address it! This made me so mad that a person could be heartless enough to not be able to tend to the needs of their own child! Other riders noticed this, as well, and you could see that they were getting visibly upset, but nobody said anything to the woman, who appeared to care more about taking an album full of selfie shots than they did their own child! This was really starting to burn through me and I got up the words and the nerve to say something to her, and just as I was trying to get her attention, the train stopped, and she got off with her child! I wanted to say something really badly! And what made it even worse was, as she got up to leave, she had one hand on the stroller and the other one, you guessed it, on that stupid phone, taking another selfie! A lot of us were mad! And one woman glared with daggers in her eyes at the woman as she was leaving! Her gaze caught the woman's expression, and she turned white as a ghost! It is my opinion that people like this don't deserve children if all they care about is themselves! That image today still angers me!

Speaking of trains, I want to share this. I've always wanted to go on one of these trains and ask people, "Excuse me. Can you tell me what time it is?" and then watch everybody pull out their cell phones, like they're some kind of a watch. It cracks me up, and I'd just want to see the reactions on people's faces, because nobody pulls out their watch anymore, but always a cell phone. I'm one of those old-school people, and I still wear a watch. I guess if they don't have their phones, they won't know what time it is! I know my watch can't text or call, as far as I know, but it does tell time. It does take a licking, and it keeps on ticking! I bought it two years ago, and it was cheap, and I appreciate it!

Late one night in February 2017, I realized I had accidentally left some important papers at a bus stop on Washington Street in Boston. I thought, *I better hurry up and go get those, I don't want to miss my curfew at the shelter!* Curfew was 11 pm, and it was after 10 pm already, so I had to hurry! I got to the bus stop, and after looking for them everywhere, I couldn't find them. I hadn't been gone for more than half an hour, and these papers were nowhere to be found! I sat down for a moment just to ponder the situation, and this guy comes up and says, "Bro, do you know when the next bus is?" I said, "I can't see the time on the bus sign, but it's right there!" He said, "Thank you, I'll check that out!" I said, "No problem, bro!" He came back inside the stop and stared at me and said, "You know what?" "What?" I said? "I'm very low on my quota tonight, and I was wondering if you can help me?" I said, "You're not making sense, what are you talking about?" I'm slowly on my guard, because I don't know what he's trying to say. He said, "I'm way behind on my quota. I'm about to kill me some boys tonight, and you might be next on the list!" I said, "What!?" I didn't like the slang of it! By this time, I am really on my guard and I am ready to defend my life any way I can! He stood over me as I sat, with an umbrella in his right hand, acting like he was going to bash it against my skull! Well, at that point in my life, I had a little bit of training in self-defense! Make no mistake, this was a big man! But my mind was racing and thinking, *If he starts to try to strike me. I have to block that umbrella and take him off his feet with a chop to his throat!* My body was shaking from pure adrenaline! I was going through scenarios in my mind! I thought, *If he thinks he's going to take me down without a fight, he's misjudged me right there, because if this is my last night on this earth, I'm going to go down swinging, and he's going to be feeling it!* He raised that umbrella above his head as if he was going to strike me!

In martial arts defense, they teach you to put your hands to your face as if you're backing up so that you appear as if you don't want any trouble, but what you're doing is preparing your defense. I surprised him when I stood up all of a sudden, and he didn't know what to think. I put my hands in front of my face and I said, "Look, I don't know what your deal is, but I don't want any trouble!" He stood back about a few feet, acting like he was going to swing that umbrella to my face! Keep in mind, the umbrella is closed so it makes for a real weapon! I prepared my hands over my face, getting ready to get in guard position to block whatever was going to come my way! He looked and smiled, putting the umbrella down! I'm confused by this time, but I still have my hands up as a guard! He might be bigger than I am, but his neck was within inches of my reach for a shot just below the jaw, or a claw strike to the side of the head. Anyway, he put the umbrella down, and he asked me this question, "Bro, do you have a dollar?" I said, "No, I don't!" I'm really confused now, by this time my body is shaking out of anger! When my body shakes like that, I'm getting ready to defend myself! He said, "Okay, I just thought I'd ask! Have a nice night!" And he left! I thought, *Thank God, thank God, thank God! I don't know what that was all about, but I thank God it didn't happen!* That was a very scary moment and you don't know if you are going to live or to die! I had been put at the point where I thought I might have to be ready to fight or lose my life, and so my defense mechanisms went up! It didn't matter how big he was! You have to know where to strike an opponent or you could be toast! I'm glad it didn't come to that, though.

I had to calm myself on the way back to the shelter and allow my adrenaline to slow down. At the point that I'm almost all the way calmed down, about 2 blocks from the shelter, another guy approaches me! I said to myself, *You have got to be kidding!* He said, "I saw you talking to my girlfriend at McDonald's yesterday! What was that all about? Are you trying to hit on my woman?" I slowly started backing away with my hands up, ready to defend! I said, "If you're talking about the woman at McDonald's last night, she asked me to get her something to eat because she was hungry! And so I gave her money to get a hamburger, a drink, and some fries! I don't know what she told you, but I didn't claim to be her boyfriend and she never told me she had a boyfriend! Not that it would have mattered, because I was concerned about getting her something to eat!"

He approached me and said, "Are you sure that's what happened? That you're not just trying to say that to save your own neck?" At this point, I'm really getting tired of this nonsense, and my anger is going up very high! I looked at him sternly and I said, "Bro, I have no reason to lie! I have no interest whatsoever in your girlfriend. I was just trying to help her out! Why weren't you there with her?" He was within two feet of me now, and I could see that he was reaching into his back pocket, like he was going to pull out some kind of a weapon, what I thought could be a knife! I took off my hoodie really quickly and put it in my left hand to block any kind of knife thrust! And I said to myself, *If he swings on me with that knife, I'm going to have to defend myself and thoroughly knock him out!* He was two feet within my reach just like the other guy was! I said, "That's close enough! I'm done with this game, bro!" I thought to myself, *As soon as he swings, I'm taking him out with a strike thrust to his neck! And then I'm going to give him a tiger claw strike on the side of his head that he's going to feel for months!* I said, "I don't know what you think you're about to do, but I do have to warn you that I can defend myself! Please don't make me prove it!" He looked at me and said, "What, are you some kind of fighter?" I said, "Look! I'm asking you in a friendly way now to back off, because I'm really getting upset! I have no interest in your girlfriend! I'm going to walk away now and I suggest you not follow me, or I will finish it!" My adrenaline level was way up, and I was thinking about knocking that knife out of his hands if he were to pull it out, or kicking his midsection! As I started to walk away backwards, he said stuff like, "Yeah, chicken! You better walk away!" And I looked at him and said, "Yeah, I better walk away!" And that was the end of that. I never saw him again! The first guy had caught me by surprise; the second guy I was ready to do something I didn't want to, at his expense. I thank my God that neither one of these things happened that night, and I made it into the shelter with seven minutes to go. I thank God for that!

It was June 2019 and I was with my friend Pops coming back from the train after going out to eat. We noticed a guy by the bus stop with two bags, one bag on each side, and he started talking to one of the bags. And he put his hand on the other bag and said, "Don't interrupt me when I'm talking to your brother!" Pops and I looked at this and I was dumbfounded! I had never seen this before and I didn't know what to make of it. I wish I knew his story, but I didn't, and I felt bad about that. I didn't know how to feel, I just felt sad, so I looked at Pops and said, "What do you think he's saying to the bag?" Pops said, "I don't know, man, I've never talked to a bag before!" He said, "I've talked to a bag lady, but I've never talked to one of my own bags!" I said, "I know, what I'm wondering is what did the bag do that he is so mad at it?" These were the thoughts that were running through my head. I looked at Pops and I said, "Pops, I almost feel like we should interrupt the conversation and see if we can find out how to resolve this?" He said, "Yeah, Ritchie!" All of a sudden, the guy looks over at us watching him, and says, "What's the matter with you guys? Haven't you ever seen a friendly family argument before?" I mean, what could I say? I looked at Pops and he looked at me. So I said whatever came into my mind! I said, "It looks like you have everything under control, so we're going to be on our way now, you have a good night!" As we were leaving, he said, "Don't worry! This one's going to get his butt beat when we get home!" Wow! I had never ever seen that before in my life in all my time in Indiana or Boston, and I didn't know how to react, so I guess you learn something new every day.

In June 2018, I was walking down to Stop & Shop, about a mile from the shelter where I still lived, wanting to pick up a few things. You're very limited what you can bring into a shelter, so you have to be careful! So I was pretty much just going to get lunch and a few cokes, and then head back. I was heading into the Stop & Shop when I noticed a lady on the bench getting ready to cry. I said, "Ma'am, what is wrong? Are you okay?" She said, "No, I'm not okay! It's my birthday today, and nobody even said 'Happy Birthday'!" I looked at her, and my face just about turned white. Being a Caucasian man, this would have been a feat in itself! It was really welling up inside of me. I said, "Nobody told this lady 'Happy birthday'!" I looked at her, and I turned and smiled and said, "Ma'am? Happy Birthday to you!" Her countenance rose up and she smiled and gave me a hug! She said, "I don't know who you are, but I'm glad God brought you my way just to tell me that!" She continued, "You see, I'm a homeless person and I'm barely making it!" At that point, I was about ready to cry! I said, "Don't you go into the women's shelters?" She said, "I was in one of them, but I got blamed for something I didn't do and got kicked out!" I said, "Oh, man, that is not right!" I said, "Can you wait here real quick? I have to go into the store for something, and I'll be right back, so please don't leave!" She said, "I won't, I'm glad to have found a new friend!" I said, "I am, too, just wait here and I'll be right back!" She said, "I promise I won't go anywhere!" I went into the store and I knew after meeting this lady what I was going to do. You probably would have too! God could have put it on my heart but he did give me reasoning to figure this one out on my own! You can probably guess, as well, but that's okay—I'll tell you! I went over to the bakery section and I said, "Pardon me? Do you have any birthday cakes available?" They said, "We have a few?" I said, "That's awesome! Can you put a 'Happy Birthday so-and-so' on the cake for me, please, and decorate it?" "Yes, we can!" I knew the lady's name, but for her privacy, I'm saying "so-and-so," as not to embarrass her in this story.

They came out with a beautiful cake! I said, "Oh, this is awesome! She's really going to like that!" The lady in the bakery said, "Yes, she will!" She looked at me and smiled, "That's very special of you to do something like this for some person!" I said, "Yeah, she's a special lady!" So I picked up the cake and I went to the ice cream section and got her a quart of ice cream! I don't know what her flavor was, so I got her vanilla! With cake and ice cream in hand, I stopped by to where I first saw her. She looked at me and smiled, saying, "That didn't take you very long." I looked at her and smiled back, "I wanted to get here before you left! I want to say Happy Birthday to you now in a proper way! This is your birthday cake and this is your ice cream to go with it, so Happy Birthday to you!" She started crying! She said, "I don't have any family! But you have made me feel like family!" She said, "No one has ever done this for me before! I don't know who you are, but to me, you're an angel!" I was embarrassed by this. I said, "God put this on my heart to make sure you had a good birthday!" She said, "I feel very special right now!" I said, "Ma'am, in God's eyes, you are!" and I reached in my pocket, where I had ten dollars left, and I said, "Happy Birthday! I hope you enjoy the rest of your day!" She said, "I'm going to share this cake with some of my homeless friends! Thank you for making my day special!" I said, "Ma'am, you're entirely welcome!" I said, "Thank God for allowing me to meet you!" She said, "I thank God!" And I went on my way, got a quick dinner, and headed back to the shelter, enjoying the rest of the day. My prayer is someday that this special lady does get housing. I hope to someday see her in Heaven, as well! You don't know who you're going to meet in life, but you hope to affect their lives in a positive way. I thanked God for this day!

My friend Pops and I were on the Orange Line train at Mass Avenue, and headed to his house to go play some cards since he had the weekend off from work. I didn't have to work that day, at the shelter where we were both employed. So we were getting ready to head over to his place to get some snacks and enjoy some friendly competition with each other. Within a few minutes after the train got going, Pops was sitting across from me, and we started talking and enjoying each other's company. There were a lot of people on the train! All of a sudden, a guy sitting next to Pops looks over at me and says with a smile on his face! "I used to be a fighter, and I was really good at it!" I thought, *That's great*. I said, "Do you fight now, today?" He said, "No, I'm retired from it," and then all of a sudden he tells me, "You know? I can knock you out in three seconds!" This got my attention and Pop's attention!" I said, "Say what?" He said, "You heard me. I said I could knock you out in three seconds from where you are across from me!" I looked at him and the smile was gone now and I said, "I wouldn't advise it!" Pops looked at him and said the same thing. Pops is an ex-boxer, and I've done a little boxing, as well, but where I excel at more than boxing is in the martial arts I've learned from a friend of mine who lived in the shelter!

I repeated to the guy, "I really wouldn't advise that!" At that moment, my mind kind of went blank. I think I was going into defense mode. And Pops said that he heard me say this, though to this day I don't remember saying this: "Don't make me angry! You won't like me when I'm angry!" This evidently got this guy's attention, because he shut up after that. Another guy across the room told the same guy, "You won't like me when I'm angry, either!" So not only did he have my attention and Pops' attention, and somebody across the train's attention, but he was getting everybody upset! I looked at him and said, "My friend and I are getting ready to get off at the next stop. We would love it if you joined us! We'll settle this three second thing you're talking about! Because I will hit you so hard your next of kin will feel it!" I told Pops, "Let's get ready to leave!" My adrenaline was pumping at a high level! I looked at the guy and said, "Bro, we're getting off the train now! If you still have a problem with me, we can settle it right on this stop, right here, right now!" And I said, "I will put you on the floor! And you might need a hospital!" I don't like fighting, but sometimes you have to stand your ground! Not everybody acts this way in Boston, but this guy did! Pops couldn't hear me because the train was noisy, but I got this guy's attention real well, and I could see the color leaving his face! I smiled back at him, saying, "The invitation still stands!" As Pops and I got off on the train, we noticed the other guy just sitting there, not even looking at us! I said, "Pops, I think we got his attention!" "I think so too, Ritchie, I think so!" He said, "Man, I've never seen you get that angry before! I didn't know you had that in you!" I said, "Pops, I guess it took for the right situation to bring it out! You and I were just minding our own business! This guy interrupted our business with his mouth!" And as we were getting ready to go up the escalator, we noticed that the other guy on the train who told that guy to shut up started walking over to him. We don't know what happened from there. Pops said, "Calm down, Ritchie, calm down! Let's go get some snacks and have some fun!" I said, "Pops, that's the best idea yet!" So we proceeded to his house and did exactly that!

You never know who you're going to meet in Boston that is going to act like this! But you have to back them up on it! You have to do what you have to do! Pops and I never saw this guy again, and if we did, I doubt he would interrupt our conversation again. After all, he had my friend Pops upset, as well! I'm pretty sure we got his attention. Another time I was close to the CVS Drug Store in Chinatown, in Boston on Washington Street, and I was talking to a disabled homeless veteran who served our country who didn't ask me for anything. He just wanted friendship. I was on a Naval Yard base through our schools Navy program as a junior at Central Kitsap HS in Silverdale, Washington, which I will document in another book later on, but this homeless veteran was out in the field fighting for our country, and that deserved high respect! He was showing me some of his service medals, and I beamed with pride just knowing him! He didn't ask me for any money at all, he just wanted friendship. I said, "Bro? You've got my friendship already, and I want to give you something. First of all, I want to thank you for your dedication and your service," and as I was saying this I could see him starting to tear up. I said, "Bro? I don't know why you're homeless now, but you deserve much better than this! I wish I had more than this," and I reached into my pocket and pulled out a ten dollar bill. To this day, I wish it would have been a $100 bill!

He tearfully said, "No one has even offered to help me since when I became homeless, and so I stopped asking for help, and here you come by, out of the blue, and give me some money!" He said, "Bro? I don't know what to say." And he gave me a big tearful hug! He said, "I'm not used to showing emotion, but I'm really grateful for this!" I kept saying, "Man, I wish I had more!" And so he saluted me, and I saluted him back! He was a former Army specialist and I was former of the Navy program. I said, "Bro? When I see you again, there will be more!" He said "thank you" and started to turn away, and I started to turn away, as well. All of a sudden, I hear, "Outta my way!" I looked back to see my war veteran friend getting pushed aside like he was some kind of ragdoll! Keep in mind, he is very disabled from war and can barely stand, and this guy going by almost knocks him off his feet, and cursing at him for being in his way! He walked right by me with a smirk on his face! I looked at my veteran friend grabbing his knee where he had been bumped; he was in extreme pain! And this was more than I could take, and I yelled out, "Hey! And the guy stopped and said, "Yeah? What do you want?" The anger was rising up in me! I walked up to this guy and said, "The guy you almost ran over back there is disabled and a personal friend of mine!" And he smirked again and said, "So? What is that to me?" I said, "It means this: you need to apologize to him right now for hurting him!" He said, "The guy was in my way, and I'm not going to apologize!" I said, "The guy you pushed is a disabled American war veteran that you almost knocked over!" I said, "You need to apologize to him. He said, "Or what?" And he raised this cane to his head in a striking position! I looked at him and said, "If you're doing what I think you're doing, then you better think twice about doing it! I have had a little bit of martial arts training and I will defend myself against that cane of yours!" I said, "You really might want to put that down before you get hurt!" I was serious, I got myself in position to defend and thrust, and after seeing what he did to a war veteran, I was ready to light this dude up, which then it would have been my fault, because I did ask him to apologize, even though he refused! So, yes, I was the assertive one, but I couldn't stand back watching this jerk knock over my new disabled veteran friend like a bowling pin!

I said, "You have two choices, since I can't force an apology from you: you can either put down your weapon and walk away, or I promise you it will get really ugly if you attempt to hit me with that thing!" I got in a defensive mode position. "Make your choice now!" He looked at me and decided to lower his weapon and smirked and said, "I hope to catch you and your friend on the street again another day!" This got my attention! I said, "Oh, this is where you want to take this, now? Threatening him and me! If that happens, and you attack us, you will find out exactly why you're walking away unscathed today! Because then there will be no excuses!" I said, and if I catch you harassing any more homeless people or disabled veterans like my friend over there, I will not hold back on you! You better remember that," and I proceeded to walk away. I'm a little disabled myself, but not like my veteran friend; I could fight, and he couldn't anymore, so someone had to take up his cause! I was glad I was there, in the right place, at the right time! And I don't regret it to this day!

As I mentioned before, I worked in a shelter that I stayed at, and during that time that I worked there, one of the employees approached and asked me if I could help her out. I said, "What do you need?" She said, "Well, as you know, I just got back to work at the shelter, and I need to get some groceries. Can you help me out?" The lady was a friend and I said, "Yes, I'll help you out!" She said, "Can I get one of your music CDs, as well? I'd like to get it over to my friend in New York who could do something with it!" I said, "I'd be very honored to do that!" So the next day, I gave her the money so she could get a few groceries. We went over to a place called Primark and got her some gloves, a hat, and a scarf, because it was wintertime! She was very grateful for that! She said, "My electric bill is coming up. I have no money for that!" I said, "I can help you out one more time. How much is that?" "About forty dollars, I think?" "Okay, I'll help you with this one, but I can't keep doing this!" She said, "I understand. Oh, one more thing," she said. "Okay, what is it now?" "I need $35 to send the CD to my friend in New York who could really help you out." I said, "Who is he?" She said, "He is a music producer who is well-known in New York and around the country!" I said, "Wow, that's awesome." I said, "This is the last time, though," so I gave her the $35! "I hope to hear from your friend!" She said, "Oh, trust me, Ritchie, you will!"

So I waited, and waited, and waited. About this time, she lost her job again, for whatever reason. I approached her one day on the street. "What about your friend from New York, has he heard the CD yet?" She said, "Don't bother me, please, I'm trying to get work." I said, "You said this guy would get back with me; he never did! I have your word that he would!" But once again, she just turned away from me! The producer's name was Twin Beats or Swiss Beats. I don't know his name, for sure, and I don't know if she even gave him the CD or not. There is no way I'll ever find this out. But I do know that I never heard from her again, and I never heard from this producer in New York! All because you try to do the right thing to help someone out, sometimes it doesn't work! I was glad to help her out with groceries but I should have seen the other stuff coming! Nothing ever came of it.

I was going to a bus stop at the same place on Washington Street to catch the bus to go to a place called St. Francis downtown. St. Francis is an awesome place where they give you breakfast and lunch, help you out with clothes if you need them, and have counselors. I can't say enough about St. Francis. They are a blessing in Boston! I was getting ready to sit down and I noticed a lady was lying on the bench. She was just getting up. I said, "Miss, are you okay?" She said, "My head hurts. I haven't eaten anything in about four days!" And by all indications, she was telling me the truth, because her face was very pale! And she hardly had any energy at all! I said, "You don't look so good." She said, "Bro, I don't feel very good!" The bus came by and went towards downtown where I was supposed to be, but it was okay, because sometimes God puts people in your lives for you to do something for. I said, "Miss, we have to feed you, we can't let you go on like this!" And so I took her by the hand. She was stumbling around and could barely get her bearings and I said, "What are you hungry for?" She said, "I'm starving for some donuts!" Well, Dunkin Donuts was right across the street, so I took her to get some donuts, those sausage egg things they have, hash browns, and coffee! When she got done eating, she was perking up a little bit. She said, "I want to thank you, nobody came along to help me at all!" I said, "You can thank God for that, because he put me in your path as I was getting ready to get on the bus to go downtown!" So I was glad He put me on Washington Street at that time! I reached into my pocket and I said, "All I have is five dollars left, but you're more than welcome to it!" She said, "Thank you very much," and she ordered some more food! She was hungry! She wasn't feeling very well, so I said, "We need to get you to the hospital to have you looked at!" She said that she was thinking that, as well, she had Mass Health insurance so she could go to the hospital anytime! She said, "I feel so weak, I don't know if I can make it down there!" I said, "No worries, we will get you there!" My body was still fairly healthy at that time so I put her arm around my neck and I slowly had her walking with me to go to Boston Medical Center, which was the hospital closest in that area. We were getting close, oh, so close, and she told me, "Ritchie! I don't think I can make it. I'm about ready to pass out!" I said, "Hold on, sis, just a little bit longer!" "Ritchie, I don't think I can make it!"

Well, at that point I think God really took over, because there came two people from the hospital with a wheelchair! I said, *Thank God, thank God, thank God!* One of those people happened to be one of the staff members that worked at the shelter where I resided at! The other was a BMC intern or a nurse! I welcomed their presence! He looked at me and said, "Bro, nice seeing you, we'll take care of it from here! We'll try to get her some help that she needs and try to hook her up with a case manager!" I was so grateful I said, "Thank you, bro, and thank you, nurse, for being here!" They both said, "If it wasn't for you, we wouldn't have known about this lady!" I said, "It's a long story how we met this morning! But the point is, now she's in good hands!" He smiled and said, "Bro, you're one of a kind. You really do try to help the people here in Boston?" I said, "When you see people down and out like this, you have to do something more than just pray!" He says, "You're right about that!" He says, "I know you're a Christian; I see how you handle yourself at the shelter!" I said, "Thank you, bro," I said, "but it's all God!" He said, "Indeed, it is!" He said, "Ritchie? We've got it from here," I said, "Thank you, very much!" They left with her in the wheelchair headed the last few 100 yards to get her the help she needed in the hospital. I looked up to Heaven, smiled, and said, "I guess I wasn't supposed to go to St. Francis today! Thank you, God!" and proceeded back to the shelter.

So you meet all kinds of people, some dangerous, some not-so-dangerous, some friendly, and some who just don't care! As a book author here in Boston, I can walk the streets and nobody would know who I even am, and it doesn't matter that they would know who I was. What's important in this is when they meet me, hopefully they would know who God is because of my relationship with Him. I thank God I didn't have to fight, but you have to stand up for yourself in Boston! You walk away if you can, try to keep a low profile, and just show yourself to be friendly!

When I'm on an escalator at one of the train stations, I always take the right side of it because of faster walking traffic that will run you over if you are on that left side! Like a car in a slower lane of traffic giving way to faster traffic! Because there are Bostonians who want to get up the escalator quickly, and I don't want to be the cause of them not being able to get by me because of a disabled knee! I also found out that sometimes these escalators are not running properly and I have reported that to their train staff at stops. I said, "Why is it that some escalators run and the others don't?" I was curious. One guy told me, and this enlightened me greatly, "Bro? It's not that they don't work, because they all do, it's simply because we get some customers in here who think it's funny that they can push a button down below and make an escalator stop running, and people like yourself will think it's broken, when all someone has to do is push on the reset button!" Wow! I didn't know that, but now I do! It's sad that some people will stoop this low to make people think an escalator is broken. I feel sorry for those that do this, because some of the people that use it are disabled or handicapped just like myself. I hope they catch who is doing this! I love living in this city, whether there are challenges or not, because it is the place I call home now! I'm a big Boston Celtics fan and a Boston Red Sox fan! And I say, I apologize to my friends and those I don't know in Boston, but I have been a lifelong Indianapolis Colts fan for a long time since I lived in Indiana! I hope you enjoyed this compilation of episodes in Life Stories.

CHAPTER 10

YOU GET WHAT YOU PAY FOR!

When I was younger I used to hear this saying, "You get what you pay for." At the time, I didn't know if that was a good thing or a bad thing. I've come to understand now, since I'm a little bit older and hopefully wiser, that "You get what you pay for" is probably not a good thing. When I was younger in Indiana, I used to hear stories about Boston, about how expensive it was to live here, or buy things here, or even survive here. I'll be honest, that kind of scared me a little bit. So any thoughts about going to Boston at that time were kind of out of the question in my mind, thinking all this might be true! So I kind of put Boston on the back-burner in my mind, wondering if I'd ever see the Celtics, one of my favorite teams, in person! But what's funny about that is that when I met someone online in 2016, she was from Boston! So I wondered, *Am I supposed to go to Boston?*

As I've already described, I started life over again in Boston, Massachusetts, and I'm very grateful for that. Things aren't as expensive as what I first heard. In fact, going out to dinner and some other places, you get more than your money's worth. There's a shoe store up here that sells clothes, as well, but the clothes don't fit me, because they don't have my size. I'm a 34 waist and their highest size, I think, is 31, which would be really small for a man's waist. But their shoes are awesome there. I can't tell you how grateful I am to be able to get shoes at ridiculously affordable prices at Primark. I have on a pair of shoes now that I purchased over there for five dollars. I've had these shoes almost a year, and they are still well intact! Which pretty much tells me it's not how much you pay for something, it's the value of what you pay for! In my case here in Boston, you get what you pay for! And that's not a bad thing, that is a very good thing!

I go to Walmart in Lynn since there are no Walmarts in Boston, and they always have good prices. There's a Dollar Tree across the street from Walmart, and they have fantastic prices. So not everything is a rip-off that you hear about, even though you might live in another state at that time. And the dinners are amazing—I could eat at many places for about ten dollars a meal, or less. You get an incredible amount of food. I will give details in another chapter about where I've eaten and the karaoke places I've been invited to eat.

I wanted to put this chapter in because not everything you hear about another place is true! I'm living proof of that right here in Boston, where I've been for almost 4 years, come April 2020. The opportunities I've had here are incredible. For instance, I didn't know you could win money if you won a karaoke contest—that's incredible! I never saw that in Indiana! There's many things I never saw in Indiana that I'm experiencing now as I get older! Keep in mind, I said "older," not "old!" There is a difference! I even run across stores from time to time up here and they have great buys! It was up here in Boston that a publisher reached out to me to do this book! They found me online somehow and emailed me, and the rest is history, as you are now reading this book. Up in Boston, you do get what you pay for.

And there are many, many places up here that reach out to the homeless, as well. I never saw that in Anderson, Indiana. They had one Christian ministries place in downtown Anderson that did help homeless people, but it's only one place, and when it's full, it's full! In Indianapolis, I heard from some friends there that a bunch of homeless people that were living under a bridge got kicked out. I would ask the city of Indianapolis, just where do you think these people are going to live? How cruel is it to do that to a homeless person? What would they do if they became homeless? After all, the homeless are just trying to get by to survive! I know because I first started becoming homeless in August 2014, and if it wasn't for David Lloyd reaching out to my friend from Lapel, Indiana, at that time I don't know where I would be today. Because the winters do get cold there in Indiana, and I don't know how I would have survived being that cold outside! But fortunately, in 2016, I only had to deal with that for a couple of months before I was invited to come to Boston. The rest is history!

You get what you pay for up here. I'm grateful and I thank God I'm here. Other than Washington State where I was raised, this has been the best place I have ever lived! I am truly grateful to God for it! I just wanted to share this with you that not everything you hear about another city or state is always true! This author is living proof of it. I also get a train and bus pass for $30 a month unlimited, to go anywhere I want! The commuter rail has a special going on ten dollars round-trip in many, many, places in Massachusetts on the commuter rail train! That, to me, is unbelievable! That's another great value! And with that pass of mine, I can go to the New England Aquarium for five dollars. I haven't even discovered all of Boston yet! I have never regretted my time here in this city, and I hope to get more books and music done, as well! I have had great respect from friends and my former employer and staff members of the Southampton Shelter! And Mario from the Engagement Center is looking to take Pops and me out to lunch sometime to celebrate our accomplishments trying to set a Guinness World Record! I told him what we have so far, and it's blowing his mind! And he's also going to give us a verification letter for the Guinness Book of World Records of how we got started and have continued towards this record! Anyway, you get the idea. If you're from another state or city reading this book, I'm just telling you, from this author's perspective, if you come to Boston you're going to find much value.

When you get a Disability monthly check like I do, you have to be smart and buy what you can purchase. I'm grateful to many specific stores and products for their value: to CVS for the Gold Emblem cheese puffs, the Arizona iced tea drinks like my favorite Mucho Mango, and man is it delicious! And the TruMoo chocolate milk, which is possibly the best chocolate milk I have ever tasted. I'm grateful for the email alerts that tell me when things are on sale, like ice cream! Yum! I'm grateful for the Bonus Bucks, which can be used on many things, but not on milk, which puzzles me, because milk is one of my favorite things to drink, and it's healthy for you! I love this new fruit candy snack I found made by Gold Emblem brand, and this snack is called Kollisions. It is a fruit snack of different fruit flavors of licorice. And man it is soooo good! And I appreciate Walgreens, for their sales, like 4 for $10.00. And they have delicious snack cakes! Like CVS, they have great sales! And Walmart has a good selection of items. I also love Dollar Tree, where I once bought a phone charger from them for a dollar, and it's lasted over two years! The only problem is, both of these places, Walmart and Dollar Tree, are in Lynn, and it takes two trains and a bus to get there. There are many other places for which I'm grateful: the Goodwill store close to Roxbury, which has really good buys all the time! Alltown convenience store on Southampton Street in Boston and constant convenience stores all over; the Roche Bros. where they have groceries and such. What really stands out to me is the Roche Bros.' awesome hot breakfast selection for about ten dollars.

In this city, you really do get what you pay for. It's amazing! Amen.

CHAPTER 11

WHAT IS THE PURPOSE?

When I lived in Muncie, Indiana, in the 1990's, I was invited to sing at many churches, and got to know a lot of people doing so. There were some really good people in these churches, and I developed a lot of friendships through God with them! One of these churches was called Glad Tidings. I got to know the pastor there pretty well. I can't remember his name now, but one thing he liked about me was not only my singing voice, but that I wanted to do something for God! At that point, I had barely become a songwriter through my church, so I was very excited to be a part of a concert that they wanted to put on at the church. There is a worldwide Gospel song writer out of Muncie, that same city where I became a songwriter. His name was Ray Boltz, who I really admired, for both his voice and his spirit. It turned out that Ray Boltz did one of his first concerts there at the place I was asked to sing! The pastor's desire was for me to get with a few people of his church and work out some kind of a musical play with the songs that God had given me that were written, but not fully developed yet. I was excited about that! Who wouldn't be? I thought to myself, *Man oh man, this is how Ray started out!* Maybe I'm getting ready to follow in his footsteps through Jesus!

So, we got together, prayed, and did a few songs to practice for the play. About the fifth day we were practicing, the pastor himself came in to see how we were doing and was very impressed. One of his congregation members had taken him aside and started whispering, unknown to us, negative things about what might happen with this concert! I guess before I came, they had some kind of a setback with some music person, and it didn't go over well. But this was different; I wasn't that guy, I was God's guy! So, the pastor listened to what this person had said, and after practice, he applauded us and took me aside, saying, "Richard, I have some real concerns about putting on this concert!" I was shocked! "Sir, what concerns are you referring to? You heard and saw our practice tonight! You liked and approved of everything you saw! What in the world is making you change your mind?" He wouldn't tell me straight-up because of the concerns of one of his congregation. He said, "I hope you understand, I'll tell the others that we won't be doing this concert!" I was broken-hearted. I felt the person that had told him there would be issues was spreading gossip, which does not belong in any church! I was very upset with him, and wanted to tell him just what I thought of him! How many people to this day could have possibly gotten something out of that concert? That concert was for God; we weren't in it to make names for ourselves! However, I knew in my heart that I had to forgive the guy who did this gossip, which I did, but it didn't make it any easier.

I cried out to God for weeks, saying, *God, why did I even have to go through that if it wasn't meant to be?* God spoke to my heart, *Son! It was very much meant to be, it was part of my plan, my purpose! But I can't force the human heart from doing evil even though they name my name! You were right to forgive the person!* With tears in my eyes, I said to the Lord, *It was hard, very hard, my flesh wanted to rise up on him!* I will never forget that incident, and the potential of how many lives could have been changed through that concert!

On December 16th, 1998, I was invited on a radio station called 98.7 FM WQME Radio, which was located in Anderson, Indiana. They asked me to come on and do an early morning two hour interview with them, and they would play my CD that was developed and then completed earlier that year, *Battleground*! As the DJ, Matt Rust, interviewed me, he was really impressed with the songs. He was just about to put them on live, when he whispered to me, "You have some really good songs!" He said, "I'm looking forward to this." I said, "So am I! So as WQME became live on the radio, he welcomed all the listeners and said, "We have a special treat for you today; we have an upcoming artist that we have invited live over the air today!" And then he introduced my name and asked me to talk about the music for a few moments! As I began to explain how the music got started in August 1994, through a prophecy, he interrupted me and told his listeners, "We'll be right back after a commercial!" And I thought to myself, *Okay, I guess that was a stopping point!* He came back on the air and introduced the songs over the airwaves and began to play them, then he got back with me and said, "Richard? The songs are so good that people ought to buy them just for the titles themselves!" That was encouraging to hear! I said, "I'm very flattered by that, Matt, thank you. It's all God!" He interviewed me a little bit longer and kept telling the audience to watch out for this upcoming music artist! At the end of the interview, he said, "How do you feel?" I said I felt really great. "Thank you so much for the interview!" He said, "Can I have a copy of *Battleground* for myself? I want to put it in rotation over the airwaves here!" I beamed with excitement. "I would very much love that, that would be an honor!" I looked up to Heaven and said, *Lord is this how it gets started? Is my life going to go somewhere through this?*

Sadly, after that interview, WQME never played the music, and I never heard from them again. They had removed their upcoming local artist segments, and replaced it with something else. They call themselves "WQME, a shade above normal," but I call them, "WQME, a shade above lukewarm!" Remember, they invited me to be on their program! I was absolutely disappointed that they did not follow through. I was also invited to Ray Boltz Studio a few years before 1995, to talk over what transpired in my life as a new Gospel Rock and Worship songwriter, and was asked, "Okay, now that God has made you a songwriter, what is your next step?" His mom was running the front desk at the time and I said, "I'm very new to this, and excited!" She told me, point-blank, "Well, we can't help you with any direction, you just have to pray about it." I thought, *I should just pray about it? Why did you guys invite me over here? To make a fool out of me? I came hoping to get some solid advice from the Ray Boltz Ministries organization and this is what you tell me?* "Let me ask you something ma'am. Is this what you told your son, Ray Boltz, when he first became a songwriter, or did you actually guide him?" I said, "This conversation's over, I'm leaving!" I said, *Lord? What was the purpose of them inviting me to their studio area here in Muncie? I didn't like what she said!* The Holy Spirit spoke back to my heart, *Richard, I didn't like what she said, either!*

Now, I don't know if this ministry still exists today or not. Ray decided to go a different lifestyle and I'll just leave it at that. He is someone I highly respected at the time, and it was him that I wanted to talk to about these new songs, but his mother didn't offer that! She wanted to take it upon herself to give that advice. There's a Scripture I have read before that basically says that if you have the power to do something for someone, then you should do it! More than just praying about it, actually doing something, which is the part I was hoping for.

After these three separate incidents in the nineties alone after I became a songwriter, I became very down-hearted and discouraged! And I kept saying to myself, *Maybe it's not God's will for me to go any further with this music! I don't know where to even start now!* So for a few years I was literally in a fog. I didn't know just what to do or how to proceed. In the early 2000's, I was in the front steps of a YMCA in Anderson when a guy came along that I thought I recognized. I said, "Hey, you're Bill Gaither, aren't you?" He looked at me with a small smile and said, "Yeah, how did you recognize me?" I said that I recognized the big hair! His smile turned upside down and said, "Okay," and started to walk away! Worldwide TV singer and comedian Mark Lowry always joked with him, and he laughed at Mark Lowry! So why was he different in the public's eye?

I caught up with him before he left the YMCA and asked him, "Friends of mine were telling me you have a studio in Alexandria, is that true?" He said, in a stern tone, "Yes," I said, "I didn't mean to embarrass you. I always thought you had a sense of humor! I apologize for assuming that!" He just looked at me. "Anyway, I have a CD called

Battleground; I'd love it if you'd listen to it and tell me what you think. After all, you are a worldwide recording artist, you and Gloria, and your Gaither vocal band! I've always admired your music! And I'd be honored if you take a listen!" He looked at me and he said, "Give me two CDs and I'll get back with you later!" I said, "Okay, here you go," and I gave them to him! "Now, I am busy, and I'm trying to watch my daughter's play!" I said, "Sorry, I'll get out of your hair!" At that point, I didn't think I believed he would watch the CDs! And, you know, he never got ahold of me again! With these stories I'm trying to make a point: God requires life service over lip service! I'm trying to be a person of life service through God.

I was to be in Lapel, Indiana, starting in August 2014. A few months down the road, I was to meet another worldwide country Gospel singer by the name of Doug Anderson, who was raised out of Lapel! He's a big-time celebrity there, and somehow or another, I was invited to one of his small music concerts, which I heard him perform. He was very, very good! After the show, I told him that I do music, as well! He said he'd be very interested in that and I said, "Okay, I'll get you a CD!" And the following week, I saw him again and gave him a CD. He said, "I'll get back with you," and about a week later, he did get back with me. I was shocked! Because after everything I had experienced with people and their words, I couldn't believe he was going to keep his word! But he said he really liked the CD, he had listened to all of the songs and said a couple of them were his favorites! I said, "Thank you, Doug! I'm very flattered by that, it's all God!" I said, "I have to be honest with you on something." He said, "What's that?" I said, "I'm not in the position to do anything with the music right now, because I'm going through a trial that God has allowed, like Job of the Bible!" He said, "Don't worry about that. I don't think any less of you. Gossip gets around in this town and I know your situation! And I'd like to get you in front of my producer so he can hear the music and see you in person!" I was absolutely floored by this! I asked, "Where is your producer?" He said, "He resides out of Nashville, Tennessee. He has a studio there and I'd like to get you in front of him!" I was shaking inside, thinking, *Maybe this is some kind of turning point now, and maybe this is what God wants? I don't know, I have to keep an open mind!* He said, "I'll get back to you on this." I said, "I can't wait! Thank you so much!" So, I waited, and I waited, and I waited, and he never got back to me! This time, I was prepared for any let-down, because I'd already been through these things.

Now, I admire southern Gospel music. But it's not my taste in music, especially after a Southern Gospel radio music host in Muncie, Indiana, invited me to sing on his show in about the early 1990's, and do some Southern Gospel songs in which I had a few soundtracks. When I got there, he told me, "Richard? Southern Gospel music is the only music that God accepts in Heaven!" I said, "What? You really believe that?" He smiled proudly and said, "I absolutely do! I did a slow burn on the inside!" I looked at him and said, "Well, I guess everybody else who writes different styles of Gospel music doesn't stand a chance in Heaven!" I continued, "What a very stupid and ignorant thing to say to someone who writes different Gospel music styles!" Now his face turned red, but I continued, "That would be like me telling someone who enjoys eating eggs and bacon and toast for breakfast, that they can only have cereal instead everyday." He said, "Young man! I don't think I want you singing on my show tonight!" I looked at him and said, "Trust me, sir, I won't lose any sleep over it!" And this made him more angry! As I was leaving I said, "I guess one day you'll find in Heaven before God what kind of music He likes!" and I walked out the door.

I was dazed. I said to myself, *Are there people really this ignorant?* Then I got in my car and left.

About 1996, I was invited to audition for, you guessed it, a Southern Rock-style Gospel band called The Homeland Boys! At this point, I'm not too crazy about singing Southern Gospel at all, but I wasn't going to turn down an opportunity to audition for them. And so I did, and they had me do six songs. Everybody in attendance loved what they heard. They took me around the back of the church and showed me their tour bus, and it was absolutely magnificent! The leader of this group asked me, "Richard? Can you be ready in about three weeks to join us on a short tour and start singing with us as a backup singer, to start with?" I said. "Yes, I can do that," and I said, "Thank you for listening to the songs!" So, about three weeks went by, and nobody showed up, no phone call, or anything! I was stunned. In fact, two years later, I came across the lead singer again. He almost didn't recognize me when I came up to him, and I said, "Do you remember me, sir?" He said, "Should I?" I said, "Yes, you should! I was the guy you had audition for your band, which I did, and you liked the music. You asked me to join you in about three weeks after that audition to be on your short tour! I waited for you, and you never showed up. I looked for that bus, and you guys never showed up! And you never even called me!" I continued, "In God's name, why didn't you get back with me? If you didn't want me to be in your band, couldn't you have had the decency to let me know at that time, instead of getting my hopes up to sing with you guys?"

He looked at me and lowered his head and said, "Please forgive me!" He said that he had told the guys after they dropped me off that day that I was a good enough singer to replace any one of them, and that it would be a mistake to have me come sing with them. I looked at him and shook my head. I said, "I trusted you guys; I trusted your words! But you didn't have the guts at that time to tell me that I wasn't the right fit for your band? I wasn't trying to show up or replace anybody! I was looking to be a part of your band, however you wanted me and do whatever you needed, but you assumed I'd be a bad fit for you, so you never got back with me." I looked at him and I said, "Of course I forgave you and them for being a part of this, I prayed that after you didn't show up! But let me ask you something: can you forgive yourself? Can you look God straight in the face one day and forgive yourself?" He didn't say a thing, and I left.

That was my experience alone in Indiana of believing and trusting people who said they named the name of Jesus. Flash-forward to Boston 2019, where I now live. I've been invited to sing in many karaoke places now, and I have that documented in the story in this very book including the fiasco of one of the guys at one of these karaoke places offering a music contract to get the second CD done that never came about. It's in the story called, "Hey, Ritchie, You're Invited!"

Anyways, in early 2019, as I'm singing and enjoying myself in these karaoke places at different times, I'm approached by three different talent scouts. Now, I have long forgiven the broken promises and words of influential Gospel people of the '90s! All I'm doing is writing it down in this book because it is true! On three different occasions, I am approached by these talent scouts, and I wasn't even aware of who they were while I was up there singing. One night, this guy named Matthew Greene approached me during the singing, and said, "Bro, you have some kind of talent!" (Side note: where I came from in Indiana, they would call you "dude!" But in Boston, they call you "bro!" I like "bro" better!) He introduced himself to me, and gave me a card! And of course, I gave him one of my business cards. He said, "I really like what I've heard from you, and I'm interested in hearing more!" I said, "I'd be interested in hearing what you have to offer. What is it that you would want me to do?" I kind of had a half-hearted interest in it after what I'd been through, in Indiana. But I said to myself, *If it's God's will, I'll give it a shot!* To this day, not one phone call has ever got back to me! Another scout that gave me her card at a place I sang at called Bell in Hand never got ahold of me! So I just threw her card away after a while. And the third scout took my card and never got back with me.

One night, a very well-dressed lady approached me at the Hong Kong. She said, "Youtube Ritchie?" I said, "Yes?" "You sing very nice, and you have a powerful voice. I'd like to give you an opportunity to join my singing group." I said, "Ma'am? Who is your singing group?" She said, "Look around, Ritchie! They're in this room right now, excellent singers I have gathered under my fold." "Very impressive," I said. So, I looked around and all I saw were the regular singers, plus non-singers in this bar, and I said, "I have no idea who they are without you introducing me to some of them." Then she got real stern with me, "You can't join us unless you clean up and shave off the moustache!" I said, "First of all, lady, I wasn't aware that I was going to be auditioning for you in this bar tonight, where I sing a lot of the time. I didn't get that memo! Second, I don't like your pompous, almost conceited, attitude! I don't care who you are,I don't care if your singers were world famous! These are my normal clothes that I wear when I sing here and my friends here like me just as I am... Forgive me if it's not a tuxedo for you or a three-piece suit from Walmart. But newsflash to you—the moustache stays!" I added, "I wouldn't join your band if they were the last one on the earth, simply because of your egotistical, arrogant, we're-better-than-you attitude! I'm a regular here, you and your bunch of singers are not. So, no, I'm not interested! Excuse me now, they just called my name to sing. So I gotta go, bye-bye." She fired back at me as I was on the stage and yelled at me, which drew attention from the crowd as they heard her screaming at me, "You will never join us, Ritchie!" And it got quiet as everybody heard her yell my name! I tried to Ignore her and get ready to do the song, but she kept on yelling!

Everybody was real quiet as she kept up with the yelling. Finally, I said something in a calm voice on the mic, "Lady? You wanted me to join your band of singers when you act like this? Is this how you really act with that attitude you're displaying, making a show of yourself?" The people in the room were cheering after I defended my position. "Just how mature are you when you act like this? I told you in person a few minutes ago I wasn't interested when you approached me, because of your attitude that is on display for all to see right now!" "Get her, Ritchie!" I heard. "So lady, I will make it clear for you again one more time before I sing. With everybody in this room who heard your rants, I'm saying it again, lady. I don't care if your band was the last one on the face of the earth, I still wouldn't join you! Why would I lower myself? You're visiting here and I'm a regular singer here that you chose to embarrass? Have a nice night, I'm gonna sing now!"

For a moment you could hear a pin drop. Then, I got a thunderous ovation as this now red-faced lady signaled her bunch of singers that they were leaving. She yelled out, "We won't be back!" The crowd yelled back, "Is that a promise?" and erupted into more clapping. The crowd started yelling my name, "Youtube Ritchie! Youtube Ritchie!"

When my song came on, the crowd quieted, and after I got done singing, I heard a guy yell out, "Three cheers for Youtube Ritchie!" And they clapped even more. I was flattered; that was an incredible night! I will never forget it. I wish the lady and her singers well, just somewhere else! I seriously doubt they will make their way over to the

Hong Kong again! Was I disappointed? Of course! But I just knew better after what I'd been through!

I don't know if any of the talent scouts I dealt with in Boston were of God or not? But the people I dealt with in Indiana claimed to know God, as well! Here's my thought on that: if you say it, then mean what you say and follow through with action! Otherwise, who are you trying to impress if you don't keep your word? To this day, I'm very leery of anybody coming up to me and saying, "Ritchie? We think you've got talent!" All I know is, if it's God's will, then it's my will to do His will! Because it's about doing life service and not lip service! If I only talked about doing these lifestories, would they have gotten done? No! Because it would have only been lip service, but God required from me life service! And therefore, this book comes forth and I thank God for it. It's been a labor of love... Amen.

CHAPTER 12

FEED MY SHEEP!

Every now and then, my mind will sometimes flash back to the near end of September 2015 and how it was one of the worst few days of a month in my entire life! Without God's help, I wouldn't have made it! You're only strong to a certain point, then you rely on the one who came into your heart! And fall back into His hands, His love, and His compassion! God spoke to my heart many, many times and constantly encouraged me that it would get better! And I trusted Him, and believed Him, even when I was literally freezing in an abandoned house! at that time God reminded me I'm still one of his sheep!

This place had many huge leaks in the ceiling and roof, and some of the windows were cracked! I had three heavy blankets sleeping on a frozen couch that was stiff as a board! In sub-zero temperatures, where the very floor would be freezing. I was grateful to my friend, David Lloyd, who let me stay in it. Early on, I would hear the Pastor and his wife of my church in Lapel tell me, "Richard! Don't get too close to that David guy, because he can't be trusted!" I don't like gossip, so I became friends with him, anyway! And over time, the opposite became evidently true—it was the Pastor and his wife who couldn't be trusted! And it was David who first warned me before I became homeless that all they cared about was money. And that was absolutely true on that fateful day in September 2015, when they asked me to leave the abandoned house that I was living in, now owned by them! And yes, you guessed it, it was over money, and I saw it up close and personal for myself. It turned out that this so-called shepherd over the church was nothing but a lying sheep disguised in wolf's clothing! And I was shocked!

Anyway, flash forward to October 2018, God is blessing my life in Boston, Massachusetts, where I now live in a place of my own, again. After faithfully living in a men's shelter for two and a half years, God rewards you with an extremely awesome one-bedroom! It's small, but it's home! I cried the first few days I got here, and was totally grateful to God that he opened this door for me again. I wouldn't change the experience I had at the shelter for anything. And I wouldn't trade Boston for Indiana if you gave me all the money in the world. And I'm serious about that! It was truly an incredible experience living in the shelter, and I was treated with respect by a lot of people. Why is that? Because I treated them how they needed to be treated. That's how people respect you. They were staff, residents, supervisors, bosses, and former employees that I worked with, and some that I trained.

My former boss, John Commanski, called me up one day and told me that he was going to send me a $25 McDonald's gift card in the mail, and he wanted to see how I was doing. I was absolutely floored by him telling me that, and so honored that he would do that! But when he was my boss, it was typical of him to do that at the shelter, because he has that type of heart, and he was awesome to work for. He saw me as his right hand man to make sure all our work got done. He would reward us with snacks, constantly! And he and Cory, who was his boss, gave us a hot chocolate and donut party one day out of the blue! Just out of appreciation for a job daily well done. And it was more than once! It was a great incentive for the other workers and myself to really do a good job daily ,and even if we were short-handed on any given day, we got it done! I truly believe what I'm about to say is true! That if you obey God and trust God he will give you a favor in different situations! He did for me many times when I was in the shelter! He would tell me over and over you are one of my sheep when I give you the ability you will feed other sheep! I never forgot the words told me that day in the shelter! His words came to pass, that through the grace of God even as a disabled person he is using me today to do just that, feeding sheep! When I lived in the Muncie housing authority in Muncie Indiana I didn't have a whole lot of money but I felt compelled in my heart to starting a feed my sheep program right there in the housing projects and feed people that needed food! I brought the idea forward to the head of the housing authority and they rejected it! I thought it was a very good idea it was God that gave me the idea! So what happened a couple years later at that same place? Lo and behold they start a feed my sheep program! I don't know if it's still there today or not? But I was grateful that they did start a program!

And I also want to give a quick shoutout to two of my former bosses, both whom I worked for while I lived in Indiana. The first one is Shawn Sherfy; he was the head manager of a place I worked for over three years, starting in 1989, called Sherfy's Big Apple! This was a really good restaurant to work at, and eat at, as well! Shawn was awesome to work for, and gave me quite a few raises, which I appreciated! This place was replaced by another business, which broke my heart, and then Bill Marr was my other employer who was good to me! His business is in Indianapolis, Indiana, where I worked before I was to become homeless. He owns a delivery van courier service called Express Delivery, and he was an awesome boss to work for. I really appreciated him. So one day, he helped me get another van at a place called Amber Motors which he wasn't really sure he trusted, and this place never fixed a strut on the driver's side, even though they kept promising to do that, but during that time, they never did, and the van also had some kind of leak from the engine somewhere. So on my last day of work, I had to be towed home from Indianapolis! I say "last day" because the van would never run again, even though a mechanic that Advance Auto Parts had recommended said he could fix it and have it running in five days. But he never got it fixed, even though I gave him what he required up-front, which was $500 dollars cash! He never came through on his promise! I was to lose my job, my apartment, and my van, all in the same month in July 2014! And I felt so bad that I couldn't pay my boss the weekly payments on the van because I lost my job.

My boss had no choice but to replace me, and that wasn't his fault, as he waited over two months to do that, because he believed what the mechanic, Randy, said he could do. But he never came through. That was a shock, knowing that I was about to lose everything I worked hard for! And I had bought an antique rug and an antique chair that was like a rocking chair, and here I was, about to lose it all! Even my landlord mocked me at that time when I shared about my van and my job, he said to me, "Where is your God now, Richard?" I said in a defiant voice, "Steve! He still lives in my heart! And He's not leaving! So mock all you want, I trust my God!" He laughed at me and said, "Good luck when you're homeless," and then he left.

The same month of July 4th, 2014, I was invited to sing the National Anthem at Anderson Speedway in Anderson where I lived, and sing on the radio for WQME radio the next night at the same racetrack. I put on a bold face at both of these events and sang at both. Little did they know what I was dealing with, and I wasn't about to share it with them, or any of the other singers that were invited to sing on the radio that night! I focused on both singing events with God's help, and I asked God to give me peace to get through both of them! And he did. I met two special acts that night, the Indy Men's Choir from Indianapolis, Indiana, who to me sounded like the Gospel version of The Temptations! And yes, they were that good, I was so impressed! And I also met the Dixon Todd Band from Alabama! And they sang Christian rock and worship songs, which they themselves wrote! I was absolutely blown away! They were so good! I had never heard of someone doing Christian Rock music before that came from Alabama! What a pleasant, refreshing surprise that these two Gospel bands would be that good! Amen.

So for two straight days, I just focused on these two events, and I thank God to this day that I got to not only participate, but focus on God in those two days, and get my mind off things. Because, on August 1st, I was about to experience just ten days before my birthday what it was going to feel like at the start of being homeless for over four years, but I didn't know that at that time! How could I? So, flash forward over four years later, by the grace of God I was to once again experience what it was going to feel like being a human being in my new place! So when I got there, I hugged the floor crying out to God in thankfulness! And it brought back memories to me of a different floor, an extremely cold, frozen floor in Indiana, where many times it was so wickedly cold there with wind constantly blowing, that I thought I was going to die! And chilled to the bone, I would ask God to take me onto Heaven in my sleep! But God would speak to me in my dreams, and speak in hushed tones in my mind and say, "Oh, Son! You have a destiny to fulfill!" He said remember my son you are still one of my sheep and you have things to do through me even though you can't see it right now! Amen...And now by his grace, I'm trying to do exactly that! I'm really grateful and thanking those He brought my way who are helping me along this journey!

A couple of my supervisors, case managers, my boss John, and night shift boss, Peter, even said, "Ritchie? We are counting on you to be an example, in the outside world of how a person is supposed to live!" I received a great compliment one night from two of the staff people and a night supervisor, as well, telling me that I should think about being an Abuse Counselor! I was floored by that and asked them what exactly was that, and why did they think I would be good at that? One of the staff people playfully tapped me on the forehead and said, "Ritchie? Bro, think about what we're telling you!" He said, "You're great with people in this shelter, you're a good listener, and you care about people's problems! It's a no-brainer, bro! You are self-qualified for the position!" I said, "Really? Wow! I had no idea!" They said, "The only catch is that you have to be living outside the shelter for two years in your own place! We all think, and I mean, every person in authority in this shelter including your case managers, thinks that you would be a benefit to the people of Boston by doing this!" I said, "Wow! Thank you for thinking of me in that way!" And one staffer looked me straight in the eyes and said, "No, thank you, Ritchie, for being who you are. Never lose sight of who you are!"

I never forgot what they said, and through God, I am trying to live up to that! Well, it's almost one year later now, and I'm still here, so I thank God for that. When I got to this place, I had no furniture at all, and barely any food. I didn't care. I was thanking God every day, so grateful in my heart that he gave me this place! I slept in a corner of my dining room with no pillow or blankets, just using my jacket as a pillow! And now that I'm here, it really breaks my heart to see homeless people in many parts of Boston that I can relate to and try to help out as much as I can, even as a disabled person. I wasn't disabled before knee surgery, but I am now. There are about 3,000-plus homeless people in Boston alone, which is far too many. And now, being in this apartment, I can see all this going on through different eyes now! I'm hoping one day just to be able to sit down with our fine mayor and see what we can do about ending the homeless situation in Boston! My prayer is that this book goes around the world! I'm not looking to be famous, but through God I'm looking to be effective! There is a big difference! Because I'm not out to make my name great, I'm out to make God's name even greater through the things that he has spoken to my heart to do that he would receive all the glory for! That's my goal, my vision, and my objective! As long as I'm alive, I embrace this!

I now want to tell you about LOI, and not to be mistaken for LOL. LOI stands for Life Outreach International, which is a worldwide feeding ministry that feeds, clothes, and brings medicine and hope to kids and adults throughout the world. This is headed up by James and Betty Robison out of Texas, and they've been doing this for many, many years. So I want to give a shout-out to them and the recognition and respect that this ministry deserves. I first got involved with them when I caught their program on TV one day, and what I saw just broke my heart with the number of kids and adults who literally starve without food every day. And I was thanking God that I got to see LOI in action as I was watching. They don't just pray for people who are hungry, they do something about it! They go around the globe and get involved, because it takes both prayer and action to do something about it! This spoke to me deeply to be a person of action! I would love to meet James and Betty someday, and let them know how valuable they are, and what they do in this world! Amen! God-willing, in the second book I will be doing a chapter on the help organizations here in Boston called

"Compassion's Touch!" As I saw their program, it touched me deeply! So I committed to help send donations when I could.

Another Outreach Ministry is called Feed The Children, and Save The Children! There are many others, as well, too numerous for this author to name, doing the work that very few do! And now I want to give a shout-out to a Rhode Island gentleman by the name of Nicholas Lowinger. If you don't know who he is, please feel free to Google his name, he is phenomenal! He was five years old visiting a homeless shelter with his mom wearing his brand new shoes, and there was no way of knowing that the kids of that shelter had no new shoes or barely even good shoes! This broke his heart and fired him up to do something about it! And do something about it, he did! He eventually started a now worldwide organization called "Gotta Have Sole!" And this incredible organization gets brand-new shoes out to homeless kids in shelters everywhere, all because a five year old child at that time had a vision! I would love to personally meet him; what an honor that would be, and he is the CEO! So for the many shoe collectors I've read about on Youtube, I hope you read this and get involved! He is an example of what it means to give, and does it from the heart!

I have also become aware of a situation in the Philippines through a friend in early 2019, and I've been doing what I can to help her situation, which was getting better at the time. She's working now

As her situation is now improving, another one is coming into play; there was an orphanage in the Philippines called God's Little Angels, on one of the islands there, which is in desperate need of someone sponsoring them! My first thought was, *Where is the government in this? Does the government of the Philippines get involved with the orphanages, at all?* I decided to Google their government and I found out some astounding things! First of all, I found out there's around 4.5 million homeless people in the Philippines alone! That number is absolutely, freaking outrageous! That's 4.5 million people too many! That needs to change. I also found out some other things, such as that there are over 7,000 islands that make up the Phillipines and about 2,000 of those islands are inhabited by residents! It makes me wonder if other people inhabit the other 5,000-plus islands! That's a tall order in feeding people.

The Philippines is the sixth- or seventh-richest country in the world! If this country is so rich, then why are there so many homeless people? I am aware that there are churches and organizations in the Philippines trying to help their own people, and I applaud them for that, because not everybody has the same goal of corruption! Many people have compassion, and it still shows! There is a guy in the government named Mr. Jimenez who is trying to make a difference in his government. And I heard they have a new President, as well. He has his hands full trying to run a better government, and how do you reach out to people needing help on 2,000 islands? I feel for him and those trying to get help out to the low-income and homeless in the Philippines! There are organizations around the world that are reaching out to the Philippines to help as many as they can, but more help is needed.

Anyways, there was this orphanage called God's Little Angels! There's only so much that a few people can do to feed 27 kids and three staff each month. But with God's help,we we're doing it! There's only so much I can do as an individual, because I had to take forced retirement disability! If I had loads of cash to help, I would have done that! But as a writer, I can get the word out to all who read this book! I also read in 2013 when they had that huge storm that leveled a city that all kinds of help came pouring in with food donations, and what happened to those donations? They found many of them in storage bins rotting away! All that food and help to people suffering at that time never got the help that they needed, and think of all of the lives that could have been saved with that food! That made me sad and mad at the same time! Jesus said, "If you love me, you will feed my sheep!" Anybody can pray, but it takes another person to act on someone's behalf! Jesus said it too, he said that you can pray and say "God bless you" and tell them "Let it be well with you," but if you do nothing for them, what have you done? That's pretty self-explanatory right there: what have you done? You've done nothing! So I question in 2019 and ask, why is it that not everyone in the Government of the Philippines is doing something for the homeless people and the orphanages of their own country, other than Mr. Jimenez and the President, and Senator Manny Pacquiao, who is also a world-famous boxer, and a few others like Tim Tebow, who was born in the Philippines? To see it and not do something about it is wrong, and goes against God's very nature! God is looking for people of life service, not lip service! So I am praying to God that there are changes to be made not only in the Philippine government, but the homeless situation there, and of course around the world, and orphanages everywhere! This author would love to hear a good report on all of this!Also involved with Pakistan since about 2018 and all the wonderful kids of the children's Home there I love being a part of that and when I can I send extra money over for little toy balls they can play with since they have nothing to play with these kids are so awesome they are grateful for any little thing they get!There are 80 of these kids and I hope one day to me to meet them in person! They call me Uncle Ritchie and I am so humbled by that! I'm hoping people will reach out to them as well, these kids can easily teach American kids what gratefulness and humbleness is all about! A lot of American kids are spoiled I wish they could see the plight of these kids overseasI I guarantee you, they would change their attitude about gratitude quickly! Then they would understand how lucky they are! as the Philippines as well as Native American nation as well as the Victor Marx organization at the end of the book! Next up is Native American Nation that's the name I give them, I've been apart of them since about 2019 these are Native American Indians that are kids teenagers older adults who need our help! The organization I'm apart of is in the Dakota's! And like the kids of Pakistan Native American children have different needs as well, and because they are in a cold region definitely need gloves jackets pullover hats! Living is not an easy task for them when they're in a freezing region! I love being a part of them wish I could do more! I can only do so much in a given month but the need is great! And then there's my email friend Victor Marx and his organization where they rescue overseas children Teens and young women from sex traffickers and prostitution rings! He is a former military man who is compassionate for Christ In taking care of these things! He is also a seventh-degree black belt not the kind of guy you'd want to mess with! And he knows how to disarm a gun up close and personal extremely fast I watched the video! It was amazing and it was quick! Him and his wife are rescuing at risk children teens and young women overseas! They both have a passion for doing this! And by the way, his wife can handle herself as well as a trained martial artist as well! There are also many homeless in Boston I try to get around to see and trying to feed them when possible! Boston Commons downtown crossing area there's a lot of homeless and Street people! I wish I had an army of people with me where we could saturate and feed them! Sometimes I see organization going around feeding them but we could use a lot more help! I do it as often as I can they know my face when they see me but there's only so much one person can do and that breaks my heart!

I'm thankful that Boston does reach out to the homeless here and has many programs to help! And there are many churches and organizations here that reach out to the homeless! If not, then I would have been still writing this book from the library, as I would have been continually living at the same shelter and waiting on housing! So I take nothing for granted where I live now! Despite the pandemic people still got to eat I don't know how many organizations and churches are open during the week like they were before covid but things have changed because of the pandemic! That doesn't change the fact that people have to eat! And 7 days a week in Boston, before the pandemic a homeless person could eat a meal at some places, more than two meals a day! That, my friends, is called compassion! And that's still not enough. I would like to see these changes made everywhere! Hollywood, if you're listening, please get involved! You have a lot of money that would be very beneficial to the cause of the homeless instead of making movie after movie to please the public! I bet one movie costing millions of dollars would make an impact on the homeless society! If I personally had the finances that Hollywood generates, I guarantee you a dent would be made in Boston and the Philippines concerning the homeless! And also Pakistan Victor Marx foundation Native American Indians!

Providence, Rhode Island, is also doing some very incredible things. They have a prison correctional institution that is going beyond what is typical for prisons; they have a thing called the MAT program, which stands for Medication Assistance Treatment! In other words, people can get drug treatment medicines to help them overcome their addictions!

And they have really caring counselors who help them through any mental, emotional, psychological, or even spiritual challenges they may be having! And they have a help hotline, as well, for those struggling with addictions! They are offered three kinds of medication for the addiction, and whichever one best fits, then that's what they go with! They have had some incredible results as many inmates are now seeing a new hope, a new lease on life, that they can actually start life over again when they get out of there! And I'm sure by now that what they've started over there has caught on in Massachusetts, as well, and other parts of the United States!

The sad part is, the way I found out about who they were on Youtube was by watching a video before that caught my eye called, "Is Seattle Dying?" This got my attention because this hits close to home. I was raised In Bremerton, Washington, and lived there until I was a teen. My friends and I would take the Bremerton Ferry across the water to Seattle. I don't know how far it was on Puget Sound, but that's where we would go sometimes on our summer vacation breaks when we weren't playing for our awesome baseball team out of East Bremerton called North Perry! I will share that story in another book sometime later called, "A Diamond in the Rough!" Incidentally, my favorite baseball player of all-time is Jackie Robinson, and in that chapter, I will share why. The thing I personally loved about going to Seattle was their awesome seafood restaurants that were close to the pier. They also have a thing called the Space Needle, which is about 600 feet off the ground! I'm sure you can find it on Youtube, as well. I'm deathly afraid of heights, but it got my curiosity up to go to the top of this thing, and so I did. What an incredible view! And they had an awesome fair that I remember from when I was a kid with many things to do!

So when I checked out the video, it really broke my heart; this was not the Seattle I remembered growing up. It is probably, from what I saw, one of the nation's worst cities to live! Drug addiction and homelessness are everywhere in this once beautiful city. And it reminded me of when I was invited to sing in the Bronx, NY, in 1998. The Bronx, NY was called the Battleground City because of its gangs, homelessness, trash, and poverty throughout the city. I saw many parts of it in the time I was there and it was eye-opening! That will be in another book called, "Unique New York!" And I will talk about my 1998 and 2000 trip invites there! It was quite an experience! Well, Seattle has become a lot like that, now! Like something out of a horror movie how run-down this once beautiful city has become! I wanted to cry watching this, and police testimonies of many officers reaching out to combat this! Many were very frustrated because people they had arrested for many crimes were back out onto the street the next day! And some officers have now quit the force, because they are frustrated that nothing changed. And I feel for them! I hope the leaders of Seattle will reach out to this prison correctional institution In Rhode Island, and get the help they need to turn around their own city! It was very, very sad to watch the once bustling city of Seattle at its very lowest point! I'm praying that guys like Russell Wilson and his Seattle Seahawk teammates can bring an impact! He is a Christian athlete and possible Hall of Fame Quarterback someday that really cares about his city! Many Christian athletes in Seattle and many others there who are praying for a change, and they have my prayers, as well! Amen.

I'm asking for those who can to reach out to those who need help, to get involved with the homeless situation in their areas, or contact me about helping those I've been working with in the Philippines. And now, there are many who do get involved, but not enough people who can help but haven't, yet! Whether you're a professional athlete, work in movies, or whatever you do, I'm just asking please,if you have the ability to help the homeless, get involved in your state or country, because they need you! Because one day, myself and others will stand before God and give an account of our very lives, and remember those high up in office and how they spent government money on themselves or others will give an account! In this life, it's not about how much wealth we accumulate, it's how we share what we've been blessed with! The homeless people, shelters, and orphanages need your help!

When re-editing this book, I caught a video of a feud between a guy named Dr. Oz and a world-famous celebrity and movie star about how one thinks eating breakfast is very important and the other one thinks it's not. It was entertaining to watch up until the last part, when I heard the ending, I got mad, and I will tell you why. It turns out that it is said that this world-famous celebrity eats about six or seven meals a day! Are you kidding me? You can't sacrifice about two or three meals a day to feed the homeless? That would still leave you about three or four meals for yourself to eat! To me, that's like shoving it in the face of a homeless person who might be lucky enough to eat one or two meals a day to just survive. I would say to this celebrity now or in person, this author challenges you to consider the homeless and donate those extra two or three meals you eat towards their cause! After all, you do make millions and millions of dollars! I do know how famous you are. It would be like me using the proceeds of this book to buy an expensive car, which I would never do. Whatever money this book generates goes to helping the homeless cause. So, I hope you will think about those that are barely surviving on the streets of Boston and wherever you live. Some of them don't survive because of lack of food, I've been to one of the dedications to the homeless who had passed away during that previous year, and it's a sad time for all as we look upon them and remember their lives and think about this, chances are before they encountered homelessness and life fell apart, they probably had a normal job like most normal people do.

To those that do contribute towards them in this world, I sincerely thank you! To those who only heap it upon themselves, I feel sorry for you! I watched an episode of MTV's reality show one time called "My Super Sweet Sixteen." I was shocked that parents had spent around over $60,000 for their daughter's birthday! I said, *Are you kidding me? You couldn't use some of that to feed the homeless?* I just read tonight that an ex-NBA basketball player had purchased a 22 million dollar home in Florida! That's well and good, I'm sure you've earned that! But you couldn't spare any of that to help homeless people? You had to keep it for yourself, or your family, all these riches? It's not just individuals that are homeless, there are whole families, as well! To ESPN and all these sports talk shows I ask you to please get involved! Not only in the Philippines but the other organizations I mentioned as well, but around the world! And it starts with change in a person's heart! that information is on the last page of the book after chapter 17 and join us in the fight to help this cause, whatever you would want to do would definitely be appreciated! This is real, and much support is needed! because this problem won't solve itself, And others might say to me, well, who are you to tell any of us all of this? And I would say to you, I'm someone who cares! Because I was there! If a member of your family not living with you became homeless, would you care and reach out to help them? Or would you tell them, you have to get out of this mess by yourself! That's how a lot of people treat homeless individuals.

And I'm challenging those who don't get involved at all, to try to become a valuable resource in this world, by reaching out to the less fortunate on this planet! To those who are involved now, I say a huge heartfelt thank you with all of my heart! I know up close and personal about the homeless, because I was one of them! That's who I was. With these billionaires would stop jetting into space and actually help trying to conquer hunger and homelessness on this Earth with their finances it would make a world impact! I would tell each one of these people before you go conquering space why don't you try conquering what's going on on Earth that's where the real problems are! And to the guy who spent hundreds of millions on a yacht? When you die you can't take the yacht with you! Why couldn't you have instead just use the money on the homeless and hungry? Do you really want to leave this world as self-centered people or do you want to leave knowing you've done something good for someone else! And I would tell each of you face to face, if I myself had the money you had I guarantee you I wouldn't be looking to conquer Mars or any other planet because that's not in my spiritual DNA! My desire is to see the hungry being fed and the homeless being housed or sheltered! I hope each one of you are ready to stand before God one day give an account of your lives and how you used your money? World-famous Gospel rock and worship songwriter Chuck Girard once wrote a song called "Don't Shoot the Wounded!" And the main theme of this song was clear. He was saying, don't shoot the wounded, because someday you might become one. Those are powerful words! And he is my favorite all time male singer and songwriter! Margaret Becker, my favorite all-time female Gospel singer wrote some very incredible songs! My favorite one she does is called "I Don't Want to Live Without You!" A very moving, powerful song about her relationship with God! And Johnny Mathis who sang "Oh, Holy Night" on Youtube! What a beautiful rendition he did! A 70s gospel song comes to mind as well, it's called day by day and it was one of the most powerful songs Back then and it still resonates today! The words are day by day, day by day, oh dear lord three things I pray, to see thee more clearly, love thee more dearly, and follow thee more nearly day by day! In my opinion one of the most simple but powerful songs with a simple message to follow God with all your heart and then treat your neighbor as yourself! Because when you do these three things and follow God, it should become automatic in your heart love your neighbor as yourself! And who's our neighbor? The homeless the hungry the hurting and the helpless!There was another favorite female Gospel rock singer I used to really like, but I saw a story on her on Youtube that really opened my eyes at how fooled I was, thinking I was following a Christian singer! And it saddened me after I saw the story on her; I immediately unsubscribed from her channel with a heavy heart, but they showed a video of her wearing a satanic robe that was pointed out to me in her video, and the devil worship signs and symbols used in her video. I almost cried when I saw it, because this was someone I respected for years! But she has fooled a lot of people, including me. She mentioned in an interview in the mid 1980's, when asked a question about how many souls would she like to save before her concert, that she wasn't interested in saving souls, she was only interested in dressing sexy at her concerts. Her argument was that Christian women can dress sexy doing concerts. This tells you right there that this woman, who confessed Christianity back then, knows nothing about being saved. And it's God's job to save souls, anyway, Christians can't save souls. However, they can lead someone to Christ in prayer, or pray for people in their prayer, close before God in their own privacy, or gather with others in church! I pray that this very popular female Christian artist back then would repent and let Christ get a hold of her heart!

And my heart goes out to a former female Christian artist who had a dynamic voice named Katy would turn back to God! She changed her name and became a very popular wordly singer from about 2005 on, and sings today. I know who she is, but more importantly, God knows who she is, and I'm praying that God will get a hold of her heart with his love and turn her life over again. I read her autobiography, how her and her brother had a very strict religious upbringing, with constant bombardment by her parents that controlled their kids, like religious torture. There's a difference between Christian parents trying to raise their kids the right way through Christ, compared to religious ones who control and browbeat their kids when they make a mistake. That's not the freedom of living for Christ; that is religious bondage, and does not belong in this world. Christ came to set us free. My heart goes out to the former Katy and her brother to get to know what real love is: the love of the Son of God! And you're both in my prayers! And Ray Boltz is in my prayers, as well. Jesus is looking to restore lost sheep as well! And in this world today we have many of them and some of them don't even know their lost sheep! Because for one reason or another they knew Christ at one time and they strayed away from him but the call is still prevalent today God is looking to restore lost sheep and add new sheep into the fold!

It would be nice to be able to give the homeless and the unfortunate the help they so desperately need. The bottom line is, I'm just asking that you think a little bit about compassion towards something that has become a worldwide epidemic, and those needing it.

It just takes a little care, it takes compassion, it takes someone like you...

CHAPTER 13

THE POWER OF DECISION!

I'm going to share something now that's been on my heart for a while. If I were in a room full of a lot of people right now and I asked you the question, how many people from the United States have had trouble trying to get much-needed money over to their friends in other countries because of these money apps? I would ask for a show of hands! And I bet you I would get a very high number responding! Now because of legalities, I can't mention the names of any of these money places that you send money through, but I'm sure it'll bring up a lot of memories of people who at various times tried to send money over to their friends and could not succeed because of these so-called judgment calls! Or the decision-making process these money apps do! A lot of the questions you would hear from these money apps would be whether you know the person. They'd ask, "What is the money for?" And I would say, "No, I haven't met them in person! But they are personal friends of mine from Facebook or social media! I followed their lives for years and I know how they live!" When they're reaching out to me for help it's legitimate!

And I would question those who refuse this money to people who are in great need of it. I could ask them the same thing! Do you know who you're declining? Have you ever met them in person? How do you sleep at night if somebody possibly dies or starves to death because of your money apps' decision-making? How many people have probably passed away in another country because they couldn't get the help that they needed? News flash to most of these money apps: not every person in a foreign country is a scammer or a drug dealer! I just don't feel you have the right to decide, and I feel a lot of people would back me up on this, about who lives and who dies! These are strong words, but they are true! I would not want to work for one of these money app countries knowing I might make a bad judgment call and the receiver on the end doesn't get the help they needed! I have talked to Congress about this, and Congress is well aware of this problem! I think they should look into the practice of deciding with these money apps about their decision-making process! I got a call back from a Congressperson, I won't mention the name, but they did tell me they're trying to work out their own money app from the United States that will have the freedom to send money to foreign countries! They said it's a few years in the process! Why I think, that's great, but it won't help those that legitimately need our help right now!

Now don't get me wrong, many of these are good money apps but some are not! And I don't think they have the right to act like internet police about who lives and who dies! I have a special friend in another country that I won't mention where but I've known them for quite a while. She is a boss where she lives, and she had problems with her car breaking down in traffic and could use the money to get a tow truck to get her vehicle out of the problem! And I thought, *No problem, I'll send some money over right away to help you out!* But it got flagged because the money app said they didn't know the person! I said, *I know the person and there is a boss in another country and they need the money desperately now!* And these money apps can't help you! I thought, *You tell that to the person that you're deciding does not get the money!* So what happened is this person who's the boss got demoted from her job because she couldn't make her important meetings for her job because she couldn't get her vehicle worked on. She got demoted and she didn't lose just her job but out of this, she lost her apartment, as well! If she would have had this money when she needed it, when her vehicle broke down, then she would have had the help she needed, and she wouldn't have gotten demoted from her job. And chances are, I probably wouldn't even be writing the story! I'll bet there's a lot of foreigners in a lot of countries who have suffered at the hands of these money apps because they couldn't get the help they needed. I'm not just talking about friends or possibly even relatives in other countries, I'm talking about whole families, as well!

I don't know how these money apps sleep at night knowing the decision-making process they do. There are legitimate people who need our help! I would say this to the money apps: what if you were those people that needed that help? And you were denied help from another money app because of their decision-making process. Just how would you feel? You need to be put in the place of the people that suffer over your decision-making process! It is my hope that Congress comes through with their own money app pretty soon!

But the good news for me is that someone referred me to a phone money App called Transferwise! I was skeptical at first, because of what I went through, but I gave them my information and they have been solid for me to use since day one. I thank God for Transferwise! They are a real blessing to use. I wish I had known about them before! But thank God I know about them now. And in this author's opinion, they are better and more reliable than any other money app in the world! That's my story, and I'm sticking to it. You heard it here first, and I'm just telling it like it is. Something for you to think about.

CHAPTER 14

ON ANY ORDINARY
GIVEN DAY

Like any other ordinary day, I was waiting for my friend Pops to show up to play some cards one morning in August so we could work on our world record, which I talked about in Chapter 2. We started playing cards right away and put on an old monster movie and got something to drink out of the refrigerator. I let him know that my acupuncturist was coming over and we would be busy for about an hour. He said, "Okay, yeah, yeah, yeah, so watch the monster movie while you're busy with her." I said, "No problem, Pops!"

My acupuncturist, Dan, is one of the finest nicest acupuncturists I know! She and Dr. Yi, her manager, are incredible human beings that care when you're suffering with pain, so I always appreciate our sessions together. She speaks really good English, though she has told me that her English is "broken." And I told her she didn't need to fix it, because it worked just fine for me! She is also the one that let me know that the Chinese language is broken up into about 50 different dialects of spoken Chinese! She said she can understand most Chinese but some people speak a different language in Chinese that she has no idea what they're saying! She said she's run into situations where she hears one person try to speak to another in Chinese and they can't understand each other because of the different dialect! I said, "Well, I never would have known that!" But that would be true in the English language, as well! There's different dialects of the English language in the United States! For instance, some people in New York may not understand someone who's from Chicago, or in my case, Indiana, because the English language is so different! Even down south, where they speak it differently! I'll be honest with you, I can't understand everybody's English because some of it is so very different! So I understand my acupuncturist's point of view!

When Dan got done, she left, and Pops and I were getting ready to eat! He said to me, "Ritchie, it's my treat today. I know your birthday was last week, so I want to treat you to your birthday lunch today!" I said, "Pops, that's awesome, thank you!" So we caught the Orange Line train to Downtown Crossing and made our way a couple blocks up the street to McDonald's. There were homeless people everywhere and it broke my heart. I give when I can, but there's only so much I make, being on disability from this botched knee surgery I had. The knee has never gotten better, but that's another story. So we ordered lunch, and had a really great time together. We also bought another guy at the table some lunch who didn't have any money, and he was grateful! Trust me, having been homeless for years, you're grateful when anybody does anything for you! So after we got done with lunch there I said, "Okay, Pops, let's head over and catch the Orange Line going back and go to Mass Ave. and stop off to PLS so I can get some money on this card to help one of my friends who needs some food." He said, "Yeah, yeah, yeah, okay!" So that was the plan.

We started walking over to the other Orange Line stop where we would catch an elevator to get to the platform where you wait for the train. He was a little bit tired and exhausted. Pops is older than I am, so he was leaning up against the wall to rest since all the benches were covered with people waiting on our train! And with my knee surgery, my knee was hurting from all the walking we did, especially the long walk down the platform! And we heard, "Attention, passengers," letting us know that our train was coming! So I said, "Pops? Our train is coming, let's get ready!" He said, "Okay! Our train pulled all the way up to the end of the platform, and I said, "Pops, let's go!" He didn't budge an inch! I said, "Pops, our train is here!" and he still didn't budge! I said, "Pops, do you hear me, our train is here!" He didn't move a muscle! I turned to look at him and his face had a blank stare on it! I said to myself, *Oh, dear God, what's going on?* I started speaking out, "Pops, Pops, can you hear me? Are you okay, can you move?" There was absolutely no response!

And then I noticed his eyes got really glassy and he tried to speak, but he couldn't. I knew at that point something was wrong, but I didn't know what! All of a sudden, he slumped toward the wall and was getting ready to fall over. I grabbed him from behind and I put his weight on mine. Keep in mind, I've had right knee replacement surgery, so any kind of weight towards it is excruciating! I kept shouting out, "Pops, Pops, can you hear me, are you okay?" He didn't say a thing but started slumping toward the ground! I grabbed him with all my might from behind, and as he started slumping toward the ground, I put all his weight on that front knee trying to give him a safe landing spot! I was going to do anything to make sure he was not going to fall and crack his head! So as he started to go down, his weight was coming down across my knee as I tried to balance him! Now, keep in mind, I can't balance him on the left knee and then try to stand on the other one because the one that was surgically-repaired would give way! And then we both go crashing to the ground! I said to myself, *I'm not going to let him fall and crack his head! I don't care how much this hurts, this is my friend and I don't know what's happening right now! I don't know if he's having a stroke or what's going on! I just know I can't let him fall!*

So as he slumped towards the ground more, I bent my knee to shield his fall, and it hurt like you would not believe. I finally got him out of position where he was sitting on his legs, but he was still leaning toward me all his weight as I was trying to stand up to keep his head from hitting the ground! It was an awkward position; fortunately, I did have the wall behind me, and I rested myself against it a little bit and I was able to sustain the majority of his weight! I don't know how much Pops weighs, but I know he weighs more than I do, and I'm around 195-200 pounds. As he's on the ground I'm still calling his name. He didn't respond, at all! I quietly said a prayer, *Dear God, you see my friend Pops right here, you know what's going on with his condition right now! Dear God, I don't know what's happening to him! I'm praying that it's not his time to go to heaven yet! Lord, I need him to wake up, he's been a really good friend! And I hope I've been one to him, as well, and God, I feel so helpless, I don't know what to do! Please show me what to do now! I don't want to see him pass away before my eyes!* I almost started crying because I felt so helpless holding him in the back and not being able to do anything else dealing with the pain in the knee! I didn't know how long I could sustain his weight but with adrenaline at that point, I was going to do it as long as I could!

Right before I got done praying, I heard a lady come up and say, "Is he okay?" I said, "I don't know, I haven't been able to check, I'm holding him from hitting his head and collapsing!" She said, "Let's try to get him to sit up!" So, with whatever strength I had left, I picked him up on that damaged knee and we got him to sit in an upright position! He was still leaning on me at that point, but just his head. I thanked God this lady had come along. Her name was Susie, and she happened to be visiting from Ireland. She asked whether anybody close by might have any water for this man. I said, "I sure hope they do!" One lady came up with a baby stroller. "Here, I have this bottle of water. Your friend can use this!" So Susie began to talk to him and say, "Pops," since she heard me calling his name, "Pops, can you open your mouth?" She lightly tapped his cheek. "Pops, I have some water for you. I need you to respond so you can drink it!"

All of a sudden, his head began to move a little bit. I said, "Oh, thank you Jesus! I know he's still alive!" She said, "You're doing really well. I have some water for you. I want you to drink it slowly, okay?" He said, "Okay." He could barely talk because he was barely coherent! But the fact that he was moving at all brought joy to me, fast! I said under my breath, *God, I thank you for bringing this lady alone and helping to revive him, and also letting me know that he wasn't going to pass away in my arms this day! That would have broken my heart if we couldn't have revived him! I would have never forgotten this day as long as I lived!* He was coming around and slowly drinking the water. I said, *Thank you, God, for allowing my friend to have life, and not taking him to heaven today! It would have broken my heart, but I know he would have been safe in your arms, God! But I'm glad you're reviving him now. Thank you, Lord, I was scared to death that I lost him!*

I think God brought Susie along to not only help me out, but to reassure me that my friend was going to be okay. I asked a man who had a phone nearby to call 911, and he did. It took them a while to get down there. If something would have happened to Pops during that time, I would have sued the city for their negligence of not being there!

Fortunately, that didn't happen! I was grateful for the two officers that showed up that offered their assistance! These two were very, very nice! I appreciated the gentleman that was on the phone helping Pops, too.

Others walking by were not so kind. Some just walked by as this was starting to happen, and I was yelling out for people to help me. One guy just looked at me, shook his head, and kept going! Nobody was obligated to help me in that situation, but it would have been nice if some people had reached out like Susie from Ireland. I am so grateful for her words and cannot even express my gratitude that she was there. If she hadn't been visiting Boston, nobody would have been there to help! But thank God she was! God knew who I needed right then and there! And I'm grateful for Trey Jones who was there with his phone handy. I want to let him and Susie know through this book how much I appreciated both of them for being there to help out my friend and ease the burden on this author's mind! And to the rest of those that walked by me when my friend needed help I say: I feel sorry for you that you had such an uncaring attitude toward someone that really needed help! Someday, when any of you need help, you better hope that someone like Pops or myself is there to reach out to help you! Some people can be so cold! But thank God for those that really cared!

A few more people gathered around by that time to see how Pops was doing, so I was very grateful for their concern. You see, not everybody in Boston has a cold heart. Some people showed me that day they really cared! And I'm very grateful to the lady with a baby stroller, whoever this was, that had the water to help revive Pops. We think he might have had a heat stroke! And it didn't help that he was wearing a very light sweater, like a jacket, because it was warm enough to bring on heat stroke! So I told him, "From now on, Pops, only bring that jacket if you need it! I don't ever want to see you have to go through that again! You scared your best friend half to death!" The police were telling him how fortunate it was for him to have a best friend to watch out for him, and I told the officers how fortunate Iwas to have them come to his aid. I said, "I'm very grateful for all of you!" I almost felt like crying right then, but I held my composure.

We got that sweater jacket thing off his arms so he could breathe.

There was a fan that was behind me blowing on him to try to get him all the way back to normal! As we were getting on the train to head to my house, he was still a little bit groggy, and one guy got mad because he didn't move quickly enough! I looked at the guy in the face and I said, "Bro, he just suffered from heat stroke!" I said, "Please lighten up on him, he's just now coming about!" The guy apologized to me and said that he didn't know! I said, "Thank you, you know now." So when we got on the train, I sat him down, and I said, "Okay, here's what's going to happen! I'm going to get you back to my building, I'm going to let you in, and you're going to go up into my apartment and rest on a chair there. You're going to watch the monster movies until I get back. Remember, I have to go down to Mass Ave. to try to help out my other friend who needs some food! And he said the most beautiful sound I ever heard, he said, "Yeah, yeah, yeah, Ritchie, I'll go up there and I'll wait on you!" That sound was music to my ears!

So, I was able to get down to the PLS station on Mass Ave., get money on my card, and send it on to my friend who needed food! You see, even when you're disabled, your mindset is still about other people needing help, as well! And as a former homeless person for many years, I wasn't going to stand by and see another friend not eat! If you're any kind of a human being at all, you can't see yourself allowing another person to suffer! And since I know what that feels like, being hungry, I don't want to see that happen to another person! I made my way back to the house and Pops was resting in the chair. He couldn't remember how to turn the remote on to watch his monster movie!

I said, "Pops? All this time you've been in that chair and you haven't seen your movie?" He said, "No, man! I couldn't remember how to turn the remote on!" I said, "Ok, now remember, it's this red little button. You just push it and the TV pops on, Pops!" He said, "Oh, yeah, okay, I will remember that next time!" I looked him in the face and I said, "Bro, I thank God there will be a next time!" He looked at me with that big smile and said to me, "Ritchie, buddy, me too!"

CHAPTER 15

SOME THOUGHTS
FROM THE AUTHOR

You know, throughout the years as I get older, I've been asked my opinion on many topics and I've thought about that, for this will become a regular chapter series in each book. Because in life, there is much ground to cover, and it's that way in my life, as well. And I also have some opinions on those things that I want to share in this chapter with you. This could be many series in other books, it just depends on how many topics I'm asked to reply to. At the end of this particular chapter you will see an email and you can respond through that directly to me or my business manager. If you have suggestions on other topics, email them to me and I will tackle those, as well. Keep in mind we will not respond to any hateful email, that's not permissible, but we will respond to every positive email, or comment, or suggestion. Anyway, let's get started on this!

I first want to share an old saying I heard years ago and it goes like this...and maybe you've heard this one, as well: Sticks and stones may break my bones, but names will never hurt me! The exact opposite is true! Yes, sticks and stones will indeed break your bones, but names will hurt you! And that's very sad, because that could have been prevented or avoided if there had been an apology or some kind of positive action required for something that someone has carried around for years eating them alive on the inside! It could be something they experienced, or something harsh that was said to them that they never got over! When I was in my younger years, I came back to Washington State from Arizona to live again. Somehow, I got hooked up with a case manager who was trying to get me settled in Bremerton, Washington, where I was raised. Somehow, she couldn't find a place for me while I was trying to get work, as well, and came upon a place called the Peninsula Lodge in West Bremerton! I don't know if this place is still there today or not, but I'm assuming it is! Anyways, I was placed in there, and I wasn't even sure what kind of place it was! I found out it was a place where people were suffering mentally, either from things they had heard or things they had seen! It was a culture-shock for me, at first, being in this place, but my natural instincts took over, wanting to be friendly with people! And my heart really went out to people that were struggling mentally over their problems, and I wanted to reach out and help! My heart wasn't right with God at that time, but he still gave me that natural compassion to try to help, any way I could! So I reached out to many people there, and some of them reached back to me. And they told me their stories, and it brought tears to my eyes, thinking about what they went through.

Even though I wasn't a Christian, I still knew how to pray for other people, because I received Christ in my heart years ago, and somehow or another, I had fallen away from what I used to believe in because of things that happened to me after I asked Christ into my heart! I was a very young believer, and I didn't know how to grow to get to know God better. That second encounter happened later on in life and I'm grateful for it, because it's stuck with me all the way until today, and it has never left my side. I felt that God had planted a seed in me in that first encounter with Him, and that seed brought me back into God's arms again in November 1987! That's why you're seeing this book now! Because of the one who loved me first and never let go of me, even when I rebelled against the love of God the first time, because I didn't know what that love was. I rarely saw that love, or very much attention, in my own family. So, at this Lodge I became inspired more and more to try to help people, maybe get them involved physically in an activity, or pray with them, or just be a friend with them, someone they could count on to just be a listening ear! In my time there, I made a lot of friends because I was willing to open up and be a friend!

That was one encounter of sticks and stones, because the stories they told were that most of them were there because they were told things that absolutely hurt them and put them in the position they were in. This brings me to this point about a neglected child and how they act. In my opinion, it's gonna be one of two ways: a neglected child will either crawl up into a ball in their mind, mentally speaking, or want so much attention that they will do just about anything to get it! As a neglected child who was told that he didn't have an opinion, and that children should be seen and not heard, I decided I wasn't worth anything, so I decided to become an introvert who was going to watch the world pass him by, because I felt I had no self-worth, at all! So, if you are a parent reading this chapter today, I encourage you to please raise your kids right. If you say something harsh to them, please let them know that you apologize and didn't mean it, because it will have lasting effects on their lives. If you only tear a person down, they will feel like they have no self-worth! So, yes, words do matter, and whoever came up with the saying, "Children should be seen and not heard" has no clue how to treat children. I know that firsthand, after dealing with the people that were in the Peninsula Lodge that I could identify with. I'm glad to this day that the State of Washington decided to assign me a caseworker and put me in there with them, because it gave me real insight to how adults who were once kids acted after things they went through.

The staff was very nice; they had a day treatment program to get the residents in the lodge involved in sports or arts and crafts, or just one-on-one talking or counseling. The day treatment program was awesome ther, and they really treated people with compassion and care! A lot of people today that have committed crimes or murders have admitted that they were treated rotten as kids. They didn't know how to reach out in love, so they reached out in anger or violence, instead, because of things that were said or done to them. So that thing about "Names will never hurt me" is a lie from the pit of hell! It will affect you the rest of your life if it isn't dealt with! Cruel things that were said or done to you that were never apologized for can affect you the rest of your life! It's never an excuse to murder someone or hurt someone but it does come from a root! As a child, I was told by my three sisters that I was ugly, stupid, and that I wouldn't amount to anything. I believed those things for years! When God came into my life again, it became a healing process. The only one of those things that I struggle with today is that I'm ugly.

So, names do have an impact on you, possibly for the rest of your life! I wasn't happy going through that phase, but I understand now that many people go through it. I just wanted to share that. Maybe you can identify with that, or with someone you know that might be struggling with it! The answer for my life to deal with that was giving it over to God in prayer and asking him to heal me on the inside! He is doing that, even today as I struggle with the looks thing! God has never left my side in the healing process that could take a lifetime! Also, something else happened to me when I was in my teenage years going into a routine physical as I was serving in a school program in the Puget Sound Naval Shipyard, which I will share in another chapter of a future book called "Following in Footsteps!"

I believe astrology is false, and I'll tell you why: in the book of Deuteronomy of the Old Testament, it talks about astrology, witchcraft, mediums, fortune-tellers. He didn't hate the people doing these things, but He hated what they were doing. They were becoming false idols to people that would prey upon with their words. In other words, trying to take God's place, predict the future, call on the dead through seances, and so on. God hates these things because He alone is God. No one can take His place and he hasn't left His throne in heaven! Think about this, for instance: let's say a person claims to be the astrological sign of a Leo, and their horoscope might say, "You're going places today!" Well, tell that to those who claim to be Leos, lying on a hospital bed, unable to move, or those who are in prison serving time behind bars. Where do you think they are going to go? What about the person lying still in the hospital trying to recover, just where are they going to go? Do you understand what I'm saying? Only God, not astrology, can guide our lives and our futures! And throw away the Ouija Board, as well!

I have been asked this a few times: Richard, what is your opinion on abortion? And that's a very tough subject. I will share this; I am a pro-life person, I always have been, and the reason I have been is because my mom didn't choose to abort me. She carried me through and I am who I am today and I'm grateful to her and God for life today! I have great compassion on those who have aborted their child and now regret it later on, or even those now considering it. I have spoken to many women who had this done in their lives and tried to encourage them that if they will just live for God they will see that child again in heaven! This has encouraged a lot of them, and so some of them did turn their hearts over to God who has given them peace of mind. Others felt like I was a fool telling them this and that their child was gone forever! I told them they were wrong and that if they would only live for God they would see their child one day. I also have great compassion for those who were raped and became pregnant with a person's child! There is no easy answer to that one! And that's all I can really say about the subject of abortion. I pray you will reconsider your decision and give it over to God.

Also, I don't like the term "OMG." I think that is a disrespectful thing that you say about God if you claim you know God! People that don't know God and say "OMG" I have nothing against, because they don't know the truth about the love of God that can absolutely change their hearts! The ones that say that you know God and use this term "OMG" would be like someone saying something against your name, the name of one of your friends, or the name of one of your family members! Would you not defend them against the people that were defacing that name? So in the same way it is hurtful to me and disrespectful to God whose name is The Great I Am! I have had Twitter battles with people who argued with me who name the name of Jesus that said it was okay for them to say that! Well, newsflash—it's not okay and it would hurt a person's relationship with God if they attempted to pray with Him knowing that you disrespected His name!

If you have a relationship with somebody, you try to protect them or protect their name! And I have a daily prayer relationship with God in heaven. People who say they are called by His name and use "OMG" with no thought or concern with what God thinks about what they're doing upset me. One day in heaven those people will have to stand before God and give an account of using "OMG." He might very well say that He never knew them and that they didn't have a relationship with Him even though they claimed His name!

We can tend to believe Judgement Day is not real, but I know it is, and it's coming one day! And whether we know Jesus or not, we will give an account of ourselves one day in heaven on the great white throne on Judgement Day! If we know Christ as Lord and savior, there will be no Judgement Day for believers, but only an account of how they lived for God. You can believe or not believe what I'm saying; it doesn't change the fact it will happen one day. That's not my opinion, that's the word of God, which was written by men and women who were inspired by God to write the books of the Bible.

There's a Scripture in there that says whoever calls upon the name of the Lord shall be saved. I listened to my foster parents, the Apelands, reading that Scripture to me, and it changed my life forever! It planted a seed in my life for who God was, but I had to still go through more things as I was learning about Him! I will always be grateful to Larry and Sharon Apeland, who reached out to me when I was a bitter, angry young teen who couldn't understand why I was where I was, when my sisters had told me the things they said back then, like a death sentence hanging over my head. As I grew up, I had no certainty of a future anymore because I listened to those words, but when Jesus came into my heart as a teen, it was going to put a fire in me that is still burning inside, even today. And it's a good thing, because I was to go through even more things after that. I pray for my sisters Lynda, Robin, and Erin, that Christ has or will come into their hearts like He did their little brother's heart. David, my older brother, passed away about four years ago, and I miss him today. I hope to see him in Heaven one day and be reunited with him! I can't wait to give him a big hug, because his little brother misses him!

Growing up as a young kid in my own house made me want to alienate myself from my own family where I rarely felt I was loved, but God showed His love for me, reaching out as a teen to me, because when I had the opportunity to call upon His name, He changed me and came into my heart. He is with me daily, even today, as I'm getting older! To me, Judgement Day is almost like a parent on the Earth who asked you to do a job or household assignment. They check on you later, and you haven't done what they asked! What excuse would you give? Do you think that the parent would be angry? I do! Do you think they would deal out rewards right then and there, or let you know that you're in deep trouble? You could have easily done what they asked you to do and been rewarded with praise from them, or money or some kind of reward, but because you've refused what they asked you to do, you're going to get the punishment, whatever that is!

Judgement Day is like that. If we live for God on the Earth and try to do things to the best of our ability through His Spirit, then we will be rewarded for it. But if we have not lived for God, then we'll get that other kind of reward, as well! If a wife sends a husband to get something from the store and he doesn't get those things for her, getting only what he wants for himself, what kind of reward do you think he's going to get when he gets back home? Would you want to be in that husband's shoes? I know I wouldn't! But if he gets what he can to the best of his ability, then she's going to be very pleased with him. And trust me, she's probably going to call him or text him when he's in the store to make sure he's getting the right ingredients! And he could very well be rewarded, if you understand what I'm saying, in either a good way or a not-so-good way, whichever way he decided to do it! So, if it were me, I would like to do it in a good way! So these are things to think about!

I ask you today, if you are a believer in Christ, then act like one by not disrespecting God saying "OMG" to your Christian friends or your worldly friends, and especially your worldly friends, because then you act like them! The word of God says we're supposed to be in the world, but not of the world's system!And saying Omg it's like disrespecting a family member, when you receive Christ in your heart you became a part of the family of God! So if you're part of the family of God then why would you disrespect his name? Plus youll probably hurt your relationship with God as well In prayer or even just talking to him you because you disrespected his name, you wouldn't want a person doing that to your name so why do it to his? You can get upset at me for saying this, but it could save you grief when you stand before God on Judgement Day! And if you hate someone, including this author, God says that is like murder in His eyes. Repent of that, as well! He will help you if you just call upon His name! Amen. ☺

And on the subject of marriage: all I can say about that is if you love someone and you are married to them, treat them like they matter, treat them with respect, treat them with love. Don't just say "hi" and "bye" to them every day, but remember you're in a relationship with them, and they're in a relationship with you! I am not currently married, but I have been down that road,but I say this from experience! If you love someone or they love you, treat them like they matter! Try not to bring baggage into a relationship or a marriage. If you do, it will hurt whatever bond you're trying to form, and always be open and honest with each other! And if either of you does bring baggage into a relationship or marriage, then deal with that baggage right then and there so it won't affect you or your spouse the rest of their lives as long as you're married! I know that from experience. Treat them like you want to be treated!

I am no expert on the subject of marriage, but I do know about a relationship with God, and it's kind of like that! If I just said "hello" and "goodbye" to God every day, then I wouldn't have a relationship with Him! And it would hurt Him deeply after all He has done for me! So it's my job in a relationship with Him to stay not only in contact with him every day through prayer, but also to praise Him! Before a child brings a concern to a parent about a problem, believe me, the parent is hoping to hear praise first, or maybe the child being appreciative for what the parent has done for them so far! A relationship with God is exactly like that for me! When I wake up every morning, I thank God for waking up, and then I begin to think in my mind about all the things He has done for me and bring those to His attention through praise and prayer. God desires our praise deeply, and for us to know Him in a relationship! This is a difference between religion and relationship! Religion has nothing to do with God, relationship has everything to do with God! religion can't get you to heaven, but a relationship with Jesus Will! This is the true gospel he is the one and only door that you have to go through it's called the narrow way or the narrow gate! And it's the only way to get to heaven not my word,but the word of God says!

Jesus came against the religious Pharisees and scribes of his day because they were constantly trying to test him! That just tells me right there that Jesus is not a religion, he is a relationship! He came against religious people of his day, he loved them, but hated what they were teaching! And I have encountered religious people in my day, as well! I will defend the word of God the best I can and defend my relationship with God, but I have better things to do than argue with people on Facebook, Twitter, Instagram or any other social media where all they want to do is argue. In that case, I just say, "God bless you," and go on, because no matter what I say, I won't change their minds. Only God can change their hearts, and they will see for themselves there is a difference between religion and relationship! And a man with an argument is no match for a man with an experience! When you have experienced the love of God, you have experienced the truth! Religion is not the truth, a relationship with God is! If you're married to someone, you don't have a religion, you have a relationship!

I have heard many churches in the city of Boston say, "We welcome all faiths to our congregation or assembly!" Well, there's only one faith, and that faith is in the Son of God! And that's the only faith that will get you into heaven! That's not my opinion, that's in the Word of God, which brings up the subject to me of denominations! I looked up the meaning of the word "denominations," and it pretty much means "to separate or divide." Do you think that God wanted believers on the Earth to separate and divide from each other over what the other believes? No, he did not! God did not make denominations, that was Man's doing! The Apostle Paul was instrumental in his ministry life In bringing believers together whether they were Jew or gentile! It would break the Apostle Paul's heart today with all these denominations on this Earth it's hard to have revival if parts of that spiritual physical body are missing! There are no denominations in heaven! Doesn't matter if you're First Church This, or Second Church That, or whatever denomination you claim on this earth. It won't be recognized in heaven, because there are no denominations! It was not God's intent to have churches divided against each other and the different things they believe! No wonder it's hard for revival to break out in the world today. You can call yourself anything you want on this earth! I myself am non- denominational and have always been. I believe in the Son of God, because he first believed in me! And it saddens my heart that this church might believe this way or that church might believe that way! And yet you can't come together as believers, that saddens my heart. More importantly, it grieves the heart of God! Instead of saying we welcome all faiths, they should be saying we welcome all races, all cultures, all backgrounds, because there is only one faith, and that faith is in the Son of God!

And priests can't save you when you try to confess sins to them, because they are not qualified to do so. The one who qualified was the one the Bible calls our high priest! His name is Jesus, and in hebrew his name is Yeshua! And that faith in the Son of God saved me. That's why this author is writing this first book, because Jesus qualified when he gave his life for a sinful world on the cross, and then resurrected again a few days later to prove who he was, so that men or women could be forgiven and receive eternal life! A Priest can pray for you,but they have no power to forgive your sins! Only through Christ are we forgiven. And for my life that's how this whole thing came to pass! That he used someone so special to me as my own daughter, to get a hold of my heart and the rest is history! That's all I have to say about denominations that God laid that on my heart to share.

I've been asked this many times: Richard, do you believe that there are hypocrites in the church? And my answer to that is that yes, no church is perfect today. There are many good churches out there who are trying to live for God! But there are also people in church playing games and just showing up and not doing anything for God, acting holy one minute in church and outside of church acting like they don't even know who God is! I have seen this with pastors who claimed holiness in church but acted like jerks outside of church, not being who they claimed to be! That right there is a description of a hypocrite, but there are also pastors who live what they say they live, and I thank God for them! In fairness, there are many churches that do try to live for God! I know that for a fact because I've been invited to sing in many of them and I know many of their people in Indiana and Boston. When I was invited to sing on TBN, Trinity Broadcasting Network, in the '90s, I saw good people who were trying to live for God, and I was invited twice! When I was invited to sing on WHMB in Noblesville, Indiana, the day before I was to get the call from my daughter, I saw good people there! Yes, there are hypocrites in church. But I know there are good people in churches, as well, who live what they say in church and live what they say outside of church! Those people God is well-pleased with.

But I want to expound on the hypocrite thing now! There are hypocrites in the laundromat, supermarket, video stores, movie theaters, playing sports. It started in the church, but it's not just in the church, it's everywhere! And there are some on social media today, as well. There are many people that don't go to church anymore because they looked at how people lived and forgot they were there for God! If we keep our eyes on Him, that's what counts, in church or out of church! God wants people to live for Him in and out of church. I'm not an expert on hypocrisy, but I've seen it up close and personal. There are hypocrites all over the place, not just church, so please understand that! This is why some people don't go to church today, because they might have gotten hurt in church by someone's comment or something that they saw or didn't like in church! And that took their eyes off what God was doing in that church! I know a lot of people today who no longer go to church because they see how some people act in church or out of church, and that is just sad! Because the important thing to remember here is whether we go to church or don't go to church, we should still have a relationship with God! You don't have a relationship with your spouse at home and then forget who they are outside the house! So why would a person treat God that way, or others that way? Knowing Jesus as Lord and Savior will change a person's heart and heal hypocrisy! God can change racial hatred in a person's heart and change the person! Some people are guided by racial hate for persons because they see a different skin color, but if you change a person's heart through Christ, then they won't see a person's skin color, they will see the love of God working through their heart to other people's hearts! That's how you beat racism or anything else, it's through accepting Christ's love into their heart! Amen... God laid this on my heart how many of his so-called people are going to miss the rapture right in the middle of their own church service and they may not even know that Jesus came back right in the middle of their service! I think the only way for sure they would know as if they had members of their own body all of a sudden missing in church! And of course if you got little kids in the church they're going to disappear and you're going to notice at that point there will be pandemonium and absolute chaos in these churches of people left behind simply because you didn't want to follow Christ but yet you played the game and now the game caught up with you in the form of the rapture you been left behind! It's not too late to get it right with God and keep it right with God and teach others how to keep it right with God! I have this bad feeling about some of these mega churches concerned with themselves they're going to be left behind but if they have kids they're going to notice they're gone right in the middle of their service if Jesus comes back during that time! Many of these millionaire billionaire pastors are deceived right now and the deception gets worse if you don't turn your life over to Christ before the rapture or during the tribulation period where they will hunt you down and find you and kill you in your own blood, because you rejected the mark of the Antichrist which will still get you into heaven you will become a tribulation saint! if you're living for God during the tribulation! I see scenarios like this people living for God during the tribulation people,or living for the Antichrist during the tribulation and the in between person trying not to live for anybody who will still die when their caught unless they shamefully take the mark then they come under God's judgments and wrath! Or if they reject the mark then the Antichrist will kill them baby, tribulation saint!

I've been asked this years ago: do you believe there will be pets in heaven? And my response is that I do believe that! And the reason I say that is that the Book of Revelation talks about white horses coming out of heaven. So, if these things are in heaven, I truly believe our pets will be there, as well! I have no way of proving that, I just have this instinct that this is true, that we will indeed see our pets one day in heaven. I have had many pets I lost in this life, and they're up there probably frolicking around, possibly with tending angels playing with them, having a good time waiting for me to see them again! I have no facts to back this up, it's just something I feel on the inside. I've asked other people about this, and many people believe this, too. Many people argue: well, pets don't have a soul! How do we know that for sure? And even if they didn't, they don't know right from wrong, they don't need a Savior, and they didn't have to repent of their sins, because pets do instinctively what each pet does! My pets were a joy to be around and I miss them all deeply and dearly. Yet, I truly believe in my heart we will one day see our pets in heaven if we live for God through faith and Jesus until we get there! plus I have heard many accounts now of people who died and went to heaven in their Spirit body while they were dead on the operating table and many accounts of them said they saw their own pets in heaven that would be truly awesome because I miss mine and I want to see them all of them! And I love the testimonies of the people who went to heaven and gave an account of what went on up there this gives us a little foretaste of just what's coming!

A lot of people today do not believe in the Rapture of the church! One particular pastor on Youtube, whose name I will not mention, does not believe in the Rapture nor believes in the Resurrection or that Jesus rose from the dead! So my question is: just what do you believe in? How do you call yourself a pastor of God if you have no basis of what you believe in? All you have is an argument. Why would you go against the very Son of God? Judgement could come in this lifetime in the way of death for some of these people because they have renounced or mocked God!All I have is an experience in the truth of God! How did these so-called pastors and preachers come up with their own Gospel contrary to the word of God? And then have the nerve to call it the gospel? I've seen programs on YouTube where I watched a few of these pastors make absolute fools of themselves nothing to do with the word of God whatsoever it was their opinion they talked about that's really sad because they're going to give an account of that before God! Maybe he's long-suffering right now because he doesn't want to see anyone perish but God is not going to be patient forever! The word of God says that in the last days, people will say, "Here is Christ," or, "There is Christ," but God warns us in His word not to follow such people, because they are false prophets and liars! His word says that they have the form of godliness, but they deny the power thereof! Then there are pastors who do believe in the Rapture who have a relationship with God and are trying to lead their people in the right way, including on the radio, TV, and YouTube!

I have great respect for preachers, pastors, teachers, evangelists, and so forth who talk about the word of God! And I personally don't like when I ask someone how they are doing and they speak back these words to me that just grind my teeth, "Oh, I'm blessed and highly favored!" I hate that saying with a passion and I hope they don't say that same saying to homeless people, because it could make the homeless person feel like they're being put down! I was homeless and I'd either feel angry or ashamed if someone told me that, I guarantee it! There's a Scripture in the New Testament that backs this up, and it talks about being so heavenly-minded but having no earthly good! That's pretty straight to the point.

God wants people to care about others, especially the widows, the orphans, the poor, the hurting, the helpless, the handicapped, the sick, and the homeless! I appreciate the truth and the blunt straightforwardness of that Scripture! There is a song with the words I want to share that say, "I listen to the trumpet of Jesus, while the world hears a different sound. I march to the drumbeat of God Almighty, while the others just wander around." Now, who are they specifying that are wandering around? Are they talking about Christians doing nothing while they alone are doing something? Or are they talking about people in the world who don't know God? It doesn't convey or specify in the beginning who they are referring to. Newsflash to the group who wrote this song—most of us are not just wandering around. So how can you write a song that stereotypes people? I know I'm not just wandering around! I hate this religious, "I'm doing something, you're not" type of song! Songs like this make me sick because it also uses the word "I." In other words, I alone hear God's voice, I alone am the only one doing something for God! Maybe if the group had written words like these instead, "*We* listen to the trumpet of Jesus, while the world hears a different sound. *We* march to the drumbeat of God Almighty, while *some* others just wander around!" If you had written something to this respect, this writer probably wouldn't have had an issue with what you wrote. There might be others who have heard this song and wondered the same. It's never about what I do, but it's about what God does through me ,and that makes it a team effort! God and myself, not me alone. Amen, you should use wisdom when writing a song like this.

I am also against prosperity preaching that just makes false teachers rich! Their bank accounts are lined up because of the money given to them. The tithe belongs to the church to which they attend. If you have a bank account, for example, at Citizens Bank, then you don't put your money into another bank account. Likewise with the tithe, if you go to church, a TV Evangelist has no right to ask you for your money that belongs to where you attend and worship. Beyond that, if you want to give to a TV preacher, that's your business...The local church you attend is that which God calls the storehouse! In this case, it's a place where you're fed the word of God. Many are deceived into thinking that giving to televangelists is giving to God because of their seducing words. If you want to prosper, then give unto your own church, or help out a widow, or an orphan, or homeless persons! This prosperity preaching has no place in God or the Gospel! Give where God puts on your heart to give and he will take care of your needs. There are false preachers today who have preyed upon believers and non-believers. They have many, many homes, airplanes, or cars, because of the prosperity preaching! They've gotten rich off many people who gave with their hearts and pocketbooks to their ministry. I heard of a well-known preacher in Houston who was called out by the media because when they had their great flood a few years back, he and his wife refused sanctuary to people in their own city who were struggling with the flood! That made me sick, watching that on the news! And yet, this pastor who claims he knows God with all the riches he has doesn't help the people in his own city? People were crying out for help from him and his wife, and they turned their backs on them, and did nothing! When you look up the word "hypocrite" in the dictionary, don't be surprised if you find their picture next to the definition.

This same so-called believer from the great city of Houston denied Christ on the Larry King show one day as he tried to hem and haw his way around giving a definite answer! Larry point-blank asked him on the show, "Is Jesus the only way to go to Heaven?" And this phony preacher couldn't answer him. Yet, this preacher has made millions with his watered-down version of the Gospel! If Larry would have asked me that question, I would have said, "Absolutely, yes! He is the only way!" This guy's father who was a Christian and a pastor of the same church before he passed away would have probably rolled over in his grave, knowing his son was a liar. He and these other prosperity preachers are going to answer to God one day on Judgement Day, just like everyone else, for fleecing the flock of God and filling their own pockets! And God is going to be very displeased with them, because they knew the truth and they didn't speak it or live it, or they used the Gospel for their own gains! There are many people that I can think of off the top of my head that I used to respect until I found out what they were all about! There is something truly wrong when you hear about millionaire or billionaire preachers or Televangelists! Many people in the United States and around the world should have been helped by that money. That shows you just where many of their hearts are.

Believers in Christ are to be selfless, not selfish! Jesus, in his life, was selfless! And he proved it with the last act of his ministry life, as he gave his life on the cross for all mankind, to a world that loved him not! That is selfless Love, and it was for others! Amen.

I wish Lester Sumrall was alive today; I guarantee you he wouldn't have put up with all the phony garbage being spewed forth today, claiming Jesus' name! Lester Sumrall was a man's man of God, a true Christian pastor and Evangelist out of World Harvest Church in South Bend, Indiana, who preached and taught the Word of God for many years. And he knew the world, as he traveled it for many years! You can find Lester Sumrall's teachings on Youtube! You won't be disappointed.

He was a man I deeply respected. I look forward to seeing Pastor Sumrall in heaven, one day, along with many others, including Evangelist Jed Metzler, and Hilton Sutton who taught us the Book of Revelation in the '90s at our church! What an honor that was! And great respect to two of many preachers I can think of today like and Dr. David Jeremiah; and Andy Wood!highly respect these men of God, because they speak truth and live it before the eyes of the World! I truly thank God for them, and you can find their teachings on Youtube!

God has given me that kind of sense about certain people and it didn't take me long to figure who many of these phony preachers were and what they spewed, which wasn't the Gospel! If I'm getting ready to go into a church and I see hungry people out on the street, do you really think I'm going to ignore them and let them know that I'll just pray for them and do nothing else within my power to help? How upset do you think God would be with me? And how much guilt would I feel inside, doing nothing to try to help them? I'm tired of hearing people say to a person needing help, "Oh, I'll just pray for you!" Ring, ring, ring! Heaven calling the person who just said this. Heaven would rebuke you big-time because faith without works is dead! If you're going to pray for them, and you have it in your power to bless them, then just do it! He said in His word that when you've done it unto the least of these, you have done it unto Him! I guarantee you, I would share that money with them or buy them something to eat, because when you see needs like these, you're going to do whatever you can to take care of whatever need there is!

I saw an article by a person of the government from Washington, D.C., and I want to comment on that; this person said that we are all made in the image of God and that we shouldn't wear the mandated masks that we are now required to wear anytime out in public, because it will hide our faces. There's a few thoughts I have on what he said. My first thought is: it would go against the law of our land that says we are required to wear these masks to protect ourselves and others. If you're a member of the Federal Government, then I would think you would want to follow your own law! If you encourage people to stop wearing their face masks, then you could be endangering their lives out in public, and those they come in contact with. And when Scripture talks about us being made in the image of God, it's not talking about our facial image, at all! It's talking about the character of God, and his personality traits, of what we are or are supposed to be on the inside. It's not talking about what we look like on the outside! God has to change our hearts on the inside to be in His likeness! His Character has to be lived from the inside out, and that only happens when a change occurs.

When God said, "Let us make man in our own image," this was before the fall of Adam, because before Adam, there was no sin, until he fell. That's why the word of God says we are born into sin; this wasn't said until after Adam disobeyed and sinned because he gave into the serpent's deception through his wife, Eve! We didn't fall because Eve was deceived and ate the forbidden fruit; we fell because Adam, whom God created first and held responsible, disobeyed God! So after the fall from grace, I have to say this: unless a person receives that new nature of God inside their heart, then they are not in His likeness. So we are not all in the image of God, because many have sinned and fallen short of the Glory of God, according to the New Testament! So that statement won't fly, because it's not true! Only through Christ can we be in God's image again! And many, many preachers who have taught the word of God rightly for years, guys like Charles Stanley, who, to my knowledge, is still around today, or Billy Graham himself, who has gone on to heaven. Charles Stanley is one of the foremost authorities and teachers on the Bible today, like the other good pastors I mentioned. He lives what he says he lives and teaches others how to live for God! Unfortunately, there are many phony preachers today, but there are many true preachers today, as well, whom I have high respect for.

And there is another pastor that I want to give a shout-out to, he is my former pastor, the head of Full Gospel Temple church in Muncie, Indiana, where I lived for many years: Pastor Denny Helton. He and his brother James, who was my first pastor that passed away years ago, were the head pastors then, and his nephew, Associate Pastor David Helton, as well. David now has his own church in Fishers, which is close to Indianapolis, the capital city in Indiana..

And a story I will share in the next book is about when we were gathered together in August 1994 before my birthday and I received a prophecy that I was to become a songwriter. That came to pass, as I mentioned before some of those songs that are on YouTube now are a result of that prophecy! Anyways, I highly respected both of my former pastors, and I appreciate and love them to this day. Pastor Denny lives as a Christian man should live, inside the church and outside the church! He is an incredible pastor with drive and passion for not only the people of God, but for those who don't know God, even more so! He would be proud of me today if he knew I were writing this book! I wanted to give a shout-out to him for being a faithful man of God, and to my close friends of the church at that time: Rick and Renae Cox, who are Christians and who are brother and sister, as well. I miss them and love them, and many others in Muncie, Anderson, and Lapel.

And I wanted to give a shout-out to Westside Full Gospel church, Pastor Charles Conley, and congregation, also in Muncie. And another shout-out to a good friend I knew in Tucson, Arizona: Stewart Reblin! He had an incredible passion for God and was a good friend! Also I wanted to mention Ronnie Mcharison, a good friend from Tuscon who went to heaven years ago. And many I knew at the Door Church in Tucson, Arizona, Pastor Harold and Pastor Mona Warner!

A lot of people asked me, we know you sing, did you ever think about trying out for *American Idol*? I thought about that, and this came to me: I don't like the word "idol," and neither does God! An idol is something you worship or pay attention to more than you do to God; I have never liked the name "American Idol" because people focus on the one they call an "idol" and I want no part of that! And I've heard there's been Christians on there who tried out, and I'm fine with that! I just have my own convictions about the word.

I have heard it said by Evolutionists that we evolved as human beings from apes, meaning that we are not created by God. Oh really? So if we are supposed to have come from apes as human beings, then my question to those who believe in evolution is: why hasn't the ape evolved even more? Why don't they have Social Security cards, or driving jobs like Uber? Do you get my point? They haven't evolved anymore than they did when they were born! And the ape was one of the created beings whom Noah and his family had on the Ark with other animals, all male and female of different species created by God. So the Theory of Evolution, in this author's opinion, is wrong! Babies don't just evolve on their own into this world; they are created by male and female.

I want to put one more thing in this chapter, and that's about the subject of what people call Easter! I found out many years ago after someone told me the truth about what the word "Easter" means! It has nothing to do with the resurrection of Jesus, at all! The word "Easter" has many definitions, and one of them is the goddess Ishtar, who was goddess of fertility, and that's maybe where the bunny and the eggs thing got twisted into this. But ever since I found out what this word really means, I have been trying to share this for years with pastor friends, people of congregations, and anybody who even names the name of Jesus. And most people want to excuse it as if it were nothing, including a pastor I talked to about this over YouTube, who argued that it was okay to use this word at Resurrection time or what I call "Resurrection Celebration Time!" I have since deleted this pastor off my email and want nothing more to do with him! Because this word is an abomination to God, especially about his son, Jesus, rising from the dead, and the more people that have knowledge about this will have their eyes opened!

I pray to God that they will listen and check it out for themselves and no longer call it "Easter," that every person that I have never spoken to will be gotten ahold of by the Spirit of God and no longer use this term since it has nothing to do with the Resurrection or the Passover! And it has nothing to do with bunnies or eggs. I couldn't bear the name of Christ in my own life if I heard the truth about this and did nothing about it. This is a counterfeit to the Gospel, which has no part in this important holiday! It probably grieves God to no end that people still use this term when talking about his son's Resurrection. You can believe me or not believe me what this word means, just look it up for yourself on Google or anywhere else, and you will find out it's true! I thank God years ago that a couple of people reached out to me and told me what the true meaning of the term "Easter" really meant!

In no way does this author claim to be a know-it-all. He is just a know-it-some! I only have knowledge in what I know through the experiences I've had and what I've learned over time. I just wanted to make that very clear! In the next book, I will share more of my thoughts.

CHAPTER 16

DO-OVERS!

When I was young, I used to play with other kids in my East Bremerton, Washington, neighborhood. We played a game called "Do-Overs," which was a game that challenged your thinking, physical body, and endurance! And what you had to do was pass the test the first time. If you didn't pass the test, you had to do it over again until you got it right. The more you had to to do it over, the more points you lost. This would be a test of trivia or a physical test of endurance! We had about five friends playing this game including me, and these tests weren't easy, especially the trivia. You had five tries (so four do-overs) to complete the assignment. If you didn't complete it, you lost points, and those points would be divided up between the other four contestants, almost like the game Trivial Pursuit, except you had to do physical things, as well! For instance, you had to do 25 push-ups in under a minute, and if you couldn't do that in the time frame, you had to do it over and over again until your five tries were up, and then you were out of the game! But if you were able to get it right within those five tries, then you moved on to the next challenge! Keep in mind, you don't want to keep trying to do sets of 25 push-ups over and over again, because your arms will feel like lead weights !Or you could quit the challenge at any time because you tried and gave your best trying to accomplish the task you were given!

The way you started the game was by rolling a dice. If that number came up, even you had to do a physical test. If it came up odd, then you had to do the trivia test! The physical part wasn't hard for me because I was in pretty good shape. Even as a kid, I had a lot of endurance and energy, and so did my friends. What kept stumping me were the trivia questions, and I would find myself out of the game a lot because I didn't have a whole lot of knowledge in that area. I rarely ever got a physical challenge test, so I didn't last in too many games. Anyway, that was a game we amused ourselves with called "Do-Overs."

We not only played this game, but we shared food, and friendship, and explored a forest at the end of our dead-end street together. I was raised in a poor neighborhood where you didn't see the color of skin of those around you, and you appreciated what you had. I didn't even have my own bedroom as a kid, because it was a very small house! So my bedroom was our living room, and I got used to sleeping on the couch for years! And even though I have my own bedroom now, out of habit, I still sleep on the couch! And sometimes, the neighborhood kids came over to watch TV with me. And while many people today have remotes to turn your TV on, but back then, you were the channel changer! If you were the closest to the TV, you were the one who was the human TV remote, and there were only about six channels you could watch because cable or satellite TV wasn't around then! So most of the time, I was the channel-changer, because I was asked to sit on the floor. And as the one on the floor, closest to the TV, I was often voted the channel-changer. If my family argued about what shows to watch, then I had to wait for the argument to stop and physically turn the channel! If there were something that I wanted to watch, it had to be voted on by family members in the room first. So I had to wait for the vote to be cleared before finding out what we were going to watch, next. And I had to get used to being a human remote! I probably would have made a great cable guy today with my vast experience of TV channels!

And back then, if a neighbor struggled because they didn't have enough food, the other neighbors would gather together and make sure they were well-fed! To see the smiles on the family faces spoke deep volumes into my heart! And at that time as a young child, I vowed that I would help suffering people when I got older, and lo and behold, it's part of who I am today! God didn't let me forget that vow back then, even though I didn't know who He was then, but He definitely knew me! So yes, God can change any heart! I want to say this to my own sisters or living relatives out there, excluding my daughter, because I know her good heart—she is like her daddy in many ways—if any of my relatives back then are racists today, this relative disowns you or any of my past relatives if they were back then...I want no part of their racial attitude or history! I will pray that God will change your heart, instead!There is no excuse for hatred or racism in this world! I heard one time that members of the KKK said they served a white God! I have news for those members: Jesus wasn't white or black, he was olive-skinned! I pray that all KKK members will receive Christ into their hearts! He loves you, and this author does too...

As a kid in our neighborhood, there were raspberry and blackberry bushes, and I'd pick those, and my mother could use them for pies. There were cherry trees, red and purple, which we picked for their big fruits in our own front yard, and if the neighbors wanted some, they were welcome to pick from the fruits we had, as well. We had many of these fruits in our own yard, and I remember the delicious strawberries that were oh- -so-mouth-watering-good! And of course, Washington is known for their big, red juicy apples! Talking about these fruits is making me hungry! I'd love to have a fruit salad with whipped cream, right about now just thinking about this.

Many times, my mom invited the neighbor kids over to eat with us! And I loved her fabulous no-bake cookies and other cookies she made! My mom would cook and bake, which she loved, and made her homemade, fresh bread and homemade chocolate pudding! Even today, I miss my mom.

Unfortunately, it becomes part of reality now as the story I'm sharing with you is a do-over, something I never intended to do! Back in early 2019, I was approached over my email by a publisher who was interested in the book that I was working on, which would be this current book you are reading now, and of course, they needed a fee to get this started. It took me a while during 2019 to get the stories together and figure out what I wanted to do with them. I guess you could call it writer's block, because I really had never done any kind of book-writing before! They gave me a deadline until December 3rd to finally get the first book done, which did get done, but barely, because my friend who works on the chapters and sends them over to the publisher had Internet trouble! So we barely got the book done in the time limit. I was relieved and mentally exhausted when it was finally finished!

All kinds of departments emailed me from the publisher saying, "Okay, now you're in our department," or this department, or that department; I had an idea there would be a lot of departments in a publishing place, but I had no idea how many, and there were a lot! I was being tossed around like a rag doll to different outlets of the publisher, and my head would get dizzy thinking about who I had to talk to next. Finally, it got down to the last department, and they were going to email me what the book would look like on the inside before it was ready for sale! I was excited about that, but the problem was, I never got to see the inside of the book, because my email wouldn't take it, for whatever reason! I loved the beautiful cover they did, and when they gave me a choice of covers to choose from, I picked out the very first one—the one on this book now—but I was having trouble with the back cover because there were a lot of mistakes in explanation of how the book came to be. Turns out, it wasn't just the back cover, it was other things that were mistakes, as well—nothing but setbacks! I was on the phone for about an hour and a half trying to get them to fix the back cover. It was finally fixed, but the inside in the foreword part before the chapters was messed up. There was no editing or spell-checking done! But after we got the back of the book fixed, I had confidence that the inside material was going to be good. My reasoning at the time was: *If they got the front cover done this nicely and we got the back all straightened out, surely they're going to make sure the inside information is correct, as well?* You would think!

I got my copies in the mail as the book was published on Amazon, Barnes & Noble, and the publisher's website. I opened the book, expecting to see some really nice things, and I was in for a shock—nothing was edited! There were misspelled words and storylines that didn't fit right because words were missing! I was shocked and angered! I had trusted them to get this right, and I told them over the phone and email that I hadn't been able to read or approve what they had sent on my email. So I had told them that since I couldn't read it, I was entrusting them to make sure everything was right, to which they responded that they'd take care of it. That was a big lie! Nothing was done to take care of things!

I was so angry that I got on the phone and talked to whatever department I needed to talk to. Another thing that bothered me was the text on the stories was very light, so you couldn't read the chapter without squinting your eyes or enlisting the help of the Hubble Telescope to see the words! They said that in order for them to make these changes and start the re-editing process, they would need another fee, which was half the initial fee! Now, keep in mind, I already paid them to publish the book in the first place! I told them this was not going to happen, and that if they weren't going to fix things that they were supposed to fix, then I would go with another publisher! And that's exactly what I did! And it is through this other publisher that you're now reading this book! I had to tell them to pull this book out of Barnes & Noble and off Amazon and their website. This was January 2020, and I told them that I wasn't going with them after all, that they had messed up and didn't fix it when I had trusted them. I told them I wouldn't make that mistake again and that I was done with them. Keep in mind, I was going to write the rest of these lifestories with this publisher if they had treated me right! I mean, who knows how many books would have been sold today if this had been done right, if it hadn't been for their mess-up and the virus world we now live in! If they would have gotten this right, I wouldn't even be talking about this!

What would you do, if you were writing your first book, and you trusted that publisher to treat you right, and they messed up on you and other potential book authors, wouldn't you feel the same way, especially if they wanted to recharge you to get the book re-done, on top of what you had already paid for in the first place? No way that was going to happen! I regret going with this publisher. Unfortunately, after that, I found out there were a lot of people who were book authors with the same publisher that got burnt, as well! So they re-published their books with other publishers! So I have to now eat the cost of getting this first book done with the former publisher and it's like starting over from scratch. The itch to get this re-edited is overwhelming; as an author, you want people to see your first, best material, not hand-me-downs from a bad publisher! And I wanted the stories done right with the first book! Here it is, May 2020, and this book was first published after December 3rd, 2019!

I have a friend who has helped me out tremendously during this time named Megan! She is the head manager of the Age Strong Commission for the Golden Age Center in Charlestown, Massachusetts, and it was her mom who works for the Age Strong Commission in City Hall that referred me over to Megan, which I'm totally grateful for! And her help is very invaluable to me. Without it, I would be stuck with nothing finished! But she referred me over to another agency where the lady's name was Carolina, who is a big blessing! This is a really good domino effect that led from one good person to the other! She is one of the managers of an agency who recruits volunteers to help people out. I received that help and I'm extremely grateful and appreciative for it! And she became a blessing when I started to run out of food until the next month! I didn't call her, she called me, and was asking how my food supply was. She had no way of knowing I was low on some food items, because I never shared that with her. So I told her the truth. What an unknown resource of a blessing from God she was! He knew my need and answered it back in the way of a phone call from Carolina, and because I never told anyone one that I was running low on food, that made it even more amazing to me, because God took care of it through another resource, Carolina!

A while back, I gave Carolina a first copy of the un-edited version of this book you're reading to look at, and she offered to buy it from me as I was selling whatever copies I had to help my friends with food in different places. I told her she could just keep the book for herself! She insisted on paying for it, so I told her, "OK, whenever you want to do that, that's fine!" I lost track of her for a little while, and lo and behold, she calls me right at the moment that I'm needing help! I'm sure that she had no idea what was going on with my food situation, but there she was, and I was glad to hear her voice! She said, "Ritchie? You kno, I still owe you for that book," and I totally forgot that she did, because it wasn't important to me, I had let it go. She offered to pay for some grocery items because she felt that she owed me, and she added three more dollars to make it $15.00. Wow! What a blessing to me! She asked me what kind things I liked to eat, and I told her. She told me that she would have one of her volunteers offer to buy the food and deliver it over to where I lived! And within two days, that person showed up with some groceries for me. And I was ever so grateful!

God used Carolina to get ahold of me right at my point of need! Scripture says that God knows our needs before we ever ask! And I didnt ask anyone, including God, because I already trusted Him for any need I might have, and look how he took care of it! Wow! God is amazing! I couldn't thank Carolina enough! In a timely manner, no doubt! And she also referred me to a volunteer, who is another blessing and is helping me out to re-edit this book! And that's where this chapter you're reading now comes into play! Because of all these changes this is where we are right now, right in the middle of the Coronavirus, which has now hindered her that she can't come over and help me on this because of the rules of what this virus dictates. But she helps me over the phone and has these stories on her own laptop from when we were able to work on them together, as she had come over once a week to my house! She is a total blessing as we re-edit these stories together, making sure they are right this time, and better than before! Amen...

My friend Brian Riley was a real blessing, as he and I were working on my own CD disc picture of the songs. Some of them are on Youtube, remember, under Richard Vernon uhi, in case you didn't recall, and the design he came up with is absolutely beautiful. The CD is called Battleground and the disc picture matches the CD case cover! I received a text from him about 3 weeks ago as, in April 2020, and he said he was having a hard time breathing, and he believed he had the Coronavirus! My heart sank reading that text, and I immediately tried to get on the phone with him to hopefully talk to him and pray! He never responded back, and it's my fear that he didn't live through it! And I cried all day and all night fearing I had lost a really good friend and great designer because of this horrible virus! This was up close and personal about a really good friend that I've never heard from again. I know I'll see him in heaven one day, because he was a Christian, it's just that I miss him now. Painfully, I have to move forward. When this CD is finally completed, it will let people know everywhere that this author lost a really good friend in Brian Riley, because I will have a dedication inside the cover of it about him. And thinking about it now just breaks my heart. He had gotten the disc picture over three-quarters of the way done, and now I'll give it over to disc makers when the time comes to finish the rest in his name. God Bless your memory, Brain, and what you meant to me. When people get this CD, they will read about an awesome friend and human being who cared about people! In his memory, this will get done, and at this time, I contacted Discmakers by email, as the CD company that I want to get this done through, this beautiful disc picture will be in memory of Brian. In Jesus' name, Amen.

I also got a call from my former case manager, Patti, the one who was instrumental in getting this place where I am today. She told me that my long-time friend just passed, as well, and that greatly saddened me. Gary Brooks was a fantastic friend who was my roommate in the Soar Program in 2016. I will share that in the next book, as well, as I will elaborate on our great friendship together! And during this time, I rediscovered a song I heard on Youtube called "Time" by the Alan Parsons Project; it is an absolutely beautiful, haunting song that fits with what we're going through in this moment of April 2020. And when we are allowed to do karaoke again, I will do this song as a dedication to my two friends I lost during this time. I cried when I started to practice it; may God give me strength to sing it on behalf of their memories when the time comes. I miss them so much. This virus does not discriminate by race. Gary was black, and Brian was white, and they were both two very good friends of mine

And another friend gets a tribute to him as well: of Anderson, Indiana, the late great Chiropractor Dr. Gary Young, whose office was on 38th Street and Main in Anderson. He was not only my doctor, but also my friend, and when he was working on my health we would also share Bible Scriptures together, and he was an awesome doctor, not only for his compassion and care, also in helping you out if you had trouble paying your bills! I just can't say enough about Dr. Young and his awesome techniques he used on me to get me better, but he was very encouraging, as well, and always smiling! I miss him greatly, and I'll see him in heaven one day, along with many others! Amen.

I also want to share that in my prayers during this time, I pray that hopefully, people will turn to God through this pandemic! I'm grateful to see many people come together and help out those who need that help. I don't have fear of the Coronavirus simply because I know who I am in God, and I'm not trying to be arrogant about that because I'm just as susceptible as anyone else to catch the virus. Not that I am better than anyone else in the faith department, either, I just know that my life is hidden in Christ. I don't fear the virus because I know that even if the virus took my life, I have a home in heaven, so there is no fear! Paul said in the New Testament, that to live is Christ, to die is gain. He simply meant that at the end of life, he was going to get eternal life and heaven! That is promised to everyone who turns to God and gives Christ a chance to work in their lives. He takes us just as we are, if we'd only just believe in Him! My prayer at this time is that many people will turn to God; if a person who knew God before this and turned away from God, my prayer is that they may turn back to God.

And to those who know God as a personal savior like I have experienced, my prayer for them is that they would grow stronger through this and be of some help to someone who might need it, maybe encouraging people to trust God through this! Now this doesn't mean that I don't follow the guidelines by our awesome governor, Governor Baker, at this time, because I most certainly do! And of course, our awesome mayor, Marty Walsh! Both men have used great wisdom in handling this crisis with expertise and skill! Thank God for these two men and all their staff! And to all our first medic and emergency responders, to all our police force, to our National Guard who helps us greatly, and our fire departments; to our doctors and nurses, to our volunteers everywhere; to our parents who have to deal with being home with their own kids, to their pets who are probably wondering why mom or dad aren't working right now and have to be home with them; to the food volunteers who make sure at-risk families eat and those families who are low on food; to the school principal from North Carolina who puts himself at risk on a school bus delivery food to his students and other kids needing much valuable food; to teachers everywhere doing the same, to workers everywhere especially grocery store workers who put themselves at risk daily and their managers; to basketball players of the NBA at this time, including my team, the Boston Celtics, doing what they're doing; to former NBA players getting involved, as well, and other sports figures stepping up; to Hollywood and what they're doing at this time; to the Age Strong Commision in Boston and their dedication not only to the homeless, but for the seniors like myself, who are dedicated to getting our laundry done, meals served daily, and people who come and clean our apartments because many of us are disabled...I don't know about you, but in my book, that's dedication! And they risk their own safety to care for others!

And I personally thank God for my case manager, Catherine, and her staff that oversee all of this! And we pray for their safety, as well! I also want to give a shoutout to my volunteer friend Jessica, who is under Carolina, and is always checking on me to make sure, like others, that I'm safe! A shout-out to many music artists like Beyonce and Lady Gaga, and others answering the call helping others; to Youtube Pastor where I have just caught his program, Chuck Missler—I love his teachings, and I feel very honored to have come across them; I found out that he went home to heaven in 2018, and I look forward to meeting him one day, face-to-face!

And a pastor who I had first caught videos of on Youtube, Justin Peters; I have a great deal of respect for this man, as he exposes those who misuse the Gospel for their own gain! And he said something on one of his videos that caught my attention; he felt one of these prosperity preachers was demon-possessed, and I often wondered about the same person he was talking about, as well, that he might be, because of the preacher in question's eyes, and the most unusual way he acts after saying a sentence! Others on Youtube have also commented on this, as well! And I thank Justin Peters for pointing that out, because when this preacher he's talking about looks at you or acts unusual after any sentence, I admit it does give you the creeps! I know it did me! When a reporter questioned some things this preacher said, he got very defensive, pointing a bony finger at her and trying to justify his answer, but they showed his eyes and that was very unnerving to see!

Keep in mind that this prosperity preacher is possibly one of the richest men in America, with his own airfield and many planes, and a ton of material things he has, just like Job of the Old Testament had, before God allowed Satan to take away all Job had, sparing his life and his wife who complained bitterly! It makes you wonder where his wife's heart was? Was her love for Job only when he was rich? It makes you wonder about the difference between Job and the false preachers of today as miles apart! Job was a righteous man who lost everything because the devil had told God that the only reason he worshipped Him was because He had allowed him to prosper. So God allowed Satan to take away all Job had. I just wanted to mention here that Job had many material goods, but the material goods didn't have Job or his heart! Job proved his love for God, but close to the end of the chapter, he started to complain a little bit, and I want to interject, he was a man of God, but he is still a human being, so he questioned God on some things, and God answered him, and Job repented of what he questioned God about. I know I would have as well; I don't know the time frame of how long he suffered, but God told him to pray for his three friends who claimed they had heard from God, which they had not, because God told Job that He needed him to pray for his three friends to restore them or he would judge them! So Job obeyed God, and he received a double portion of everything he had lost before his great test was to occur! That's a startling distinction between the love of things and the love of God!

When I lost all my material goods, including an antique chair and furniture that was worth money in my house, my heart was still for God, even when my former landlord Steve in Indiana mocked me then, saying, "Richard? Where is your God now?" before I was to lose everything. I told him that things I had acquired in this life did not dictate my love or trust of God! My faith was my trust in God, and whatever was going to happen I just knew that I was in his hands, and that same faith kept me going during the homeless years.

There is a big difference between faith and feelings; feelings will let you down, and your emotions will rise and fall because of how you feel, but faith in God will hold your heart forever, because it doesn't rise and fall with emotional tides. Faith is steadfast and will lead you through even the most dire of circumstances, because it's grounded in God! My faith never left me, all the time that I was homeless, because I didn't depend on feelings. And regardless, if circumstances and changes happened or not, my faith was in God, and that never changed! There is also a big difference between being happy and being joyful; happiness is directed by our feelings, and can change in an instant! But being joyful is something that comes from knowing God and is not dictated by feelings or emotions, because in even the worst circumstances of life, I can know that God has control of my life in His hands, and I can be secure in that, by knowing that He does! He took care of me in different ways and means through different people He had brought my way after I became homeless, and He rewarded faithfulness in my life to Him, even when life as a homeless man became very challenging and difficult! And He has rewarded me now with the nice place I live in.

So it makes me wonder: if God took away all these prosperity preachers' wealth and material goods, would they serve Him, or would they bitterly complain, like Job's wife did then, and say, "Why, God? Why?" This would expose the real motive of so-called servers of God and show the world what these preachers are all about, that their god is money! I hope God does send a test to them like He sent to Job! But remember this: Job was a righteous man who didn't do any wrong. This is the vast difference between a heart longing for things, and a heart longing for God! So, if God did it against Job, who was in right standing with God, He can even more so do it against corrupt and false teachers and preachers in this world!

I've also heard some preachers say that if a person has some kind of disability or handicap, that they don't have enough faith to believe

God for their healing? What a false bunch of doctrinal garbage that is! Where does that line of thinking come from? It isn't in the Bible, and it sure isn't from God! And I hate when these prosperity preachers talk about faith in God! When you have huge wealth and are prospering, it doesn't take faith to talk about what you have, it takes faith to talk about what you don't have! If God takes away all their prosperity and wealth, then will they see which one of them has faith? I guess these self-absorbed preachers, teachers, and false prophets who claim this haven't read the Old Testament or New Testament accounts of God using men and women of different ailments, shortcomings, and disabilities throughout the Bible to do His will!

For example, Moses was a stutterer when it came to speech, and was afraid to speak to Pharaoh, and God used him mightily in his older years! Elijah was afraid of the Queen; Elisha had a quick trigger temper; Jonah was reluctant and wanted vengeance; many had physical impairments, as well. A person's age doesn't matter to God, but availability of a person's heart is what matters to Him, because age is not defined by what you see on the outside of a person; what defines them is what God puts in their hearts and what they do with it!

There are way more examples of how God used less-than-perfect people to do His will, and you're looking at one of them! Many of them had different defects or faults, yet God uses the willing, not the self-absorbed perfectionists. The preachers of today who spout false doctrinal garbage have made fools out of those trying to serve God the right way! They do it by manipulating a lot of people to give with phony promises, and it goes right into their accounts! And many people gave out of the goodness of their hearts. If you don't take my word for it, you should look up Justin Peters on Youtube, he is awesome! And many others Christian or non-Christians who have commented on the same person who did the COVID-19 video. It is eye-opening stuff, and try telling the handicap preachers and teachers of today and many others that they don't have enough faith in God. They are doing tremendous works of God and it humbles me to the core that many have handicaps and disabilities far worse than my own. I should be grateful that God uses imperfect vessels, such as myself.

Amen, and some of them are also physically blind, so I'm grateful that I even have physical sight! This shows me that we should be thankful for what we have, and the ability we have to do it with, compared to those things of what we don't have! This is why I won't be envious or want to covet what another person might have, because God gives me what I need, Amen...

I wonder if there will be consequences for the preacher saying the virus is gone? I wish he was gone, off TV, radio, Youtube, and whatever else, because he is a liar! He said, "I command the heat and the wind to blow this thing away!" Only God has command over heat and wind, and no one can take His place! How dare this phony- baloney preacher give America and the whole world false hope and assurance that COVID-19 was gone at his command! Newsflash: at this writing, this virus is still taking lives. This preacher needs to be disciplined for putting out such misleading, false hope garbage! I'd love to say it to his face. I'm not saying he's possessed, as some have suggested, but there is something really strange about his eyes. This author would have no problem talking to him, on-camera or off-camera! I'm sure many would, as well!

I would love to have one of those false preachers or teachers tell this author that I don't have enough faith for my healing. God uses me even more through this now disability that I have, and has opened my eyes to many things! So these people who say this stuff need to just be quiet before they make even greater fools of themselves, starting with their own lips! And unfortunately, we have Coronavirus scam artists trying to prey on people's money! You really don't have a conscience of any kind, or a decent heart, when you try to take advantage of people who are suffering with loss of loved ones, or even finances! This kind of stuff irritates this writer to no end! And if you're a scam artist reading what I just said, you may try to fool people, but you can't get away from the eyes of God, who sees every wrong act you're doing, and if you don't stop, you could well come unto His judgments on this Earth! So remember that next time you try to pull some kind of scam, because you'll reap what you sow! That's in the Bible, so quit while you can, so you don't come into His wrath! I really appreciate the things I have found here on Youtube, and being able to do music there, as well.

Just to clarify to all of the readers, I am not against wealth or prosperity when it's earned, received, given to or inherited in the right way, I'm against those that use it only upon themselves instead of reaching out to help others, and those who manipulate with words at the expense of others to make themselves rich!

Enough of that,I want to give a huge shout-out to former White House Representative Elijah Cummings, who was a real man of God who was in the Senate, and a man who loved his family, his city of Baltimore, and had great compassion for the Constitution. He also had a booming voice when he wanted to be heard. Great wisdom and knowledge this dynamic man had in life, and he loved people! He made his wife, who I believe is also in the Senate, and his family, proud for knowing him! I thank God for his life! And to the black leaders who are all stepping up all over this country, I say thank you! Leadership does not have a color tag attached to it, they are called leaders because they are those who lead by example! A leader can be any color or age; God will use people who are willing to step up and be accounted for and let's not forget a tribute to John Lewis the man who was responsible for good trouble when he and others crossed a forbidden bridge they weren't supposed to cross they were beaten but he and the others did not give up they went to cast their vote and nothing was going to stop them including white racist and kkk members, I don't know too much about but you have to absolutely applaud someone who refuse to be stopped or shaking in their faith! He continued on through life including the Congress and became a very well respected gentleman and leader!

And to the statewide mayors gathering together by internet, using knowledge and making plans, coordinating with each other: that's wisdom, and a shout-out to the morning show of Joe and Mika, I say you're doing a great job, and I watch your broadcast. I appreciate Joe's honesty about his own shortcomings. Joe, you both are in my prayers, thank you for being an honest man over the airwaves. There is one thing though, you should let your talented co-host Mika do more talking and share the mic with her, I've read many comments on this! You're doing a good job please share the mic don't let it go to waste. A shout-out to Chris Cuomo,Nightly newscaster,msnbc news, hopefully who gets better after having contracted the virus and joins his fellow newscasters Jake Tapper, Lawrence O'Donnell, Anderson Cooper, Don Lemon, Ari Melber, Wolf Blitzer ,Brian Williams, Chris Wallace, a high shout-out to all of you. These are my favorite broadcasters who define the word "professional!" I only ask Ari to let his guests finish what they're saying before interjecting his thoughts; I have deep respect for them all!

And to those news broadcasters I don't know about, please forgive me, but these are the people I really appreciate! I trust MSNBC on Youtube; they are a very reliable and accurate source of information, as well as some others, and they report accurate news as it's happening! I appreciate our Boston News Stations and broadcasts on Youtube concerning updates from our own Governor and Mayor.

To Dr. Fauci, if anybody can find a remedy to fight this virus, I'm betting it will be him! We in the United States appreciate you, and I'm sure those around the world do, too! To kids everywhere who haven't quite driven their parents out of their minds yet, thank you! To those everywhere stepping up and making a difference and caring about others, this author says a heartfelt thank you for caring! People are stepping up everywhere answering the call to help. To former Navy Captain, Captain Crosner who now has the Coronavirus, you are deep in my prayers and you have my highest respect! I pray you recover well and get to command your ship again! The Navy which I was a part of years ago, needs men like you! And prayer for the men on your ship. I say "your ship" because it does belong to you, and that is your crew! And to many others I know nothing of and your continued good works, I say a heartfelt thank you! And those around the world in every country making a difference in lives, this author says a big thank you! Also to The Russell Wilson family, the Andy Dalton family, and the Drew Brees family, a huge thank you.

If I didn't call out a name, it's because I'm not aware of who they are, but I definitely know about these three families! And I believe this virus is something former President Obama and his wife had warned us about after his administration was through that might come to pass. I have great respect for both of them! We were supposed to be prepared to deal with it, and obviously, we weren't, just like the Titanic, which didn't listen to warnings before this massive ocean liner sunk! They did not heed the warnings, and in this time of 2020, we didn't, either! We could have started preparing for this virus after former President Obama's administration, but it was ignored, and now we're paying the price! Whoever wins the next presidency I pray that God will guide them in everything! We need wisdom from them, and common sense! A massive amount of people's lives could have possibly been spared and prevented death if we had prepared! Who knows how many more lives this virus will take? It's horrible to even think about, and I especially want to get a frontline shout-out to courageous doctors and nurses helping patients everywhere! And a special shout out to a courageous New York female doctor by the name of Lorna Breen, who had overwhelming compassion for all her patients and those who worked long side of her,she worked many, many hours and even contracted the virus herself, but when she was cleared to work a week after that, she was on the front lines again! I'm sad to report that she lost her life during this time, and I cried bitterly when I heard the news of her passing; she is a hero, a person who gave her life willingly so that others might live! Dedicated people like this are what make our nation great! I look forward one day to seeing her in heaven!

I never thought that I would be adding one more chapter during this "Do Overs" period, but here it is! All because the first publisher couldn't get it right, henceforth the name, "Do-Overs!" And during this time, I was able to locate music of a group I listened to a long time ago called The Way, a southern Gospel rock and worship band of the '70s! I was so overjoyed to find their music that I got re-acquainted with it for days, and I thank God for them, because they were one of the first Gospel music groups to influence my life as a songwriter, and I'd love to meet them. I have great respect for them and the awesome music they did back then! One of their songs called "Can It Be?" is one of my very favorites! And another song they do is a song called "Song of Joy," and that's the song this author sings, a song of joy because God allowed me to find their music again!One of their founding members emailed me one time,and I was overjoyed to see that! Thank God! There are other Gospel artists who influenced my life as a songwriter, and I'll share them in the next book.

In these days of COVID-19 it is very different, and what is so really surreal about this is when I went to CVS about three days ago. A normally-bustling Boston population was nowhere to be found, except a homeless guy who was trying to provoke me into a fight, because I didn't have two dollars. I looked at him and just shook my head, and walked away. It's not worth fighting over two dollars. And during this time, because of the Coronavirus! It was like something out of a horror movie, with empty sidewalks and almost empty streets of cars! Everything but zombies! This is the reality of where we are today, and like many other states and cities, we are now under a curfew from 9 pm to 6 am to stay inside; this is where we are in society. And it's mandatory by law now that we have to wear face masks to protect ourselves and others. But that doesn't stop me from going out in the daytime and trying to feed some homeless folk! And it doesn't matter to me if they might be carriers of the virus or not, because they have to eat! Could I get sick or possibly die doing this? There's always that possibility, but I'd rather give my life doing something that makes a difference compared to being at home, instead, all the time, watching TV!

God has been watching over me during this time with pretty good health as I follow the mandates of our state law, and I will continue to do, and continue with my own concocted meals for any homeless person I might run into. My prayer is that they will find a cure for this thing and get back to normal society, which they are calling the "New Normal!" It is very weird to walk down the streets and not see very many people around, because this is a big city with a good-sized population! From a writer's point of view, it feels like something out of the Twilight Zone! But our government in Boston is very good. We have a really good governor and mayor, and both of them deeply care for what's going on and the people under their care, including the homeless, who are the most vulnerable. How long this will last, only God knows!

This New Normal has given me time to catch new shows once in a while as on Youtube, where I found a cartoon called *Simon's Cat*!

There are many extreme episodes of this cat who literally makes a fool out of its owner! I absolutely love watching it! And I have also seen a commercial I caught one time while watching an action movie. You will get a kick out of this; it shows a scene where an Egyptian Pharaoh is putting together a small list of things he needs, so he calls out, "Alexis? We need toilet paper!" So the guy who is Alexis, their version of what we now use called Alexa, he starts tapping out on the wall with his hammer and chisel a picture of what a roll of toilet paper is supposed to look like! And while he's attempting to do that the Pharaoh yells out in the room, "Is there anything else we need?" "Yes, we need some goat milk, and this, and that, blah, blah, blah!" So keep in mind, Alexis isn't done chiseling, yet, and hears these other order requests and he just stares for a moment. He then takes his hammer and chisel and drops it off over his left and leaves the room! Alexis has exited the building! I thought this was absolutely hilarious to watch! Poor Alexis, being bombarded with new orders, and frustrated beyond belief! I was eating chips at this time, and almost choked on one, because I was laughing so hard over what I'd just seen!

As I was saying, like many of you, I am cooped up in my own place, as well! I keep getting phone calls from this one college saying my student loan is due but there's loan forgiveness? If you are the people from that college reading this book the guy that you are calling is not that kind of senior? More past the 50s age bracket which qualifies me to be an older senior, not a college senior! So I don't know if the phone call is a scam or if it's really sincere, but I'm telling that college right now whoever they are I am not that kind of senior!And what's really hard is that I have to stay active in this house doing different things so my mind doesn't get complacent! So, henceforth I work on this book and hopefully will be working on other books to come! And my prayer life is on high alert for others. As this virus has taken us all by surprise, and hit us like no enemy ever could! This is so much to think about because it has stunned our nation and the entire world, and has made us feel absolutely helpless and powerless! And that's a hard reality to swallow for all of us; I wish I could pray for people online right now, but this is all I can do right at this moment in time

I'm hoping to get started on the second book soon, which is going to be called *Life Stories Volume 2 Continuation in Boston!* I'm grateful for Megan's help in sending Carolina and the beloved volunteer my way; they have been very resourceful with me and for me! As a young senior, I just feel like I'm not over the hill, but rather I'm still learning to climb it! I'm grateful for the laundry service who does my laundry every two weeks, as I am a disabled person who was used to doing his own laundry when I could walk. Now, keep in mind, a young senior, but still a senior! I'm grateful for the Age Strong Commission, who gave me a case manager named Catherine who oversees the laundry detail, my house-cleaning person they send every two weeks by the name of Ebi; he is a real blessing and he's pleasant to talk to! He does whatever needs to be done in the kitchen and bathroom, and sometimes he'll shop for me, if I need it. You never realize how much you need these people until your mobility is gone! Before all that happened, I thought I didn't have to depend on anybody, as far as the physical things are concerned! So when you don't have that mobility temporarily or permanently, you are humbled by it, and you're grateful to those that reach out to you! And also I thank Catherine for the one a day meals that I receive daily Monday through Friday! These are some of the perks you receive from the city when you become past age 55! Not to mention, I'm also disabled from surgery, which really helps my eligibility for these benefits, as well.

I never planned to be disabled, but it helps knowing that these services are here for you. I never thought in 2020 that the world would be going through a wake-up call like this! But this virus has also brought fear with it around the world, and that fear dominates a person's thinking about what might happen next with uncertainty! And however long this is around will determine when this book gets back out on the market to be, again, re-sold! So life right now is at a standstill almost like the movie *The Last Man on Earth* with Vincent Price! Except he had to fight zombies; I'm grateful I don't have to do that! I can't run from a zombie, so I would have to stay and fight! Because if I tried to run it would be like a sideways crab running, and nobody wants to see that!☺ Fortunately, it hasn't come down to that! So you would have to win your fight to stay alive! So I'm glad that part hasn't taken place! Anyway, that's where we are in this world right now.

I went out to feed some homeless folk on the day of this writing and when I got done, I felt this prompting in my spirit,and it was telling me to turn and go across the street to Walgreens! *Walgreens? Lord, I know that's you talking to my spirit, but what's at Walgreens? I only have about 12 or 13 dollars left.* The prompting continued in a hushed voice. *Son? Go to Walgreens. I said, Yes, Lord, and so I did.* I thought that I might as well go to their frozen food section and see if I can find some more of their chicken taquitos to buy, which are a little under four dollars, but man, these things were so good! I thought, *I'll get a box of 12 of them and use the leftover money on snacks!* So,that was the plan, but I still kept wondering why God's Spirit led me into Walgreens. I approached the frozen food area, and I couldn't believe what I was seeing! The sale I missed out on two weeks ago was back again this week, and I couldn't believe it; I was blown away! *So this is what God was prompting me to do!* And I would have missed it again if I had insisted on going where I was headed to originally, CVS. God did not want me to miss this sale again! And there it was, right in front of my eyes! The four items for ten dollars sale was back again and I couldn't believe the selection of choices I saw before me!The chicken taquitos were there, plus 40-piece pizza rolls, plus boxes of 6 corndogs! Oh man! I was in food heaven! I was so grateful I hadn't missed out on this again! Wouldn't you be? I've learned when I get that in my spirit I need to listen! Hopefully, without questioning next time, and like the Nike saying, goes, "Just do it!"

When I got home, I decided to catch Youtube and see if anything was different in the news. Nope! Just the same. So I decided to check on my email account. And what did I find?But that televangelist praying loudly on a Youtube video, telling the Coronavirus to go, and blowing it away with his breath! I just hope he had a breath mint in his mouth when he did it!He didn't blow,he spat!There's a big difference between blowing and spitting,watch the video for yourselves! And by the way, this probably bruised his ego, but his breath of wind didn't kill the virus! It is still taking lives! This is the reality of it all today. That was all a show, for nothing! I hope he and his bunch don't get the virus, but if they do, then this will show them that this virus is real! And I believe in the power of prayer, that's my power source daily, but the guy praying was one of those prosperity preachers that I've shared about that just wants your money! And attention: Oral Roberts made a claim one time to his TV audience, I think it was, that said that God would take him home to heaven if he didn't get 7 million dollars from his supporters! So what happened? God took him home! Did he get his 7 million dollars before that? I doubt it! God does not work in manipulation tactics! Why Oral Roberts said this on TV, I'll never know! That's why the guy praying on the video who is a billionaire preacher with more than one home, boats, cars, a couple of airplanes, etc., you name it, absolutely made a fool of himself doing this flesh act on Youtube! And he is one of many who got rich exploiting the Gospel for his own use! He obviously loves the spotlight! Why he couldn't have prayed about COVID-19 in his own prayer time is beyond me, instead of making a fool of himself in the public's eye on Youtube. The Bible says to pray in secret and your heavenly Father who sees you in secret will openly reward you. We're supposed to let our light shine before men, but boasting is not light, unless this light boasts about God! I guess he never read that particular New Testament Scripture!

Just a quick reminder to the readers—I don't put down where you can find these Bible references I share because it will give you the opportunity to look them up for yourselves, because if I gave you the info where to look them up, do you really think you would? Or would you just take my word for it that what I'm sharing is a Biblical reference? That's why I ask you to check it out for yourselves. Guys like this make me sick, preying on people, most of them Christians, and some of them not, trying to give them false hopes of prosperity, but at the same time manipulating them to sow a huge money seed straight into this and other preachers' bank accounts! I would have a hard time standing before God one day on his Judgement Day, giving an account for my own life lived on the earth, knowing I had made money from ill-gotten gains of untold wealth. I couldn't manipulate people to give money to me by using false doctrine; it is not in my spiritual DNA to do such phony baloney garbage! My job is to share those things God has given to me to share with others. It's for sharing, not hoarding it all for myself! If you ever saw the Christmas movie *Scrooge*, you will know what I'm talking about

What God gives us in life, whether talents, abilities, etc., is for sharing and caring, not keeping it all for ourselves! What good would that do me? His word asks in the New Testament: what does it profit a man if he gains the whole world and loses his own soul? That's a chilling warning of a Scripture! That's why I'm not going to hide what God has given me if it benefits someone else's life! If I had the wealth and material things that many in this world have, including prosperity preachers, I guarantee you I would be sharing it for those less fortunate than myself! For that is what's in my spiritual DNA! If I had a fleet of cars, I would be giving them to others who needed them, or I'd sell them to help the homeless, because in my rational way of thinking, I would only need one car to drive! Plus, I can't drive a fleet of cars at one time by myself, anyway! When I was a courier in Indiana, I could only drive one delivery van at a time. Do you see my point? Why hoard it if I can share it!

When my daughter said to me in September 2013, "Hey, Dad? I think God wants you to write a book!", I could have easily processed that in my mind as information and then put it on the back-burner of future things to do! If I do that, it's possible this book you're reading now would never have gotten written or even published! Christian songwriter Steven Curtis Chapman brought this out in a song he wrote one time that said, "Whatever you do, do your very best for God!" And I totally agree with my Christian songwriting brother that you should do all you can do for God, whatever it is! I think the song was called "What about the Change?" So why not be a blessing for someone else? If you have the talent or ability to do that, then I would encourage you to do that! Amen...

If in the late 1990's I would have signed with a Christian Music Recording Label to be one of their artists, I would have used that money that the music would have earned to help the unfortunate ones in life! But as you can see, that never happened due in part to people who were about lip service, and not life service !I want my life, dear reader, to be about life service through God! There's enough "Yes" men in this world, but not enough "Yes, Lord, I'll do it," men in this world! There is a difference. Anyways, as this guy is supposedly praying in this video on Youtube, there is what sounds like mocking music and voices in the background. It made me nauseous just watching it. If this guy really wanted to do something good for America, then why not donate one of his big planes, or a few of his antique priceless cars, or one of his big boats or throw in one of his mansions since he and his wife can't live in two or three mansions at the same time, and donate or sell them so that people won't have to suffer without food? Then this author might change his opinion about his self-righteous greed! Or as they say, just do the right thing! Otherwise, to this guy, I say: you're just full of self-righteous religious phoney baloney hot air, spouting yourself just to be heard on Youtube! Well, nobody's buying what you're selling! And God knows it! Even if God told you to donate the items mentioned for the good of feeding people, I seriously doubt you would listen or even comprehend what spirit is talking to you! You can take a lesson from a man named Bill Gates and his wife to see what real Christianity is all about. They are givers, not takers! Something, sir, you have no clue of! Even when news stations tried to interview you, you ran away from them and wouldn't pay attention to them, unless you decided to point your bony finger at them!

My Pastor told me one time this saying and I've never forgotten it: If you point a finger at someone accusing them of something, then know that at least three fingers are being pointed back at you! So I know for a fact that more than three fingers are being pointed back at this Youtube video COVID-19 preacher, and his people that were partakers of this, as well! This guy has made himself before the world an absolute object of mocking and scorn! And well-deserved, I might add; the real problem that really matters, is he shamed the name of Jesus before the entire world, like the Prophet Samuel told King Saul, "Thou art the man!" In other words: King Saul, you're the guilty one, and Saul heard the truth, and now the Youtube preacher who did this shameful video exposes what we already knew about you! You are more concerned about fleecing the American public, with more hoarding of wealth than you could ever spend in five lifetimes! I feel sorry for you and your prosperity preaching buddies! And the timing of this video makes me wonder why you had to wait for over 45 thousand Americans—and counting—to die to do this Youtube video? It's really hard to pray for people like this sometimes, but God gives me the strength and the command to do it, anyway; I'll make room on my list for them in my prayer time. They really shouldn't name the name of Jesus because they have no idea what a real believer in Christ is all about!

Now, I want to share with all these prosperity preachers just what God laid on my heart to say to you all this morning; God spoke this into my spirit when I was praying to him to say this to all of you: *What if the Lord himself blew his breath on you and that breath wiped away all your finances, your bank accounts, your houses, boats, planes cars, motorcycles, jewelry, expensive clothes, stocks and bonds, and anything else of value?* The Lord is asking: *Would you serve him like Job of the Bible did, saying the Lord giveth and the Lord taketh away, blessed be the name of the Lord? Or would you do like Job's wife suggested you do saying, Curse God and die! And would your wives turn on you, saying the same thing? Would God still be your God that you claim to know when it's like this? Would you worship him, or would you curse him?* It's easy to smile and put on a big religious front when things are going well, but remember—God knows all of you and all about you! And he can very easily expose what's behind the mask you have hidden behind. You might say all is well, but in that moment when it's all taken away from you, will you live for God? Or is mammon and the love of money your god? Something to think about, because God put this on my heart to ask you! Do you serve God when all is well? And would you serve Him if He blew it all away with his mighty breath, because that could happen to all of you! God is trying to wake all of you up with these questions. That's why he laid it on my heart to convey this message to you!

And just to let you know from personal experience, God asked me two questions before I was to lose my job, my delivery vehicle, and my home, and become homeless for over four years. But, I served my God that whole time and I am where He has placed me today because I served Him, no matter what condition my life was in after that, and that's the mark of a True Believer in Christ! That's when real Salvation is put to the test! When you think you've got it all, you could lose it all in a moment's time. God is no respecter of persons, great or small! If He did it to me, He can also do it to you. Pride goes before a fall! Scripture says, be not deceived, God is not mocked. For whatsoever a man soweth, that he shall also reap! And one more Scripture to all of you that says: to whom much is given, much shall be required. I pray in Jesus' name that this haunts you in your very sleep! Your very lives have come up into the nostrils of Almighty God! This could very well be your appointed time before God! He says in His word again: I would rather you be either hot or cold, but because you are lukewarm, I will spew you out of my mouth! Everything I have said was spoken to me to say by the Spirit of the Almighty God, and I didn't say God said He would do it, what He is saying to all of you prosperity preachers and televangelists is that God can do it if He chooses to do so. Your wealth won't make it into Heaven, but your soul will, if you're right with God!

The Bible says that God uses the foolish things to confound the wise. And I guess I am one of those foolish things. I guarantee you that I didn't wake up thinking I was going to be talking about this and now sharing what God put on my heart to say. Because God got no glory out of it; you mocked Him, and you mock your brothers and sisters who are trying to live for God! And this author is one of those that God spoke to this morning to warn you how you live before the spirit of the living God! Don't let him say to all of you, thou fool! Thy soul is required of thee this day! I would seriously think about what the Spirit of God is trying to tell you and the condition of your souls before Him today! I do not claim to be all-knowing all-wise, that's God's job, but when His voice prompts me to say something or do something, I will obey that, because that voice deep inside of me is the spirit of the living God! And if you've done nothing wrong, then God will show that. I have spoken what God has laid on my heart; this might be a word for your lives to heed to the Spirit of God and repent. Or, you could just ignore what this writer is saying, and say, "It is well with my soul." But, is it? And it wont bother me if you're mad at me for sharing this, because there is a Scripture that says that it is better to obey God rather than man, so that's why I shared it, what you do with what was said is now up to you! Maybe God is calling you to the carpet, which is a term used when someone is in trouble with the Big Boss or about to get into trouble with the Big Boss! This phony preacher of the COVID-19 video should be barred from TV and radio And never allowed to share again!

I also want to share about an employee who works for the same Televangelist who put out the COVID-19 Youtube video, of the wonderful thing that she did! She gave her very own car one day and handed it over to a college student who no longer had a car. Now, that's how the Spirit of God works! I praise God for that employee, that God in Jesus' Name would bless that woman abundantly for doing such a selfless act! Take notes, prosperity preachers, of what the woman did! That's real prosperity! Amen...

And to those pastors going against the law of the land gathering together for church—how foolish are you? I found out some members of these churches that gathered together contracted the Coronavirus and died, because the pastors wouldn't listen to wisdom, and now some of those members have paid that price with their very lives! And that's sad that they bring a reproach on the name of God when they don't listen to what is good and safe for us. Plus, it gives law enforcement a hard time. Didn't we learn anything from the preachers that brought snakes, you might as well say serpents, into their church congregations and dared to handle these poisonous snakes? All because they wouldn't listen, mis-using the Scripture that says that they shall take up any deadly thing and it shall not harm them. When the Apostle Paul was bitten on the island by a poisonous snake, the crew of the ship was watching to see if he would die! To their amazement, Paul shook the snake off his arm. The Scripture I mentioned was a show of God's power over his consecrated life. Paul did not tempt the snake to bite him, yet the snake came at him and bit him, and Paul shook it off like he was brushing away a fly. This must have really freaked out the ship's crew, but Paul knew who he lived for and what he lived for and had no fear, and the crew saw it, as well! The Scripture means, if something comes upon you, then it shall not harm you. And I saw in a documentary on

TV that some church members who did this, including some pastors, died from the snakes' poisonous bites. I don't know if they still do this practice today or not, but I would say to them, stop tempting God's grace on your life, putting it on line with a foolish test!

I saw a sign on Youtube from Texas saying, "We will not take the mark of the beast." Are they talking about government rules about gathering together in defiance of not wanting to listen, or something totally different that I'm not aware of? Because in the future, there will actually be a mark of the beast that's talked about in the last book of the Bible, the book of Revelation! I also read that a female college student is not taking some kind of thing that they want every student to have, some kind of tracking device that shows your whereabouts! And I think she thinks that's the mark that the Book of Revelation is talking about. I want to encourage that student that what her college is trying to institute is not talking about the mark of the beast in the Bible. Maybe this is a pre-sign of things to come? I don't know, but I applaud her stand for truth. The Bible talks about when, during the last three and a half years of the seven-year tribulation, a person will not be able to sell, buy food, or live in peace without that mark on their head or back of their hand! But if you take the mark of the Antichrist then you have doomed your soul to an eternity in hell! This is not make-believe, this is real, in the near future! Those who refuse the mark, whether they are living for God at that time or not, will be put to death! There is a movie on Youtube that is very eye-opening and scary called *New World Order!* I ask you to watch it, as it was very realistic about the near future! If you decide you're going to live for God during that time, then you will pay for that decision with your own life through your own blood, but you'll make heaven your home!

Those who take the mark during that time will also have to face God's wrath on the earth and all its judgements, and again stand before God on Judgement Day where He sadly cries over each soul who rejected His love to them in life! I believe you will see His tears as His heart breaks after their lives are being played back like a giant video screen showing that they had rejected the one who had died on the cross for them and their sins, the Lord Jesus, when all they had to do in life was ask Jesus to come into their heart and ask forgiveness of their sins. God will have no choice but to judge them into hell! God does not send people to hell; hell was created for the devil and his fallen angels. We are the ones who send ourselves to hell, because we refused the free gift of God through salvation through Jesus! So we are the ones that have the choice of either heaven or hell. This writer chooses Heaven. Before the Tribulation takes place, you will hear of billions of people disappearing around the world, for the Tribulation is not for the believer in Christ! It is for those who rejected Christ in life! You can believe what I'm telling you or not, it's scriptural, but that doesn't make it less true, because you believe that way. It is true and it will happen, and it's my prayer that God gets a hold of your heart so that you can go when Jesus comes back!

And now I'll share another Youtube video I saw. There's an action movie comic superhero actor who, it turns out, now has the Coronavirus! He has a wife and child who I am sure depend upon him, so he has to quarantine away from them to try to fight this thing. So how is he going to fight this? By taking nothing but gin while he has this virus. Your wife and your child are hoping and praying that you get better, so how is this easing them, knowing you're going to do non-stop drinking while having a killer virus? How selfish Is this of you, not only putting your health in more jeopardy, but now having your family wonder and worry if they'll see you alive again? How stupid and selfish this is. I couldn't believe it when I saw this! You have people counting on and caring for you and all you can think about is indulging into a drunken stupor with a virus that kills normal people who have no conditions, and you want to egg it on by doing something this foolish? You know, for someone who has played an action hero, you're not very smart! Do you have a death wish, putting yourself at risk like this? Or are you so upset because you have the Coronavirus that you have to numb yourself by trying to drink it away? You need to wise up and put your family first, and be a leader of your house and do the right thing! My prayer is that God will get ahold of that head of yours and talk to you! You have a family to think about; it's not just about you! You have to consider them, as well.

In real time at this stage of this virus, New Yorkers had lost over 10 thousand during this pandemic in New York City alone, and that's more than they lost during the 911 terrorist strike! And who knows how many more will add to the death toll in the state of New York itself? I shudder to think about it! And that's extremely sad to me, because that's our neighboring state on one side, as Rhode Island. Even though we don't know all of the people from these states personally, I consider them all as our brothers and are sisters in this same virus war! And many who have passed away from this over there just breaks my heart! As the United States death toll has climbed, we may surpass the amount we lost in the whole 12-year Vietnam War! And it took less than a month to do it here in 2020! This is horrible beyond any scale I can think of at this point in our very lives! I don't know about the virus epidemics of the past, which took a lot of lives, but I know it was many! But in my lifetime writing this, I'm sure a person never would have dreamed our world would be dealing with something like this, and I know many lives have been lost around the world, as well! And because it took my friend Brian's life, like many of you, I can't even pay my respects to him, or my friend Gary, or others! And I feel for those survivors who have lost loved ones and can't even pay their respects. My heart goes out to all of you, wherever you live, and we're all in this together, since we have to do these stay-at-home orders for our own safety! Even though not all are following the law of it, and some are protesting it. Like many of you, I have to occupy myself at home trying to stay focused and busy, and that's not easy when you live on your own. And I'm sure many singles can Identify with what I just shared...

And we don't know what the so-called New Normal is going to feel like. This is an uncertainty, and a scary time here in Boston and Massachusetts, the United States, and the entire world! We don't know how we're going to feel whenever this thing is dealt with and over with! Being cooped up in my place like many of you, I'm not just on my laptop all the time doing these stories, I have also once in a while caught some things to watch for which I pay about 14 dollars a month and get an incredible array of TV shows and movies to watch because of my Firestick TV. And Youtube's endless amount of action movies, comedy TV shows, and comedy movies, including British comedies that I love to watch that you can get on there! There is an incredible array of stuff that I catch once in a while when I'm not occupied with other household things to do. If you haven't caught an episode of Aaron's Animals you're in for a treat it's amazing what they do with these two cats! One episode after another absolutely hilarious stuff!And if you're a Wipeout fan like I am you would love to see that program! If you're a contestant on there your stamina will be challenged! Plus all the silly amount of gadgets you have to go through traps! And on YouTube you can catch Undercover Boss,I have always liked that program! One of my favorites dry sense of humor comedy programs of all time has got to be silent library MTV comedy! Absolutely hilarious! Some things are a little risque to show overall it's very funny dry sense of humor wise!

It just numbs my brain of the many things we could normally do before, but we can't do now, and that's sad. Lately, I have caught some movies on Prime Video, like *Rambo: Last Blood*! So you know it's going to be good. I didn't like the language, but it had a lot of action. If you watched the movies of *Home Alone* in the '90s movies and saw all the traps the crooks had to endure, then you would enjoy this version of Stallone alone, with deadlier consequences! Another movie I highly recommend on Youtube is called *Brother's Keeper*, and it was awesome! It was based on a true story, I believe, and you have to catch another movie called *The 5th Quarter*, another true story of a brother's vow and dedication! Watch the movie, and you'll see how this title got its name! I also can't say enough about *Wonderlawn*, another movie! And it, too, is based on a true story of what God can do when He is allowed to do what He does! And I want to bring up two special movies I saw at Christmastime. One of them is called *The Bells of Saint Mary's*! The producer of the movie decided to do it and make the picture as a true life account based on his own sister who was a nun. And I've never seen Bing Crosby in a better movie than this one! Incredible movie!

The other movie is a true life account called *Christmas for a Dollar*, and is about life in the Depression times during Christmas! It is an incredible, inspiring movie about compassion and love. It's on my Christmas list to watch now, every year! I saw a movie this year absolutely incredible called Translated! It's about a scenario where is the Apostle Paul is sent into the future it gets really good from there! And a comedy called Mayor Cupcake, I don't like a few words in the movie, but overall I thought it was funny! I highly recommend, as well, a movie called *Chariots of Fire*, which is also based on the true life account of the early 1900's Olympic years and the people that were in it and their impact in doing so! It is absolutely amazing from start to finish. On Youtube, there's a documentary that was amazing called, *Finding Noah*, which is about searching for Noah's Ark on Mount Ararat! They didn't find everything they were hoping for, but they did drill and locate wood fossils that were attributed to the history of the Ark, absolutely an amazing find! The journey up a cold, steep mountain made a believer out of skeptics, as well as Christians, who came away, amazed at what they had found! And those who were just thrill-seekers also came away amazed, as well!

There is one more movie video I want to share that I found on the Tubi Movie App, called Noah's Ark! Avoid this movie like the plague! It lies at the end of the movie and said more than eight people survived on the Ark for the flood that was about to come, and that people outside before the water came decided that it was a good idea to get on the Ark and banged on the door to get in! That is a lie distorting from the real truth! Only Noah and his wife, his three sons and their three wives survived, another son they had rebelled and perished with others in that great flood! And this movie made no mention of animals to be brought forth two-by-two onto the Ark, male and female. Another lie! What a crappy movie and a joke! I don't recommend it. I can't believe that the British would put out such a farce of a movie about Biblical history and turn it into some kind of make-believe fairytale! If I knew nothing about Old Testament Bible history, I would have fallen for the same crap and lies I saw on that video. What a waste of British filmmaking! And shame on the actors who played in it! Guess none of them read the real account of Noah's Ark back then in old Bible days! What a sham of a movie. If no animals would have been brought forth on the Ark back then, then you wouldn't have any pets at all, because your cat, your dog, your bird, your snake, your gerbil, or anything else are descendants of those animals brought on board and the legacy they had!

I want to share a couple more things real quick. I know why they call them Smartphones, because mine is way smarter than I am !And I never knew the big apartment complex where I live has a backdoor on the first floor! I had always gone through the front door, not knowing it. When one of the residents approached me one day before this Coronavirus pandemic happened, and told me that this place also has a backdoor, it was just like blinder scales fell off my eyes! I had never ever seen anyone walk to the back and use such a door before, and most of these residents are older than I am, so there was no reason for me to believe that one did even exist! It was a totally new revelation to me! And I'm grateful that the resident shared that with me, just as I'm close to finishing this final chapter, I received a knock on the door and it surprised me! One of the male building nurses named Tom was at the door. He and I had a phone conversation yesterday, and he was asking me how I was doing and if I needed anything. Embarrassingly, I replied, "Yeah! I'm out of toilet paper!" I said, "I tried to buy some last week, but they were wiped clean off the store shelves!" We use toilet paper to wipe with, so I used the pun that it was "wiped clean right out of the store!" I was grateful that there were boxes of hand tissues on sale, but no toilet paper left to be found! In these kinds of situations, you have to be innovative as to what you can do, so I grabbed a few boxes of tissue paper, and I was grateful to even find that! When I opened the door, he had with him bundles of rolls of toilet paper. I couldn't believe it!

Another blessing from God during this time that I really needed it! I'm sure heaven was laughing with me when I made a vivid search on my quest to find toilet paper at two stores a week ago and found nothing but the tissue boxes! I'm grateful I even found that, because in times like this, you really don't want to have to use something like paper towels, not on your life, if you can help it! No scratchy bottom backside for me, no, thank you! You don't wanna be that guy! And one day I received a call from California from a friend of mine who I had first got to know in early 2019. Those who are in martial arts will recognize this name; it was none other than my friend, Paul Vunak, who is recognized throughout the United States and the world as one of the foremost trainers in martial arts! He has trained many in the branches of the military, and many police forces in the United States! His videos can be captured on Youtube and they are incredible! That's how I first heard of him, last year. He's very pleasant to talk to, and I've talked to him on the phone. For a guy who knows as much about martial arts as he does, he is a very soft-spoken and a humble guy! And he has been doing this training for others for a long, long time! And as he is getting older, he is still training people! So, I answered the phone, and was very relieved to hear his voice at this time, to know he is safe and his family speaks volumes to me! He wanted to know how I was doing and reminded me that when this is over that he still wants to train a disabled guy like me when I'm ready to come to California! What an extreme honor this would be, to be trained by one of the foremost authorities on self-defense in the world! And someone I highly admire and have great respect for.

He is phenomenal, and he has trained assistants like Chris Moran of New York, in whom I have had the pleasure to speak to, as well! Chris Moran also offered to retrain me in the little I know of martial arts! I know some of it, but I don't know the majority of it, as a couple of years ago before I had the surgery, I was able to train a few at the shelter I had lived in, so that they could defend themselves! And what an honor to be a friend of a man I have extremely admired since I found his videos last year on Youtube! And now the offer to hopefully soon fly down to California, and not only meet him but to be retrained by him just leaves this author absolutely speechless! Wow! And I pray my friend Chris Moran and his family are safe, as well; I hope to meet him one day in New York! And who knows how many others Paul has trained? Wow—I can't wait! And he has been called one of the best street fighters in the world! That's extremely impressive! And I want to give a shoutout to one of our Congress Representatives here in Boston; her name is Ayanna Pressley, and she is absolutely incredible! She has great compassion for not only Boston, where we are, but for the state of Massachusetts, as a whole! I don't know what all she does in Congress, but I know it's a lot! I don't know alot about our other Congressional Representatives here, other than Senator Warren, who I hope gets to be the running mate for the Vice Presidency in November! And a shoutout to Senator Markey! I hold our Senators in very high acclaim with much respect, and it's an honor knowing that one of them, Senator Warren, is a person of high importance for the Vice Presidency position. And I know they care for our lives, as do other Representatives of Boston whose names I'm not aware of. I thank God that we have them and the people that watch over us in this state! They have incredible leadership! And if you have some kind of complaint or comment, they do have a phone number and answer you back. I appreciate that very much about our representatives. They really do get back to you. And the outstanding leadership of the other women in Congress, as well!

There is one last thing I want to share with you all: whenever I've gone out on a sunny day, I would wear my sunglasses, which are really good at keeping out the bright light from my eyes ,but when the order from our mayor came about to wear the face masks that we do, I tried putting on my sunglasses again, and found out that the two don't mix, the hard way! When you're walking with the face mask on with your sunglasses, you will find out in about 30 seconds or so that you cannot see a thing, because the breath of your nose and mouth under that mask is clogging up the vision in your eyes, and it's like you're walking into a fog bank! Wow! I even tried to adjust the mask a little bit lower on my face and try to push up the sunglasses even a little bit higher on my head, and that trick didn't even work! There is nothing like a blast of fresh warm air coming from your very nostrils,and giving you a dose of reality as to where you are trying to go to, and what you're trying to see? You might bump into someone or something and not be able to realize it until it happens! That's a scary thought! Can you say, "Uncertainty with cloudy and fogged-up vision?" That doesn't sound good to me! Reluctantly, I put my sunglasses into my jacket pocket and was very disgruntled over what had just taken place! I needed windshield wiper glasses like Elton John had used in his concerts; then I would be able to see! No such luck, though; I wasn't aware that my mask and my sunglasses would not get along with each other and I would have to separate them both! Woefully, sigh-fully, and reluctantly, which almost sounds like a disheartened bad weather forecast, I ventured out into the bright sun where with my vision I was barely able to see anything at allI It was so bright out that I felt like I was seeing sun flares before my eyes! But I'll take barely seeing anything at all over not being able to see anything at all, anytime!

I'm grateful for those reading this book. I hope you found something in the chapters you enjoyed, or even could identify with! I hope we come out of this soon and try to experience life again! That is my hope, and I guess we will all see what the New Normal looks like. Hopefully soon, be it weeks or even months, I pray, but over with! And how different things might be then; I'm hoping people will still be considerate of others in this New Normal! As more and more people are being taken out of life from this deadly virus, my heart grieves, especially for kids and teens that have to experience what is taking place right now and are wondering what their lives and future are going to hold for them? My heart as well goes out to the survivors and to those who have lost loved ones during this time, here in Boston, and our State of Massachusetts, the United States, and around the world. Who knows how many of us will be left after this devastating interruption into our lives has run its course, since life has no guarantee, and it is really sad...It has been devastating and eye-opening! This writer is just as human as you are, because what affects you, affects me, as well, as we are all in this together! My prayer is that during this time, this will pull us all together as more and more people are being considerate of one another! And hopefully, I will see you in the next book, since this is my first effort through God that I have been attempting to write for some time now...

Sincerely yours, the author, Richard [Ritchie] Vernon, signing off for now, saying: please be safe and know that my heart is with you. All of you are in my prayers during this season of unknowns. God Bless You, and I'll see you again in the next and final chapter of this book... Please be civil and cordial with your comments, when emailing this publisher about the author or any other products we have,because we will delete spam. And spam, as the author puts it, isn't just for breakfast anymore; it can be deleted, as well! Richard shared with us that he was forced to eat spam as a kid, so we guarantee that he hates both kinds of spam! So please feel free to contact us about our upcoming books or his uhi music here. His Youtube music channel is Richard Vernon uhi, or email us to get more info for book or music information. All replies will be answered back...We invite you to check out the music he does, as well. We are proud to have him on board with us.

CHAPTER 17

THERE IS STILL TIME!

You know as an author you think you're done when you've gotten chapter 16 and you think that's it for the first book but I was so wrong! God spoke to my heart to get a chapter 17 done and some may like it some may not but regardless I do have to answer to God whether I listen or don't listen! I choose this day and every day to listen! I want to share with you about possible future events coming up that some may know about and from what I've read on YouTube others definitely know about and I want to share that same sentiment with you dear readers as this chapter unfolds! With the way things are going in this world there is no certainty of how long this world might last and so it's always good to be prepared as if you were getting ready to go over a cliff and you would hope somebody would be there to pull you back from falling over! It is my desire to be that type of person that would keep someone from falling off a cliff hopefully! You know myself as an author I am definitely not a perfect man, I have never claimed to be so, and I've been ashamed of my own self through action and attitude in the past but that person is not the one sharing with you right now! I was abused physically sexually mentally emotionally and socially when I lived somewhat in Washington Arizona and Indiana! I will go more into detail in another book about what happened sexually in another book but for now I want to share this I went to a doctor to have a physical when I was in the Puget Sound Naval Shipyard as an introductory high school student into the Navy introduced to all kinds of people there from sailors on up and the wonderful CO's that I had! What happened to me when they sent me for a physical to join a Navy softball team that they had it up because they felt that I would have talent as one of their players became an absolute living nightmare for me! The doctor I went to the physical for I don't know what was wrong with him mentally, but something definitely wasn't right about him and he did more than just a physical on me, introduced to me the world of sex before I as a young teenager even knew what sex was and that's the truth! I was so shocked so stunned and looking inside of myself I said what did I do to deserve that? This took me from a world I'm not knowing anything about sex as a young teen to being introduced to something I wasn't ready for! I have long since forgiven this doctor I'm sure he's probably passed away that was years ago! If my Co's would have known what this doctor did to me, I'm sure they probably would have court marshalled him out of the Navy! Or had him prosecuted for child abuse! I had four co's that looked out for me on this base where we were part of a repair and deploy unit to get ships that were in and get them out through different paperwork and I was one of their runners on the base! When this happened to me on that particular day, I tried to cry deep inside but I was too stunned to what happened to me I didn't understand why it happened but it happened nevertheless and I could not shake It loose and it had far-reaching effects as I got older! And not in a good way! I was to have a long battle with sexual addiction after what this man did to me! And not with other men but with women! I was going to be in the Battle of my life just to try to keep my sanity! It changed my whole attitude about what love and sex were and at no time in my life should I have ever gotten married because I wasn't prepared for it my mind was tainted and driven because of this! I was never going to experience what real love or what a real marriage would look like because of this doctor's actions and even today why he did this I have never figured out! I just know that he left an indelible imprint on my life going forward and I was going to carry it out the rest of my life even against my own will! God had not abandoned me I just didn't know how to reach out to God after that happened, I felt so lost and lonely an abandoned inside I didn't know how to reach out to anyone including my bosses! So I held it deep inside I was so ashamed I felt used on the inside, and so later on in life I was going to be used again and I was going to use again, but there did come a point where Christ was really introduced into my life again and let me know that he loved me that he didn't hold it against me what happened to me but that he could heal me take away the deep scars and wounds from that day going forward because I was so ashamed of myself and there were times I wanted to end my own life because I felt absolutely useless to mankind after that! Because back then when you were a young teen like myself you were trying to figure out life you didn't need something like this happening to you to help you decide a path you were going to go on later on!

The only thing you knew from that point you felt like you were damaged goods to the world not just from that day but every day after that, and later on in life that made me wonder how could God still love me? I was so stunned to what happened that I could not get my mental emotional or psychological bearings in my mind! Not only after what I've been through but what happened to me after that and what I experienced with others as well! I regret to this very day not knowing what real love was even in my own family! And I will get more into the Washington stories in a later book where I was raised after California! And that I would never experience another normal marriage in my life, I felt like I was being poured out like water everywhere I went I felt no meaning no purpose no desire no anything! I felt no life on the inside and I thought sooner or later life is going to end because it was so Hollow so absolutely meaningless no desire whatsoever to continue on no fire inside of me no path to choose because I felt like my path had been chosen whether I liked it or not! As I got older God really spoke to me and showed me that not only did, he loves me and that he would forgive my sins again and then if I would let him, he would wrap his arms around me spiritually speaking and start trying to heal me on the inside! He spoke very kindly, very compassionately, very softly, that I was his child and he saw a wounded child even if some man deep scars on the inside that he wanted to heal! It also became something to the point where I could identify, other people having to deal with abuse especially in the sexual sense men and women children and teens! I'm not saying I'm at a spokesman for this but I definitely have a lot to share about it now when you've been through it and you're starting to heal eventually after years you want to share with people, I understand what you went through or what you're going through now and I myself will pray as well for your situation! This was one of the worst experiences of my entire life next to the death of my father my stepfather my mother and my brother so far that I know of in this life I don't know anything about my sisters or their kids or anything how they're doing because my three sisters never got back with me once I left Washington! I definitely would have been an unwilling spokesman then or any kind of abuse because when you're going through it you're angry bitter mad on the inside I'm willing to forgive unwilling to share, but as I got older and God reached deep into my heart again the ability to forgive was there, and it made me not only realize not only the shame I had been through but the shame I had put others through since having to do now with a sexual addiction I did not want never asked for it never desired it and never knew what sex was until that happened! But now I can speak freely about it and I would also say this to those I hurt I pray that they will forgive me once they hear my story at no time should I have ever gotten married because I didn't know what love was or the difference between that and sex because your mind becomes so warped after that you don't think about anything else! Because after a while you don't feel like you have a right mind to think from! I couldn't get one positive thought together by trying during that time, because there's absolutely nothing positive about sexual abuse or any other kind of abuse only learning experiences come after that and they are very painful trust me! I thank God that he pulled me through later on in life even before I became homeless, he had gotten a hold of my heart and started healing the broken parts inside of me made me aware of what other people go through then and even now and now all I want to do is pray for people and pray for those I hurt and pray especially for those that hurt me because after the doctor it continued and the abuse increased even more! When I found out that Jesus died for people like myself who were so ashamed of their own lives because of what happened to them or what they did to others I didn't feel like I could be forgiven ever I felt dirty rotten and low on the inside and I said I will never ever have a normal life feeling the way I feel now carrying this burden on me I never wanted in the first place! But God has a way of removing especially heavy burdens too heavy to carry by yourself you need someone else to carry that burden and Jesus is the one that carried my burden and let me know even back then how much he loved me how much he cared for me, and most importantly to me how much he wanted to get rid of what I was dealing with on the inside that I was always ashamed to tell anybody what I was dealing with! I was married a few times in my life after my teenage years and I even shared what I was going through and I was told to get over it! I found out in my last marriage that my ex-spouse I just as many faults as I did and kept them hidden until I found them one by one some of them before I got married to her, I was warned that we shouldn't have gotten married I should have listened because it was painful! Especially when she committed adultery twice on me and possibly married my former best friend whom I trusted with my life and got him an apartment next to me when he was struggling on his finances in another town! So, we all have faults in marriage and we carry baggage into it but we got to get rid of the baggage before marriage preferably or it's going to be a marriage of hell or both of you! It really turned me cold when she said just get over it? You don't tell someone who has been through abuse to just simply get over it you pray with them you love them you have compassion on them and you try to tell them or show them how to become a normal human being again if possible! We ever rarely got along in that marriage because of my faults and her faults, I take the blame for it though because I was the one who was struggling with what happened to me before I even met her and I thought marriage might be the cure but it never is! And so, because she and I didn't get along, her kids and I wouldn't get along, and then of course in any argument we had naturally her kids would side with her whether she was right or wrong because kids will side with the natural parent! Maybe in the future book I'll go more into that but it was painful most of those thirteen years! The pastor that married us warned us, that he saw all kinds of red flags in this marriage I wish I would have listened maybe I could have gotten the professional help I need it at that point I don't know? But it was a learning experience that was painful! When you come to find out your marriage partner has just as many faults and addictions as you do or more you become very conscience of your own partner even though you're still trying to deal with what's happening inside of you from years ago! And even though she committed adultery on me twice I still loved her even at that time that's why God dealt with me to pick her up in another state with my former best friend to rescue her from being homeless because the other guy was getting tired of her and was ready to kick her out on the street in Jackson Georgia even though I lived in Indiana I felt the tug of my heart go get her with my van and so we did an my former best friend now was to meet my separated wife for the first time and once I got her back to Anderson Indiana she latched on to him quickly and was over at his house every day I brought her back so she could start a new life with her kids away from me hopefully because even though I forgave her and I still loved her I wanted nothing more to do with this marriage wise because she already made her stake in this and I was looking forward to getting a divorce I'm sure she was too after she met my former best friend I'm sure they're married today! I hold nothing against either one of them and I pray they will live for God while they still have the chance, they might hate me and be bitter with me because of our horrible marriage but I forgive her and I forgive him and I'm just going to let it go at that whether they we choose forgiveness or not? I can share this now and I would pray with anybody I don't feel that God has made me a spokesman for sexual abuse but at the same time if he did, I will not ignore the call! I'm just glad he loved me all the way through this and there's people out there possibly reading this book now or those going through abuse of any kind I just want them to know the same God that is bringing me through this day by day with his unfailing passionate long-suffering love for me has that same for others whether you are the abuser or you're the one being abused!

That love of Christ does not change and never will! His word says Jesus is the same yesterday today and forever which simply means he never changes! And God is reaching out on planet Earth today to those who don't know him, to those who might have known him but turn their back on him, and also to encourage those who do know him trying to live even stronger lives as believers in Christ! God is reaching out to mankind in these last days as the Bible says we are in the final days if not the final weeks or even the final years of what is going on in this planet! And the love of God's desire is to implant his love into every single person's heart whether you've been abused or you're the one doing the abusing, or maybe just someone who you consider yourself a good person, and maybe you are but you still need the love of God to come into your heart to prepare you for heaven! Any one of us could die tomorrow and the question would be did they know Jesus as Lord and Savior? Many people dying from covid today and since this first took over in early 2020 I hope they reached out to God in their dying days and I hope those surviving with covid or without covid would reach out to God today take his hand and ask Jesus into their hearts! We live in a very corrupt society today unfortunately and there's no guarantee of life from one day to the next! So, it would be well to be prepared in case it happened to anyone of us! You might say to this author, Ritchie I don't know how to pray and ask this Jesus in your talking about to change my life and forgive my sins! And I would tell that person all you have to do is be sincere before God and let him know that you sinned before him, and let him know you're sorry for those sins and ask him to come into your heart and make you a new creation where old things are passed away and new things come! If you will do that with a sincere heart because remember God knows our heart he will come in to your heart and change your life like he has done this author! There would be others that say I don't believe in God? Well to those I would say he believes in you and he still believes in you while you have life in your body ask him to make himself real to you and he will if you will but have a sincere heart and ask him in by faith, he will do it! The word of God specifically says God is not willing that any should perish but that all and he means all would come to repentance! Because every one of us whether you admit it or not need the love of God deep down in our heart, we can feel our lives with everything drugs sex outside of marriage alcohol smoking anything, to try to fill that void in our hearts and our lives but only the love of God can do that! Even this corrupt government we have today in the United States can be changed by the power of God and there are some decent Republicans and Democrats in this government who either know God or they love democracy God knows who they are, and then there are other individuals in this government and in the former Administration as well who could care less about the love of God and the love of democracy in these days and would completely destroy all if they had the chance? And God is watching these people right now even talk show hosts which I call mock show hosts, think they are clever with the God jokes and think they can get away with anything putting down Jesus or God or even Christians and because they haven't been struck by lightning, they think they're safe! I would say to all these talk show hosts that are doing this, stop doing this while you have life in your body just because you haven't been hit by lightning doesn't mean you're going to escape this life without facing the wrath of God because of defaming his name there's an appointed time for every one of us and it's called judgement day and it's coming in the near future where everybody including myself have to stand before God one day and give an account of our lives! When the Christian stands before God one day on that day he or she will not be judged for sins because Jesus forgave them and cleansed them of all unrighteousness! So many of us will not be judged before the creator of the universe, but however we lived our lives for God after he saved us that is going to be accounted for before a Holy God!

And then there's judgement day for those who don't know Christ who rejected him who despised him who wanted nothing to do with his sacrifice on the cross and raising of the Dead for our sins, those I believe will have their whole lives played over before them and it could be a life full of shame for a life full of so-called good works but the good works Don't mean a thing unless Christ was involved in them! It's sad to say and it breaks my heart that those who stand on judgement Day will be cast into the lake of fire forever in the bowels of hell! By an angry but sad and compassionate loving God who didn't want to do that gave them chances in life that they threw away and now it's payday! I believe God is going to be crying with great tears every person that has to go into hell that could have avoided it by receiving Christ in their heart! And remember this those people can't blame God for doing what he had to do because they chose to live that life outside of Christ so by their own decision-making, they cast themselves into hell against the wishes of a very loving God! I know it's going to break his heart when he has to do this on judgement Day for every person that comes before him in judgment! If you don't know Christ in your life right now, I encourage you to ask him into your heart and you will see his love is true for you even now and in the future and he will never leave you nor forsake you his word says this and he backs it up with me every day! Because in the very near future there is one coming on the scene called the Antichrist and he is going to kill people left behind when the rapture of the church takes place and those who are believers before the tribulation are the ones called The Church, I just want to make that clear, we're not talking about a building or an establishment we're talking about actual human lives that received the love and forgiveness of God! The word rapture is not in the Bible, but the word caught up or catching away is and that meaning in Greek for rapture is the word harpozo, I'm not sure I spelled it right but that word means rapture! There is no guarantee of life from this day forward you could live one day and perish the next through covid or anything else so it would be awesome to have an insurance and that insurance policy would be asking Christ into your heart! This Antichrist will kill tribulation believers those left behind from the rapture, and if you're a doomsday prepper reading this and you're thinking this is not going to affect you because of all the preparation you will make during that time, remember this technology is growing even more so in these days to where they could find you just by the heat of your body or your heartbeat they could locate you in the bowels of the earth if they needed to and they would find you and they would ask you to take the mark of the beast which is the system of the Antichrist! The beast is simply the league of ungodly Nations that the Antichrist will head up in the

European nations! And like the Trinity of Father Son and Holy Ghost the devil will have his own unholy Trinity himself the Antichrist and the false prophet make up the unholy Trinity! The tribulation period will last for 7 years! The first three and a half years will be a false peace giving you false promises and false hopes that you will see that none of it is true after the other three and a half years kick in of the tribulation where people will be forced to take the mark of the Antichrist if they want to continue living! Those especially tribulation saints at that time will be given a choice to renounce Christ and take the mark and continue living or die in their own blood because they live for Christ now! For many of us today who are believers still alive on this planet all we had to do was die to ourselves and allow Christ to take over our lives! But at that time, you will give your life in your own blood if you refuse the mark on your hand or your forehead! Once you receive that Mark there is no turning back! I heard a well-known preacher say one time and this absolutely disgusted me when I saw this video, he was asked a question in the 90s if a person receives the mark of the Antichrist can they still be forgiven? And he said yes, they could ask Christ back into their heart! This is a lie for many reasons because once you received the mark there is no more forgiveness there is no returning to Christ or turning to Christ may be the first time in your life because once you had that Mark you've sworn allegiance to the Antichrist in his bunch and think about this as well once you receive that Mark on your hand or forehead you will take on the devil's nature you won't even think about salvation or forgiveness or love or anything because it won't be a part of your spiritual DNA because something has invaded that and taking over! This pastor has repented since saying that but how many people did, he hurt during that time with this dangerous false doctrine God awful words that came out of his mouth and that lie? In these days especially if those of us who are going to live for Christ then we need to live for Christ be careful what we say and what we do and try to honor God in every way possible daily! During the other part of that tribulation, it will become so bad and it maybe become bad even before that that you won't be able to buy or sell anything because you don't have that Mark because you don't belong under the one world order government of the Antichrist! Do you remember me early on in the story saying would you avoid a cliff if you could? This is that cliff! You could avoid this cliff and the tribulation period if you will but accept Christ into your heart and let him change your life you will see the difference and so will others you can still do it while there's still time! Nobody but nobody has to go through the tribulation period if they will ask Jesus into their heart then you will be ready for heaven when Jesus comes back for his people his church! As the author of this book, I'm trying to help you avoid that cliff! The tribulation and the antichrist and all his followers are that cliff so you're being shown there is a choice even now! Think about this covid could take a whole lot more lives before Christ comes back will you be ready to go, I hope you do because I want to meet you all in heaven one day! No matter who you are or what you've done in this life Christ will make the difference in your life you can even save a corrupt Congress if they will but turn their lives over to him but I have a feeling that many of these people are going to go to jail or prison before it's over and done with including many of the former Administration! And you if you're reading this and you have racial issues with anybody ask Jesus into your heart and he will take away all of that! I see that because of all the things that have been happening to those outside of the white Caucasian gender they are! It's not too late to change no matter who we are if you avoid the cliff, I just shared with you if every person in America or even around the world received Christ into their heart there would be nobody the Antichrist could kill or that he would force to worship him! Think of it beloved it's not too late to change it's not too late to receive the love of God no matter who we are! I saw a program on TV one time called the good place! And it talked about people being accepted into this so-called heaven that we're good people but that's not reality heaven is not for good people in their own works or their own ways heaven was created for those who came to know Christ and they will live in his kingdom forever! If you have watched this show I just mentioned I want you to know such a place that's not exist between Heaven and hell you're either for Christ or you're against Christ there is no middle ground! That show is a lie from the pit of hell! There is no such place and there never has been and there never will be there's only two choices that can only be accessed through either our own way or the way the truth and the life which is Jesus! Hopefully my friends in Boston read this as well and understand we're not guaranteed life but we are guaranteed eternal life through the Son of God who took an extreme excruciatingly painful punishment for your sins and mine! Don't let the sacrifice of what Christ did on the cross go by the wayside it was for us he died that was for us that he rose again and it is for us if we know him that he will one day return and bring us to his home in heaven! You can believe what this author is telling you or not but please I pray in the name of Jesus please avoid the cliff because once you fall off that cliff there is no turning back! But remember this, as long as we have life in our body there is still time! God bless you all and be safe I pray in Jesus name!

Thank you! We hope you enjoyed this first series of books to come! The second book will be called *Life stories Volume II: Continuation in Boston!* Please email us and stay in contact. Thank you. Be safe and may God bless us all...

I Richard "Ritchie" Vernon would like to encourage you to support the following organizations that I endorse, it takes passion to care! A Portion of the proceeds from this book will be given to these organization to support the underprivileged and those in need.

Look for the second future book entitled-Lifestories Vol 2 Continuation in Boston!

The word of God says, God loves a cheerful giver!

Pakistan Living for Christ Home in Pakistan
Contact Person:
Rukhsana Sadiq
Punjab Pakistan
Sobiasadiq1122@gmail.com

All Things Possible in Burma

Victor Marx
All Things Possible Ministries &
The Victor Marx Group
info@victormarx.com
https://victormarx.com/

Rene Tuñacao
Patricia Rojas
Poblacion Tabogon Cebu
Godiskeepingmealive02@gmail.com

Erin Hibbs
Native American Heritage Association
540-636-1020